Charles M. **REIGELUTH** Jennif

VISION AND ACTION

Reinventing Schools Through
Personalized Competency-Based Education

MARZANO
Resources

555 North Morton Street
Bloomington, IN 47404
888.849.0851
FAX: 866.801.1447

email: info@MarzanoResources.com
MarzanoResources.com

Visit **MarzanoResources.com/reproducibles** to download the free reproducibles in this book.

Printed in the United States of America

Library of Congress Cataloging-in-Publication Data

Names: Reigeluth, Charles M., author. | Karnopp, Jennifer, author.
Title: Vision and action : reinventing schools through personalized
    competency-based education / Charles M. Reigeluth, Jennifer R. Karnopp.
Description: Bloomington, IN : Marzano Resources, 2020. | Includes
    bibliographical references and index.
Identifiers: LCCN 2019040251 (print) | LCCN 2019040252 (ebook) | ISBN
    9781943360185 (paperback) | ISBN 9781943360192 (ebook)
Subjects: LCSH: Competency-based education--United States. | Individualized
    instruction--United States. | Educational change--United States.
Classification: LCC LC1032 .R45 2020 (print) | LCC LC1032 (ebook) | DDC
    371,39/4--dc23
LC record available at https://lccn.loc.gov/2019040251
LC ebook record available at https://lccn.loc.gov/2019040252

Production Team
President and Publisher: Douglas M. Rife
Associate Publisher: Sarah Payne-Mills
Art Director: Rian Anderson
Managing Production Editor: Kendra Slayton
Production Editor: Laurel Hecker
Content Development Specialist: Amy Rubenstein
Proofreader: Mark Hain
Cover Designer: Rian Anderson
Editorial Assistant: Sarah Ludwig

ACKNOWLEDGMENTS

The authors would like to thank Paul Jaeger and Layne Sherwood at the Minnesota New Country School and Nikolaus Namba and Barry Sommer of Lindsay Unified School District for their descriptions of their respective school systems, which provide powerful examples of personalized competency-based education.

Marzano Resources would like to thank the following reviewers:

Emily Batchelder
Assistant Principal
East Clayton Elementary School
Clayton, North Carolina

Jennifer Evans
Principal
Burnham School
Cicero, Illinois

Shanna Martin
Social Studies Teacher and
  Instructional Coach
Lomira Middle School
Lomira, Wisconsin

Brian Stack
Principal
Sanborn Regional High School
Kingston, New Hampshire

Chris Stogdill
Principal
Otte Blair Middle School
Blair, Nebraska

Visit **MarzanoResources.com/reproducibles** to download the free reproducibles in this book.

TABLE OF CONTENTS

PART I: VISION

PART II: ACTION

ABOUT THE AUTHORS

 **Charles M. Reigeluth, PhD**, is professor emeritus at Indiana University, Bloomington. He is a distinguished educational researcher and consultant who focuses on paradigm change in education, including the design of high-quality personalized competency-based education, the design of technology systems to support such education, and the process for transforming school systems to the learner-centered paradigm of education. When he was sixteen years old, he walked out of a classroom feeling disillusioned with his educational experience and decided to dedicate his life to making education more enjoyable and relevant to students' lives. He taught high school science for three years, was a professor in the Instructional Systems Technology Department at Indiana University for twenty-five years, and was chairman of the department for three years. He facilitated a paradigm change effort in the Decatur Township Schools in Indianapolis for eleven years to advance knowledge about how to help school systems to transform. He has devoted forty years to advancing knowledge about both what a school system should be like to better meet students' needs and interests and how to help school systems to transform to such a different paradigm of education. He is internationally known for his work on instructional methods and theories.

Charles has been a long-time member of the American Educational Research Association (AERA), Association for Educational Communications and Technology (AECT), Association for Supervision and Curriculum Development, Phi Delta Kappa, and the Aurora Institute. He received the Honored Alumnus award from Brigham Young University's School of Education and the Distinguished Service award from AECT, where he founded the Division for Systemic Thinking and Change. He has published twelve books and almost two hundred journal articles and book chapters on those subjects, and six of his books received outstanding book of the year awards from AECT. He also received seven awards for outstanding journal article or book chapter from AERA, AECT, and International Society for Performance Improvement. His books include *Reinventing Schools: It's Time to Break the Mold* (2013) and *Instructional-Design Theories and Models, Volume IV: The Learner-Centered Paradigm of Education* (2017). He has given keynote addresses to a variety of organizations around the world, including the National School Boards Association and the International Conference on Media in Education in Japan.

Charles received a bachelor's degree in economics from Harvard University and a doctorate in instructional psychology from Brigham Young University.

Visit www.reigeluth.net or www.reinventingschools.net to learn more about Reigeluth's work.

 **Jennifer Karnopp** is completing a PhD in education leadership and policy studies at Indiana University, Bloomington. Her dissertation examines the implementation of a districtwide change initiative in a rural context. Her experience as founding principal of a small, independent charter school in New Hampshire, which provided a personalized, competency-based learning experience to students in grades K–8, inspired Jennifer to earn her doctorate to better support other communities as well as policymakers in their efforts to engage in student-centered change. Igniting the curiosity of children through quality learning experiences has been the driving force behind Jennifer's varied career in education. For over twenty years she has worked in a variety of traditional and nontraditional learning environments, from developing and providing educational programing through children's museums, to being a classroom teacher in traditional public and charter school classrooms, to working as a special educator. She also developed curriculum and training experiences for early childhood educators across the country through a curriculum development and training company that she founded.

Jennifer is the coauthor of *Reinventing Schools: It's Time to Break the Mold* (2013). She is also the author of three books designed to help early childhood educators create child-centered learning environments: *Focus on Babies*, *Focus on Toddlers*, and *Family Child Care Basics*.

Jennifer received a bachelor's degree in anthropology and a master's degree in special education from Indiana University.

To book Charles M. Reigeluth or Jennifer Karnopp for professional development, contact pd@MarzanoResources.com.

INTRODUCTION

Educators are well aware of several serious problems related to the United States educational systems.

1. **Equity:** The quality of education differs greatly, based largely on the socioeconomic status of the school community. The resulting lack of opportunity for poorer citizens is not only a grave social injustice, but it also deprives society of their immense talents, limits perspectives among people in positions of power, and exacerbates the growing gap between the haves and have-nots, which, if unchecked, is likely to cause serious social unrest.

2. **Survival:** The very existence of a public education system is under threat. Some people are so frustrated at the inability to improve their public education system that they believe the only solution is to privatize education through vouchers. This would have grave consequences for equity and would aggravate the growing problem of tribalism in the United States.

3. **Ethics:** Schools currently are at best neutral regarding ethical development of our youth, given the persistent bullying and cheating that occur in schools. Unethical practices of housing lenders were instrumental in causing the Great Recession that began in 2007, causing widespread suffering throughout the U.S. and the world. Unethical practices of drug manufacturers, distributors, and even doctors caused an opioid crisis that has killed more U.S. citizens than died in the Vietnam War and has had devastating effects on the lives of millions more people.

4. **New needs:** We are living in an increasingly complex and interconnected world, and that is bringing huge changes to all aspects of our lives. Hence, the kind of education that was needed in the industrial age—including the hidden curriculum of "sit down, be quiet, and do what you are told to do"—is no longer what's needed. This not only results in student disengagement and under-preparedness for success in life, but it also places our whole society in peril.

5. **A devaluing of teaching:** Teaching has become a much less attractive job, resulting in shortages of teachers and high turnover rates, with inevitable consequences for the quality of education.

These problems cannot be addressed with piecemeal reforms in our education systems—they require fundamental changes. Business as usual doesn't cut it anymore (New Commission on the Skills of the American Workforce, 2007). Teachers, administrators, and parents have the intuitive sense that the traditional approach to teaching isn't meeting the needs of today's students. But what will meet their needs and dramatically improve their schools, and how can *you* make it happen? The purpose of this book is to help teams of educators (teachers, administrators, staff, coaches, facilitators, and even board members), parents, and students to answer these questions. Personalized competency-based education and other aspects of the new paradigm of education that we call Education 3.0 are the most promising ways of effectively addressing the serious problems with U.S. education systems today. We offer proven ideas and methods both for a *vision* of personalized competency-based education (PCBE) and for the *action* (or process) for transforming your school or district to that vision.

This book is an extension of our previous book, *Reinventing Schools: It's Time to Break the Mold* (Reigeluth & Karnopp, 2013), which introduced six core ideas essential to personalized competency-based education. Although you need not be familiar with that resource, it contains valuable insight into why PCBE is so badly needed, and provides guidance for state and federal governments to support the local transformation of school systems. This book elaborates on those six core ideas and provides detailed guidance for how to incorporate them into your own vision and change process. This book is also a companion to *A Handbook for Personalized Competency-Based Education* by Robert J. Marzano, Jennifer S. Norford, Michelle Finn, and Douglas Finn III (2017). It builds on what has been learned at the Lindsay Unified School District in California (see *Beyond Reform: Systemic Shifts Toward Personalized Learning*) and several other pioneering schools and districts around the United States.

Why Transform to Personalized Competency-Based Education?

There are many reasons why you should transform to personalized competency-based education. There are many ways PCBE can be done, some of which are not very effective. If done well, PCBE will:

- **Improve student learning**, retention, transfer, and motivation (Guskey & Gates, 1986; Haynes et al., 2016; Haystead, 2010; Means, Yoyama, Murphy, Bakia, & Jones, 2009; Pane, Steiner, Baird, Hamilton, & Pane, 2017)

- **Improve what students learn**, with a greater focus on what they need to be successful in life and what their families and communities need to be healthier (Collins, 2017; Lash & Belfiore, 2017; Pane et al., 2017; Reigeluth & Vogt, 2018)

- **Provide more flexibility and options** for both what and how students learn (Reigeluth & Karnopp, 2013; Thomas, Enloe, & Newell, 2005)

- **Empower students** to be more self-directed and intrinsically motivated in their learning (Thomas et al., 2005)

- **Improve equity**, not by closing achievement gaps in a one-size-fits-all curriculum, but by helping all children to reach their potential, given their individual talents and interests (Aslan & Reigeluth, 2015; Thomas et al., 2005)

- **Lower the cost** of education, especially by lowering administrative costs (Egol, 2003; Reigeluth, 2018)

- **Reduce the bureaucracy**, empowering teachers and empowering parents to play a larger role in their children's education (Reigeluth, 2018)

- **Improve the quality of life for educators**, and consequently reduce the teacher shortage and improve teacher quality (Reigeluth, 2018).

So how can you do PCBE well? This is a matter of vision.

What Is the Vision?

In today's fractured society, it is not easy for your school system to come up with a shared vision of education that will meet students' needs as they face an uncertain and rapidly changing future. To tackle this task, it is important to think about changes in both *what* students learn and *how* they learn it.

What Students Learn

What students need to learn has been changing dramatically as we evolve deeper into the post-industrial age, partly because information is so readily available through the internet, partly because knowledge work is replacing manual labor as the predominant form of work, and partly because our society and its institutions and tools are becoming so much more complex.

We suggest that the major criterion for deciding what students learn should be its relevance to students' current and future lives—what they need to learn to become happy, successful adults who contribute to their communities. Several influential educators (for example, Collins, 2017; Prensky, 2016) propose that the curriculum should focus on helping individual students find their passion, cultivate their individual talents to pursue that passion, and develop the skills necessary to achieve their goals, such as the ability to think critically, problem solve, and learn how to learn. This requires more than piecemeal changes to the curriculum—more than just adding some new courses. It requires a fundamental change, which we describe in chapter 3 (page 57).

How Students Learn

How students learn has also been changing dramatically in the post-industrial age, partly because learning sciences and instructional theory have greatly improved our understanding of how people learn and how best to help them learn, and partly because technological tools that can personalize learning have become more powerful. We suggest there are three keys to maximizing student learning: (1) student motivation, (2) scaffolding to support learning, and (3) a supportive learning environment.

1. **Motivation:** You can't make a student learn. To maximize student learning, you must motivate the student to learn. Psychologist David McClelland (1987) identified three powerful motivators in his Three Needs Theory: the need for achievement, the need for affiliation, and the need for power. Instruction is more or less motivating to the extent that it addresses all three needs. PCBE addresses the *need for achievement* through a competency-based approach to learning that emphasizes real-world accomplishments. Student progress is based on mastery rather than time, so every student feels a sense of pride and accomplishment, and students learn by doing authentic projects that impact their world. PCBE addresses the *need for affiliation* through collaborative learning in a supportive environment. It also fulfills the *need for power* through self-directed learning with agency, voice, choice, and development of grit (Dweck, 2016).

2. **Scaffolding:** Motivation alone cannot maximize learning. Students also need personalized support that empowers them—*scaffolding*. This scaffolding may entail *adjusting* the difficulty or complexity of each project, *coaching* the student during performance on the project, or *tutoring* the student in new knowledge, skill, or understanding just before it's needed in the project (Reigeluth, Myers, & Lee, 2017).

3. **Supportive learning environment:** Finally, a caring, supportive learning environment is essential to maximize student learning. It's been said that if a student doesn't think that you care, the student doesn't care what you think. This requires building relationships that endure over more than just one year and includes relationships among students as well as relationships between students and the teacher. Caring means that the teacher knows about personal difficulties each student faces and helps the student deal with them. Trauma-informed teaching, a growing school movement that places students' social and emotional needs at the center of the schooling experience, is an example of this.

Systems Thinking for the Vision

Transforming what students learn and how they learn it requires systems thinking. Educational reforms have often focused on changing one part of a school system at a time: open classrooms, personalized learning, self-directed learning, project-based learning, collaborative learning, computers in the classroom, site-based management, and the list goes on. Each of these is good. The problem is that most of these individual changes are incompatible with the other parts of the school system, thereby reducing their potential benefits and endangering their sustainability. For example, we know an elementary school in the Midwest that decided to move to competency-based learning and placed students in math classes according to their skill rather than their age. But the school still used teacher-centered, large-group instruction. As a result, all students in the class moved on to a new topic at about the same time. So, the competency-based approach had become a form of large-scale tracking, and poor test results killed the effort.

To successfully maximize student learning, we must pay attention to which other parts of the school system must change to support any important shift we want to make. As Marzano and colleagues (2017) put it in *A Handbook for Personalized Competency-Based Education*, "For a PCBE system to be effective, it must be designed so that each piece works in concert with the other pieces" (p. 10). This is the essence of truly systemic change, or paradigm change (Reigeluth & Karnopp, 2013). A *paradigm* is a completely different pattern and structure for a system. It is more comprehensive than a model—there can be many models within a single paradigm. In educational systems, the one-room schoolhouse is one paradigm (for the agrarian age), the current teacher-centered factory model of education is another (for the industrial age), and the personalized competency-based paradigm is a third (for the information or digital age).

Only paradigmatic change can help teachers maximize student learning and prepare students for the future. Paradigm change is not new to education. The one-room schoolhouse, or agrarian-age paradigm, was different from the industrial-age paradigm that predominates today (Reigeluth & Karnopp, 2013). We call these *Education 1.0* and *Education 2.0*. The personalized competency-based paradigm, or post-industrial paradigm, is *Education 3.0*.

What Are the Actions?

It will not be easy to implement the vision for personalized competency-based education that your team develops. Many aspects of your school or district will need to be changed at once, because the success of each change depends on the other changes. Fortunately, much has been learned about how to succeed at paradigm change. For example, the actions (transformation process) must include many stakeholders and give them ownership over the process to reduce resistance to the changes. The process must operate by building consensus, rather than by majority rule. Finally, the process must recognize that changes in mindsets and other kinds of learning are the most important outcomes of the effort.

Transforming to PCBE is a difficult and treacherous process. The guidance we offer in this book will help your team succeed in this essential undertaking for the future of our children. We offer guidance about the transformation process for a whole school district and for individual schools. But we caution that it is not wise to try to transform an individual school within a school district, because it will become incompatible with the rest of the district, which will then automatically try to change it back. Many successful pilot schools have been unsustainable as a result.

What Are the Criticisms of PCBE?

As described in the preceding sections, personalized competency-based education has a laudable and needed goal: all students achieving mastery of whatever they are attempting to learn. Yet some people are critical of it (Herold, 2017b). Why? At the root of the criticisms is a lack of conceptual clarity. PCBE is many different things to different people. There are many ways to do PCBE, and many of them don't work well.

Personalized learning alone is a one-legged stool. So is competency-based education alone. There are four parts of competency-based education—competency-based approaches to (1) student progress, (2) student assessment, (3) learning targets, and (4) grading and student records—but they are not always used together. To work effectively, all four parts of competency-based education should be used together, along with personalized, collaborative, project-based, and self-directed learning—all supported with appropriate technological tools and teacher training. If you try to implement one of these at a time, your stool will fall over long before you can assemble all the legs.

Table I.1 shows some conceptualizations of PCBE that are destined to disappoint, along with remedies to those flawed conceptualizations.

Table I.1:

Flawed Conceptualizations of PCBE and Corresponding Remedies

Flawed Conceptualizations	Remedies
Students working alone on computers	Also using collaborative projects extensively
Competencies as small, separate objectives	Using more comprehensive objectives that are more meaningful and address higher, deeper, integrated, and sometimes unmeasurable kinds of learning
Assessment and remediation as separate events at the end of a considerable amount of instruction	Integrating assessment with the instruction, so the instruction provides whatever remediation may be needed
Using traditional bell-curve grading when evaluating mastery of competencies	Moving to records in the form of proficiency scales and lists of competencies mastered
Maintaining time-based student progress where competencies must be mastered within a specific timeframe	Changing to continuous (learning-based) student progress for each student
Assessing a whole set of competencies at once and passing a student if 60 or 70 percent of them are mastered	Identifying critical competencies and ensuring mastery of each one

The lesson of these criticisms is that PCBE requires *full commitment*. If your team is not going to implement PCBE fully, then it will be a waste of your time and effort. If you are committed to doing it well, this book will help you get where you want to go.

How Is This Book Organized?

The purpose of this book is to help a team of preK–12 teachers, administrators, and other stakeholders to improve its school or district by transforming to PCBE. We offer ideas and transformation processes for the classroom, the school, and the district. This book is intended for a team of educational stakeholders because the transformation to personalized competency-based education cannot be done effectively in a single classroom—it must be a schoolwide or districtwide effort.

Part I is about the PCBE vision. Its chapters offer ideas about what changes you might want to consider for your PCBE classroom, school, and district to better meet students' needs in this post-industrial, digital-age society. All three levels of change should be done together (if you are an independent public charter school or private school and don't have a district or central office to deal with, then obviously only the first two kinds of changes are important). Your team should consider six core ideas while developing your vision, each of which is addressed in a separate chapter (chapters 1 through 6). Chapter 7 presents two comprehensive case studies that exemplify the core ideas—one for an independent public school (not in a school district or charter network) and one for a school district.

Part II is about the change process. These chapters address the difficult challenge of how to transform from what you have now to what you envision (with the help of part I) to maximize student motivation and learning. Chapter 8 helps you to decide on the best scope for your change effort and describes a framework for the change process that applies to every scope. Chapter 9 offers detailed guidance on sequential activities for a school district, while chapter 10 offers such guidance for an independent public school (not part of a school district or charter network). The appendices offer criteria for assessing readiness for transformation, as well as detailed lists of helpful resources for enhancing your success.

Now that you have some understanding of PCBE, recognize that complex paradigm change is the only way to achieve strong outcomes for students, and have a sense of how to navigate this book, let's move on to the nuts and bolts of making PCBE a reality in your school context.

PART I:
VISION

*Core Ideas of
Personalized Competency-
Based Education*

Part I provides ideas based on research and practical experience for you to consider building into your ideal vision of PCBE. You should form a team of teachers and other stakeholders to develop your vision (see steps 1.2 and 2.1 in chapters 9 and 10, pages 159 and 189, for guidance). We suggest that your team explore six core ideas while developing your vision (we originally introduced these core ideas in our previous book, *Reinventing Schools: It's Time to Break the Mold* [Reigeluth & Karnopp, 2013]).

1. Competency-based education

2. Learner-centered instruction

3. Restructured curriculum

4. New roles

5. A nurturing culture

6. New organizational structures

Please note that all six core ideas are important and interdependent aspects of PCBE. Chapters 1 through 6 address each of these core ideas respectively. However, they do not constitute a model because they can be implemented in very different ways. Rather, they constitute a different paradigm of education, within which there can be many different models. The challenge for your team is to figure out what features are best for your school or schools. Also, your team should not attempt to create your ideal vision without consulting part II: Action, first.

Each chapter begins with principles that identify features of PCBE based on research and the sciences of learning and instruction (National Academies of Sciences, Engineering, and Medicine, 2018; Reigeluth, Beatty, & Myers, 2017). Then, each chapter offers some detailed guidance for your team to consider in developing your own vision of PCBE. The detailed guidance sections take a question-and-answer format to help you conceptualize your vision. Many changes you decide to make in your classrooms may require that changes be made on the school level and even the district level, so we address all three levels within each chapter.

The first time you read part I, we recommend that you skip the detailed guidance sections, to give you a better understanding of how the principles in each chapter are interrelated and interdependent. Once you've read through the principles in part I, return to each chapter to delve into the detailed guidance. Also, be sure to consult part II before designing your ideal vision. This will give you a more holistic (systemic) view for your vision. At the beginning of the first six chapters, we provide the following "map" (table P1.1) to help you keep track of where you are in this scheme.

Chapter 7 presents two case studies that span all six core ideas—one for an independent public school that includes changes on two levels (classroom and school), and one for a school district that includes changes on all three levels (classroom, school, and district).

Core Ideas	Principles
1. Competency-Based Education	A. Competency-based student progress B. Competency-based student assessment C. Competency-based learning targets D. Competency-based student records
2. Learner-Centered Instruction	E. Learning by doing F. Instructional support G. Personalized learning H. Collaborative learning
3. Restructured Curriculum	I. Relevance to students' current and future lives J. Whole-child education K. Balance of universal content and individual strengths L. Sound progressions in content
4. New Roles	M. Teacher as guide N. Self-directed student O. Parent as partner P. Technology as a tool for students
5. A Nurturing Culture	Q. Strong and caring relationships R. Multi-year mentoring and multi-age grouping S. Motivational learning T. Family services
6. New Organizational Structures	U. Small school size V. Professional organizational structure W. Student choice, teacher incentives, and accountability X. Administrative structures Y. Governance structures

Table P1.1:

PCBE Core Ideas and Principles

*Visit **MarzanoResources.com/reproducibles** to download a free reproducible version of this table.*

As an introduction to part I, we offer the following vignette that describes PCBE in action. The real classroom in this scenario represents only one of many ways the principles or guidelines can be implemented. Every community—indeed, every neighborhood—has different needs and resources, so its classrooms should differ correspondingly. Such diversity among classrooms is in sharp contrast to teacher-centered classrooms, which we have typically strived to make identical to each other—a relic of the industrial-age mindset of standardization and one size fits all.

Note: This vignette is based on one of the authors' experiences in a charter school. We recognize that charter schools are controversial in some circles, but because they often have more flexibility than traditional public schools, many have experimented with PCBE.

Housed in a small charter school, Ms. Clark's lower elementary classroom is a large, wide-open room with large windows. The walls are bare except for a framed poster of Van Gogh's *Starry Night* and a large framed image of Earth. Carefully arranged shelves divide the room into four distinct areas representing different content areas—mathematics, language arts, the sciences, and social studies. Each shelf displays a variety of hands-on materials accessible to the students. One table in the science area is set up with materials for learners to conduct a science experiment with magnets, either individually or in small groups. Child-sized tables for four students and a few individual desks are dispersed around the classroom. There is also a large open space in the center of the room with an area rug and a small easel and whiteboard. To the right of the easel is a low table where Ms. Clark places a large stack of photocopied work plans, and under the table is a bin full of clipboards.

On this Tuesday morning in November, Ms. Clark and her classroom assistant, Ms. Santos, welcome their twenty-four lower-elementary students (grades 1–3). Two students, Clara and Travis, walk to the whiteboard to see if their names appear in any of the lists of lesson groups scheduled for the morning. Clara notices her name in a geometry lesson group. She flips through the bin of clipboards until she finds the one with her work plan, which she started yesterday. She grabs a pencil and settles down on the floor to copy the words *geometry lesson* onto her work plan under the column marked *Tuesday*. Two other students enter the room and seek out a puzzle map from a shelf in the social studies area. They bring it to a mat on the floor and sit down with it.

Travis, a second grader, grabs a clipboard with his work plan from the bin and heads to a low table where a laminated card with his name on it is sitting out where he left it next to a box of wooden number tiles. He sets down his clipboard and carefully copies the words *stamp game multiplication* from a list of choices written on his work plan. Ms. Clark notices this and smiles. Travis had been asking her for a lesson on the stamp game material ever since his friend Andres had started using it last month. On Friday, she had watched Travis help another student work through a challenging six-digit addition problem, so she knew he was now ready. On Monday, she invited Travis to join three other students for a stamp game multiplication lesson, and he spent most of the afternoon working through multiplication problems. He was in the middle of one when the school day ended, and when he protested at the suggestion to clean up and put away the materials, Ms. Santos reminded him that he could mark it with his name card and return to it in the morning.

Because this is a new activity for Travis, Ms. Clark wanders over to watch him for a minute as he works. She notices he made a mistake in the way he grouped the tiles, and she watches quietly to see if he will notice. He pauses when the tiles don't line up together as he had thought they would. Travis checks his paper, and then looks at the tiles again. After a moment, he finds his mistake, corrects it, and continues with the problem. Careful not to distract

Travis from his work, Ms. Clark opens her tablet, pulls up his digital learning record, and makes a note that Travis independently found and corrected a mistake and was using the material correctly.

Ms. Clark then scans the room to make sure all the students are purposefully engaged in some activity. She notices a group of three friends who are laughing and chatting with no learning materials in sight. She walks over to them and whispers a reminder that the day has started. One student grabs her work plan, looks it over quickly, and then asks one of the other students in the group if she would like to complete a word study task together. They head to the word study material. The third student watches the friends walk away and shows no indication of selecting an activity to begin the day. The teacher asks him what he would like to accomplish today. When he shrugs in reply, she asks him if he has any goals that he has not yet met. He thinks for a minute and remembers a goal he had set to identify every state on his paper map of the United States. The boy smiles, runs his finger down his work plan until he finds *Label U.S. Map*, and then stands up and walks to the atlas on a table in the social studies area.

This scenario clearly demonstrates the six core ideas of PCBE.

1. **Competency-based education:** Ms. Clark has students follow a specific learning progression, and Travis moved on to the next standard or learning target when he was ready. Ms. Clark observed Travis working and noted observations in a digital system.

2. **Learner-centered instruction:** When Travis demonstrated motivation for learning multiplication, Ms. Clark verified that he was ready and capitalized on his motivation by setting up a lesson for a small group of four. This classroom environment gives students freedom to choose what to work on next and nurtures responsibility. Ms. Clark provides tailored instruction on concepts and the use of materials when each student is ready. Students practice independently or with guidance from a friend (or the teacher when necessary), using materials that are designed to be self-correcting, freeing the teacher to work with more students.

3. **Restructured curriculum:** Ms. Clark utilizes her entire classroom environment as a learning resource that integrates traditional content learning with social-emotional learning. Her careful curation and presentation of resources in the room allow students to engage with different content at different levels of complexity to meet their needs and interests. For example, two students explored geography through a simple puzzle map, while another accessed an atlas and paper map of the United States to identify all the states. The classroom environment also provides opportunities for teaching self-direction skills, as when Ms. Clark guided a child to remember and act on personal goals (labeling every state), or when Ms. Santos reminded Travis of a strategy

for redirecting his frustration at having to stop an activity at the end of the day by placing his name card with the material as a reminder that it will be there for him the next day. In this way, the curriculum addresses the needs of the whole child.

4. **New roles:** Rather than delivering curriculum to the class, Ms. Clark choreographs and guides student learning by carefully selecting the materials that will be available to students on the shelves or tables, arranging small-group minilessons, checking for student understanding through observations, and directing student attention to ensure expectations are clear. Her students are responsible for deciding which learning option to take on and when, whom to work with, and where in the room to work. They are empowered to advocate for moving on when they think they are ready.

5. **A nurturing culture:** The classroom, with a mix of ages in grades 1–3, allows multi-year mentoring, which helps build strong and caring relationships and reduces unhelpful comparisons or competition among students. Students are encouraged to help each other, and they can interact with each other throughout the day. Hands-on, activity-based learning with a degree of student choice results in a high level of motivation.

6. **New organizational structures:** At the time of this scenario, this public charter school enrolled just under one hundred students in grades K–5. Parents chose to enroll their children in the school for a variety of reasons, ranging from the school's pedagogical approach and mission to convenience of location. Teacher voice is strong, with teachers meeting regularly with the school leader to determine how to best align the Montessori curricular components with project-based learning. The small school size facilitates teacher and parent engagement.

Competency-Based Education

CHAPTER 1

Core Ideas	Principles
1. Competency-Based Education	A. Competency-based student progress
2. Learner-Centered Instruction	B. Competency-based student assessment
3. Restructured Curriculum	C. Competency-based learning targets
4. New Roles	D. Competency-based student records
5. A Nurturing Culture	
6. New Organizational Structures	

This chapter discusses four principles for competency-based education that are universally helpful for maximizing student learning and guiding all students to reach their potential. It then offers detailed guidance to help your team develop this aspect of your vision for your classrooms, school, and district. While this core idea focuses on competency-based education, please keep in mind that the remaining five core ideas are essential and interdependent aspects of the PCBE paradigm of education.

We do not offer these principles and guidelines as a blueprint for what you should do. Rather, we offer them to assist your team as you engage in rich discussions and collaborations to design an ideal PCBE system in your unique context. For guidance on forming your team, see steps 1.2 and 2.1 in chapter 10 (page 189) for an independent school or steps 1.2 and 2 in chapter 9 (page 159) for a school or schools in a district.

Principles for Competency-Based Education

For an education system to be focused primarily on learning (rather than sorting), student progress must be based on learning (not time). This requires learning targets to be clearly established, student assessment to measure what each student has actually learned, and student records to indicate what each student has learned, rather than comparing students to other students. Thus, competency-based education is a four-legged stool. The four legs are the four principles within this core idea.

Principle A: Competency-based student progress

Principle B: Competency-based student assessment

Principle C: Competency-based learning targets

Principle D: Competency-based student records

If any one of these legs is missing, the stool will fall. So, what should each of these legs be like? The following is an introduction to each of these principles.

Principle A: Competency-Based Student Progress

In a competency-based system, students move on when they have learned and can demonstrate the understandings or skills. If it's important enough to teach, it is important enough to make sure students learn it. Thus, no student moves on before mastering the current topic, and each student moves on as soon as he or she masters the current topic. Student progress is based on *learning* rather than time (Bloom, 1984). This means many students in a classroom are working on different topics at any given time, which requires a *personal learning plan* for every student. This may seem like too much for a teacher to manage, but that's only true if you try to do it within an Education 2.0 system. The use of different teaching tools (such as the self-correcting materials in the classroom vignette at the beginning of part I, page 11), the use of technology to track student progress, and a totally different way of organizing learning in a PCBE (Education 3.0) system actually make teaching easier and more rewarding for teachers, as well as better for student learning (Kulik, Kulik, Bangert-Drowns, & Slavin, 1990).

Principle B: Competency-Based Student Assessment

For a student to move on as soon as he or she has learned the current material, the teacher must know when the student has mastered it. This is a very different purpose for assessment than in Education 2.0, which is typically norm-referenced assessment, designed to identify how much a student has learned compared to other students (Gallagher, 2003). Hence, PCBE requires a different paradigm of assessment—*criterion-referenced assessment*—which compares student performance to a standard (or criterion). Competency-based assessment requires a completely different set of psychometrics from norm-referenced assessment, making it a truly different paradigm of assessment.

New Hampshire

"Students across New Hampshire are evaluated not on pop quizzes, but on demonstrated competency tied to teacher-driven, performance-based assessments" (Dintersmith, 2018, p. 24).

This kind of assessment must be performed on each individual competency, or learning target (see Principle C: Competency-Based Learning Targets), when the student is ready for it. This is in contrast to the current practice of a large test that covers many competencies—whether or not the student is ready for it—and students pass even if they have not mastered up to 40 percent of the competencies (Marzano, 2006, 2010). In fact, competency-based assessment does not have to be in the form of a pencil-and-paper test. Rather, it should be performance-based and follow the motto of *practice until perfect*—the performance on practice becomes the test (Patrick, Worthen, Frost, & Gentz, 2016; see Principle F: Instructional Support, page 29). Furthermore, it is important to assess the student's ability to combine many smaller competencies into broader competencies, or standards. This fits the concept of badges.

Badges are an assessment and credentialing mechanism to validate learning in both formal and informal settings. Like scouting badges, they are a way of certifying mastery of a set of specific competencies. Digital badges are being used increasingly in K–12 and higher education settings.

Principle C: Competency-Based Learning Targets

To know when each student has learned the current material, the teachers have to define the content in the form of learning targets, which are more detailed than typical state and national standards (Educational Impact, n.d.). A good target is a kind of learning goal or objective that provides enough information for the teacher—and the student—to judge that the student has achieved mastery. Criteria for mastery are key. Even deep understandings and social-emotional learning can be formulated as learning targets.

People are right to caution that breaking down standards can lead to fragmentation in instruction (Wiggins, 2017), but learning by doing (principle E) places the learning targets within a holistic, meaningful context, while instructional support (principle F) allows the teacher to assess mastery in a broad range of relevant, realistic situations. This means that state standards must be broken down into learning targets that have criteria for mastery. Furthermore, there are different levels of mastery for most learning targets, and those levels constitute a *proficiency scale* (Marzano, 2010), which Marzano defines as "a series of related [learning targets] that culminate in the attainment of a more complex learning goal" (p. 11).

Principle D: Competency-Based Student Records

To make decisions about what a student should learn next, one must know what the student has already learned. Current student records (report cards with a single grade for each course) tell you nothing about that—they only tell you the courses the student attended and how well the student did compared to other students. What you need instead is a list of individual learning targets the student has mastered, often accompanied by a portfolio, rubric assessment, or other proof of mastery, sometimes called a *digital backpack*. Student records should also provide information about who the child is as a learner—interests, strengths, weaknesses, preferences, and so forth.

Technology can make this more comprehensive kind of student record easier to maintain than the norm-referenced report cards commonly used today. When students take a tutorial on a digital device while they are working on a team project, the results can be automatically entered into the record-keeping system, as is already being done by Khan Academy and many other learning management systems. Even when teachers need to observe student performance (for example, public speaking) and enter information about mastery into the record-keeping system, a handheld device with a rubric or set of criteria can ease the task of keeping detailed records of competencies mastered by each student.

Some skeptics worry that changing student records will be a problem for college admissions. However, according to Ken O'Connor, Lee Ann Jung, and Douglas Reeves (2018), "a growing number of college admissions officers find grade-point averages to be of little use (Marklein, 2013). . . . Grades do not typically represent student achievement but rather an amalgam of achievement, behavior, compliance, and test-taking skill" (p. 67). Many post-secondary educational institutions have developed alternatives to the grade-point average (GPA) for deciding on admissions, due to several factors. One is the growth of the homeschooling movement, which has no GPAs. Another is the growing number of high schools, districts, and even states that have adopted competency-based report cards (see Competency-Based Report Cards for an example). Furthermore, more than a thousand accredited colleges and universities are "test optional" or otherwise de-emphasize the use of standardized tests (FairTest, 2019). Some parents feel compelled to compare their student to others. To satisfy this need, they can compare the number of competencies mastered by their student in a given period.

Competency-Based Report Cards

From 1998 to 2004, New Hampshire launched competency-based education pilots in twenty-seven high schools. In July 2005, the New Hampshire State Department of Education allowed school boards to award credit based on either seat time or demonstrations of mastery of the required course competencies. For the 2008–2009 school year and beyond, the state required local school boards to adopt policies for all students to earn high school credit by demonstrating mastery of required competencies for a course, as approved by certified school personnel. For example, at Sanborn High School in Kingston, New Hampshire, all courses use a competency-based grading and student record system. Throughout this process the department sought to respect local control.

Source: New Hampshire Department of Education, n.d., 2016.

Systemic Requirements for CBE

Chris Sturgis and Katherine Casey (2018) identify the systemic nature of competency-based education by identifying sixteen design principles for CBE in three categories:

A. Purpose and Culture

1. Center the school around a shared purpose

2. Commit to equity

3. Nurture a culture of learning and inclusivity

4. Foster the development of a growth mindset

5. Cultivate empowering and distributed leadership

B. Teaching and Learning

  6. Base school design and pedagogy on learning sciences

  7. Activate student agency and ownership

  8. Design for the development of rigorous higher-level skills

  9. Ensure responsiveness

C. Structure

  10. Seek intentionality and alignment

  11. Establish mechanisms to ensure consistency and reliability

  12. Maximize transparency

  13. Invest in educators as learners

  14. Increase organizational flexibility

  15. Develop processes for continuous improvement and organizational learning

  16. Advance upon demonstrated mastery

Source: Sturgis & Casey, 2018.

Detailed Guidance for Competency-Based Education

We recommend that you read all the sections titled Principles in chapters 1 through 6 before reading the Detailed Guidance section in any of those chapters, because the principles are so interrelated and interdependent that it is crucial to understand the big picture before getting into specific details. Any effort to move to PCBE that focuses on one core idea without making changes in other core ideas is likely to fail.

We begin with considerations for implementing the principles in the classroom, followed by school-level considerations, and finally district-level considerations.

The Westminster Public School District in Colorado is one of the leading school districts in the United States for implementing PCBE. It uses the *New Art and Science of Teaching* instructional model designed by Robert J. Marzano (2017). You can visit www.westminsterpublicschools.org/Page/9094 to learn more.

Westminster Public Schools

Classroom-Level Considerations

To implement competency-based education at the classroom level, your team must make decisions about student progress, assessment, learning targets, and student records. First think in the ideal for a long-term vision (step 2.1 in chapter 10, page 196), and then compromise as necessary for your initial implementation (step 2.3 in chapter 10, page 200).

Principle A: Competency-Based Student Progress

Your team needs to decide about moving from time-based student progress to learning-based student progress. Here is the main question you should consider.

Q **How can we foster and assess each student's learning individually, rather than having everyone learn the same content at the same time and take the same test at the same time?**

Ideally, the teachers should find or, if necessary, create learning resources that students can use on their own. Several organizations provide a wide variety of learning resources, both free (called *open educational resources*; see Open Educational Resources) and for a fee. Teachers should also try to integrate their assessments with their instruction, as is done in Khan Academy (Thompson, 2011), where students practice a competency, progressing through five levels of mastery, until they reach a criterion of, say, ten practice items correct in a row (Khan Academy, n.d.). This way, the practice is the test—there is no need for a separate test.

Teachers can accomplish this by using online resources such as Khan Academy or Engage NY. If technology is not available for teachers, a second option is to have students work in pairs with explanation and demonstration sheets and practice worksheets accompanied by answer sheets with rubrics. One student uses the worksheet to do the practice, while the other student uses the answer sheet (with a rubric) to judge mastery and provide immediate feedback when the performance does not meet the criteria. To do this, teachers would need to find or prepare several sets of worksheets with at least twenty items on each, so that the second student wouldn't use the same worksheet that the first student used. Generally, the faster learner should answer a worksheet first, because the slower learner will learn a lot while assessing and giving feedback to the other student.

If technology is not available to use online instruction and it is not feasible for teachers to create the needed worksheets for all the learning targets, then teachers will need to use large-group assessment and instruction, which will significantly weaken your move to competency-based education. You might consider holding off until a more suitable solution is feasible.

Open Educational Resources (OERs)

Amazon Education (https://amzn.to/2MaVsGZ) offers a variety of services, including Amazon Inspire, which provides educators—regardless of funding or location—access to free digital teaching resources with rich features such as search, discovery, and peer reviews. It also allows schools to upload, manage, and share OERs.

Engage NY (www.engageny.org) is sponsored by the New York State Education Department and offers a free online library of Common Core–aligned curricula funded through a $700 million federal Race to the Top grant in 2010. As of 2019, it has about five thousand lessons, modules, units, primary resources, and texts.

GoOpen Campaign (tech.ed.gov/open) is sponsored by the U.S. Department of Education's Office of Educational Technology, and provides information about the twenty states and roughly one hundred school districts that it supports to offer OERs.

Khan Academy (www.khanacademy.org) provides a wide range of tutorials that include explanatory videos and practice to mastery. It also provides an automatic record-keeping system for keeping track of student progress and mastery.

OER Commons (www.oercommons.org) is a nonprofit organization sponsored by the Institute for Study of Knowledge Management in Education (ISKME) and offers free OERs and fee-based services.

Open Up Resources (openupresources.org) began as the K–12 OER Collaborative, a thirteen-state initiative to provide free, high-quality, standards-aligned educational resources. They also provide support to districts and schools for implementing these resources by offering such services as professional development and printing.

Summit Learning (www.summitlearning.org/guest/courses) offers a complete, standards-aligned curriculum for grades 4–12 in core subjects. It comes with projects, teaching and learning resources, and tests.

Principle B: Competency-Based Student Assessment

Your team should decide about moving from norm-referenced assessment (comparing student learning to that of other students) to criterion-referenced assessment (comparing student learning to a standard to determine mastery). You also need to develop those assessments. Marzano and colleagues (2017) offer detailed guidance and tools in *A Handbook for Personalized Competency-Based Education* for unpacking standards into essential topics with their associated learning targets and proficiency scales. Eric Hudson (2018) proposes that you consider the following questions as you develop competency-based assessments.

What competencies should we assess?

Competencies are typically expressed as learning targets. As such, we will discuss that aspect of assessment under the detailed guidance for principle C: competency-based learning targets (page 23).

What criteria and evidence should we use to assess mastery of each competency?

We suggest you form a task force of teachers for each level of learning (as described in step 2.3 in chapter 10, page 200) to determine what criteria are appropriate for each competency. With the criteria in mind, the teachers can decide what evidence would best demonstrate that the criteria have been met. Then the teachers should create a *rubric* for each competency to help them and the students to assess mastery. It is unwise to begin your implementation of PCBE until you have decided on criteria and evidence for each competency.

Q&A

What tools should we use to keep track of competencies mastered?

In addition to decisions about competencies and the criteria and evidence for mastering them, you will need a way to keep track of the competencies that students have mastered. *Digital badges* are an excellent choice for doing this. They are an effective and flexible tool to guide, recognize, assess, and spur learning (Muilenberg & Berge, 2016). Digital badges can also recognize the soft skills not captured by standardized tests, such as critical or innovative thinking, teamwork, effective communication, and social-emotional learning. They are an indicator of accomplishment, along with evidence of that accomplishment, and are housed and managed online. Research shows that they enhance student motivation and self-direction skills (Dyjur & Lindstrom, 2017; Grant & Shawgo, 2013). David Niguidula (2019) offers field-tested guidance for using digital badges to demonstrate student mastery. Many badges have already been created that teachers can use, and many public schools use badges.

Badges in Public Schools

The 40,000-student **Aurora Public School District** in Colorado initiated a digital badging program in 2014 within its college- and career-success department based on discussions with local employers about important skills for their graduates to have (aurorak12.org/category/digital-badges). There are now different sets of badges in grades preK–2, 3–5, 6–8, and 9–12. Each badge represents one of the 21st century skills in Colorado's state standards, and a set of four or five "journey" badges amounts to one "summit" badge. Evidence accompanies each badge, so others can judge whether the student has met the criteria for mastery. More than twenty badges have been externally validated by community partners. The school district has a badge ambassador to build relationships with community partners.

The **San Diego Unified School District** started using digital badges in 2016 in their elementary, middle, and high schools (www.sandiegounified.org/badges).

Boston Beyond is piloting skill badges for middle school and high school students. Their website (bostonbeyond.org/initiatives/digital-badges) has some useful information.

These are just three of many public schools using badges.

Digital Badges

Open Badges (openbadges.org) is a technical standard for issuing, collecting, and displaying digital badges that includes such contextual information as what the badge represents, how and when it was earned, who issued it, and the criteria for awarding it.

Credly (credly.com) is an online web service where teachers can design, manage, and share digital badges.

Accredible (www.accredible.com/digital-badges) offers a free comprehensive guide and tools for designing and awarding digital badges.

HASTAC (www.hastac.org/initiatives/digital-badges) offers a collection of digital badges and webinars.

Principle C: Competency-Based Learning Targets

Competency-based assessment requires clear specification of competencies to be assessed. So, you should consider this question.

How can we break down topics and standards to the level of detail required for assessing mastery of each individual competency?

This can take a great deal of time, but it is likely that others who have transformed to PCBE have already done this work. Your challenge, then, is to find it and adapt it to your setting. See Resources for Learning Targets for some resources that may help. If you can't find a detailed list of learning targets (preferably with criteria for mastery), your teacher task forces will need to take the time themselves to develop these essential tools. If you can't afford the time, you should hold off transforming to PCBE until you can. Grant Wiggins and Jay McTighe (2011) offer guidance in the form of the Understanding by Design framework for creating your own learning targets.

Resources for Learning Targets

Marzano Resources offers a set of proficiency scales for learning targets in English language arts, math, science, social studies, and such additional content areas as metacognitive skills, cognitive analysis skills, knowledge application skills, life skills, and technology (www.marzanoresources.com/educational -services/critical-concepts).

Center for Curriculum Redesign supports the **Assessment Research Consortium** (curriculumredesign.org/assessment-research-consortium), a collaborative entity whose goal is to redesign systems of measuring students' progress, aligned to 21st century competencies and desired education outcomes.

Competency Works (www.competencyworks.org) is an online resource dedicated to providing information and knowledge about competency education in the K–12 education system.

Mastery Collaborative (www.masterycollaborative.org) is a network of New York City schools that are transforming to mastery-based, culturally responsive education. It includes Living Lab, Incubator, and Active Member schools.

Performance Assessment of Competency Education (PACE) (www.education. nh.gov/assessment-systems/pace.htm) is a New Hampshire state initiative that offers a reduced level of standardized testing together with locally developed common performance assessments.

Principle D: Competency-Based Student Records

You need to decide how to keep track of what learning targets each student has mastered. You may find the Mastery Transcript Consortium (www.mastery.org) to be a helpful resource. It is a growing network of public and private schools that are creating a high school transcript to capture the unique skills, strengths, and interests of each student. Here are two questions you should consider.

How can we arrange to replace the traditional report card with a new student record that keeps track of each individual learning target that each student has mastered, including those for social-emotional learning and creativity?

If your school district will not allow replacing norm-referenced report cards, you will need to consider having both kinds of student records and decide how you will generate the grades on the norm-referenced report based on the targets mastered on the competency-based record. Marzano and colleagues (2017) offer advice on several ways to do this based on proficiency scales for each measurement topic. A common way is to give grades based on the number of learning targets mastered within the grading period, so that higher grades are given to students who have mastered more targets.

How will we maintain the record of learning targets mastered?

A digital *learning management system* (LMS) will greatly reduce the amount of time teachers need to spend on this task. We earlier explained that assessment should ideally be integrated with the instruction, so every student continues to work on a target (or set of targets) until it is mastered. Record keeping should also ideally be integrated with assessment so that the LMS automatically enters the learning target into the student's record when it is mastered. Such a system can also keep other valuable data about student progress, performance, and interests. There are many learning management systems available, both for free and for a fee. A few are listed in Learning Management Systems, but we encourage you to explore other options, too.

Learning Management Systems

Edio facilitates project-based learning for teacher-designed, co-designed, and student-designed projects. It supports self-directed learning as students plan, manage, and revise their project work via movable taskboards and visual checklists. Every student's progress is tracked through customizable reports, dashboards, and transcripts.

Empower delivers curriculum, instruction, and assessments and tracks, reports, and monitors progress for every student. It also has the Learner GPS, a tool for students to set goals and track their progress.

Moodle is a free, open source, modular LMS with a plug-in-based design. It has instruction, assessment, and reporting modules. It can be customized or modified through modular, interoperable plug-ins, and commercial and noncommercial projects can be shared without any licensing fees.

Canvas is a cloud-based learning management system that allows teachers to build lessons, set learning objectives, give feedback, and communicate with students. It contains a variety of resources and integrates with many other digital tools to simplify the logistics of teaching and learning.

Blackboard Classroom promises to personalize learning, increase student engagement, and boost teacher productivity with its Personalized Learning Designer and ability to use mobile devices. It also offers seamless integration with such productivity tools as Google, OneDrive, Dropbox, and Box.

D2L Brightspace helps teachers personalize learning by supporting self-pacing and pacing based on mastery, creating lessons aligned to standards using an intuitive course-building tool, tracking student progress through the school year with simple dashboards and reports, and integrating seamlessly with your existing tools, among other features.

Khan Academy provides a wide range of free tutorials that include explanatory videos and practice to mastery for student assessment. It also provides an automatic record-keeping system for keeping track of student progress and mastery.

Project Foundry, while not a complete LMS, scaffolds project-based learning with tools to help students plan, manage, collaborate, assess, and report their own learning.

Schoology is a K–12 learning management system that includes instructional tools and assessment management, allowing teachers to personalize learning for students.

More information about using competency-based education on the classroom level can be found in *A Handbook for Personalized Competency-Based Education* (Marzano et al., 2017), *Making Mastery Work: A Close-Up View of Competency Education* (Priest, Rudenstine, Weisstein, & Gerwin, 2012), *Breaking With Tradition: The Shift to Competency-Based Learning in PLCs at Work* (Stack & Vander Els, 2017), and *When Success Is the Only Option: Designing Competency-Based Pathways for Next Generation Learning* (Sturgis & Patrick, 2010).

School-Level and District-Level Considerations

As an individual school within a district or even an individual classroom within a school, you can implement competency-based learning targets and assessments. However, competency-based student progress and student records require some fundamental changes on the school and district levels. In PCBE, students should be able to move on to learn content at the next-higher grade level as soon as they are ready, and teachers should avoid reteaching content that a student has already mastered (though periodically reviewing or refreshing competencies is beneficial). For example, students who complete fifth-grade math halfway through the school year should be allowed to move on to sixth-grade math right away and not have to repeat it the next year. This requires that PCBE be implemented across classrooms in a school and even across schools in a district. Similarly, changing to competency-based student records must be done schoolwide, if not districtwide. Your change team should address that scope of change (see chapter 8, page 147 for guidance on that).

Q How will we allow students to move on to learn content at the next-higher grade level as soon as they are ready, and how will we avoid reteaching content that a student has already mastered?

Your classrooms will need the resources to help students learn content one or two grade levels higher than their current grade. Multi-age classrooms help in this regard, but teachers should perhaps also collaborate with teachers at the next-higher level. They can offer some of their resources to the next lower level and forward information about what the students have already mastered when they move to the next level. For students in their last year at your school, a teacher would need to collaborate with teachers at their next school or post-secondary institution.

Q How will we change the student record-keeping system for our school and district, so as not to overburden teachers with two systems?

Your team should work with stakeholders in your school, other schools in your district, and your district's central office and school board to develop a districtwide (or at least schoolwide) competency-based record-keeping system to replace the norm-referenced report card. We recommend that this new system have two major parts: (1) a list of learning targets mastered and (2) evidence of such mastery (for example, portfolios, videos of performances, observer ratings, test scores), along with such information as date of mastery, who certified mastery, and so forth. In addition, you should consider bundling mastered learning targets into badges, certificates, certifications, licenses, or other kinds of credentials that are more useful than a huge list of individual learning targets.

Q What if we are unable to bring about change of that scope?

You can move toward that ideal in a single classroom or school by having teachers keep their own records of competencies mastered by each of their students, and then convert those records to the school or district format at the end of each grading period. However, the work of keeping two systems will overburden teachers, and, therefore, failure to implement competency-based student records districtwide will endanger the sustainability of your PCBE transformation.

Summary

This chapter described four principles for competency-based education that are universally helpful for maximizing student learning.

Principle A: Competency-based student progress

Principle B: Competency-based student assessment

Principle C: Competency-based learning targets

Principle D: Competency-based student records

It then offered detailed guidelines to help your team develop part of your shared ideal vision for your classrooms, school, and district.

Learner-Centered Instruction

Core Ideas
1. Competency-Based Education
2. Learner-Centered Instruction
3. Restructured Curriculum
4. New Roles
5. A Nurturing Culture
6. New Organizational Structures

Principles

E. Learning by doing

F. Instructional support

G. Personalized learning

H. Collaborative learning

This chapter discusses four principles for PCBE related to learner-centered instruction. It then offers detailed guidance to help your team develop more of your shared vision for your classrooms, school, and district.

We do not offer these principles and guidelines as a blueprint for what you should do. Rather, we offer them to assist your team as you engage in rich discussions and collaborations to design an ideal PCBE system in your unique context.

Principles for Learner-Centered Instruction

Competency-based student progress requires instruction to be personalized—customized to each student's learning needs—rather than standardized. But how can this seemingly difficult task be managed? It requires learner-centered instruction, along with new roles for teachers, students, parents, and technology (core idea 4). Learner-centered instruction has two major parts:

> A focus on individual learners (their heredity, experiences, perspectives, backgrounds, talents, interests, capacities, and needs) [and] a focus on learning (the best available knowledge about learning, how it occurs, and what teaching practices are most effective in promoting the

highest levels of motivation, learning, and achievement for all learners).
(McCombs & Whisler, 1997, p. 11)

Four principles for learner-centered instruction have strong research support (Bransford, Brown, & Cocking, 2000; Lambert & McCombs, 1998; McCombs, 1994, 2013; McCombs & Miller, 2007; McCombs & Whisler, 1997; National Academies of Sciences, Engineering, and Medicine, 2018; Weimer, 2002).

> Principle E: Learning by doing
>
> Principle F: Instructional support
>
> Principle G: Personalized learning
>
> Principle H: Collaborative learning

These principles are highly interrelated and interdependent with each other and with the principles for competency-based education. The following is an introduction to each of these principles.

Principle E: Learning by Doing

Generally, the most effective way to learn is by doing, especially for younger students (American Psychological Association, 1993; Bransford et al., 2000; Freeman et al., 2014; National Academies of Sciences, Engineering, and Medicine, 2018; Newman, 2003; Preeti, Ashish, & Shriram, 2013; Schank, Berman, & Macpherson, 1999; Strobel & van Barneveld, 2009; Vega, 2012; Walker & Leary, 2009). Types of learning by doing include project-based, problem-based, inquiry-based, task-based, maker-based, and hands-on learning. We collectively refer to these forms of learning as *project-based instruction*, which enhances motivation, retention, and transfer to the real world.

Some people are concerned that project-based instruction may hurt students' college admissions. However, efforts such as the Reimagining College Access project (Gewertz, 2018) are underway to change college admissions to focus more on students' projects. Students from project-based schools, such as the Minnesota New Country School, are having great success with college admissions (Aslan & Reigeluth, 2016; Thomas et al., 2005).

In project-based instruction, each student chooses or designs a project as a vehicle to master specific content. Projects may be of many different types and scopes, as long as they are chosen or designed by the student and serve as a vehicle to master a predefined set of competencies, or learning targets. Giving students choice increases their motivation, but teachers and even parents may influence the choice or design of a project, especially for younger students. As students grow older, projects should increasingly focus on bettering the student's world, not just the student (Prensky, 2016; Wagner, 2012)—see Principle I: Relevance to Students' Current and Future Lives (page 58). This is sometimes referred to as community-based learning, service learning, or place-based learning.

- The projects are typically **collaborative** to prepare students for the way most projects are executed in the workplace, home, and community; but some are occasionally done individually.

- The projects are typically **interdisciplinary** because that's what most authentic projects are like.

- They are of **significant scope** for the developmental level of the student, ranging from hours or days for preschoolers to months or years for high school students.

- The projects are also bound by time and space. They may be done **in the classroom** if they only require resources and activities available there, or they may be done **in the real world** (place-based and community-based learning) if they require resources and activities only available there. It seems likely that many real-world projects will eventually use augmented reality (Bower, Howe, McCredie, Robinson, & Grover, 2014), which superimposes virtual images, text, and sounds on a mobile device's camera screen and speaker (for example, the game *Pokémon GO*), to support performance of the project. Projects may be done **in a virtual world** through computer simulations if such resources are available. The popular computer game *Oregon Trail* is an example of this, and schools will probably utilize virtual reality as that technology becomes less expensive and more powerful (Freina & Ott, n.d.). Presently the classroom is where most projects are conducted, and this will likely continue to be the case, especially for younger students.

In situations when such projects are not the best options for learning (as in the cases of literature and reading skills and some math skills, for example) other kinds of activities should be used.

Lab Atlanta

"At Lab Atlanta, a community makerspace in Atlanta run by a private school, high schoolers can take a semester-long course to invent projects that promote sustainability for their city, such as addressing air and water quality and improving public transportation" (Dintersmith, 2018, p. 24).

Principle F: Instructional Support

Gaining the ability to discover new knowledge and skills on one's own is important, but using the discovery approach for all learning is highly inefficient (Kirschner, Sweller, & Clark, 2006; Sweller, 1994). Scaffolding accelerates learning and helps all students reach their potential. It can take the form of adjusting, coaching, or tutoring.

- **Adjusting** entails tailoring the complexity or difficulty of the project to the level of the student. To use a familiar, concrete example, imagine a project that entails learning to drive a car. The complexity or difficulty of the project could be adjusted by requiring a standard versus automatic transmission, requiring driving in heavy versus light traffic, requiring parallel parking or not, requiring hill starts or not, requiring rainy or icy road conditions or not, and much more.

- **Coaching** includes giving suggestions or hints to the student while the student is performing. For example, imagine a young student is having difficulty adding two fractions that have a common factor in the denominator, like ⅔ and ⅚. Upon seeing the student struggle, the teacher (or digital assistant) could provide a hint reminding the student to look for the common factor.

- **Tutoring** involves teaching the student a competency, preferably just before it is needed in a project. For example, imagine a team of three students working collaboratively on a project that is being conducted virtually. At a certain point in the project, the students need to use a competency they have not yet acquired. The three students pause their work on the project and go to their individual tablets, where a digital assistant explains, demonstrates, and provides practice in the skill with immediate feedback. The program is tailored to each student's interests and learning preferences. This also frees up the teacher to provide more personalized mentoring for every student (Murphy, Gallagher, Krumm, Mislevy, & Hafter, 2014). When each student has reached the criterion for number of correct performances in a row, the program certifies mastery and the student is cleared to continue to collaborate with teammates in the project's virtual world. The project's immediate needs provide powerful motivation for the students to master the needed content (learning targets). This scenario is but one of many ways that tutoring can be provided just before it is needed in a project.

Principle G: Personalized Learning

To accelerate learning and help all students reach their potential, it is essential to customize the learning experience (Hanover Research, 2015). Personalized instruction does *not* mean that students must learn alone. In fact, teacher guidance and collaborative project-based learning are common parts of PCBE. A good way to personalize the instruction is to help each student make good choices in all the following areas: goals, projects, scaffolding, assessments, and reflections (Watson & Watson, 2017).

- **Personalize goals:** All students should have their own long-term learning goals (taking years to achieve) and short-term learning goals (taking weeks or months to achieve). Their goals should be tailored to their individual needs, interests, talents, and prior learning.

- **Personalize projects:** Teachers can use many different projects to teach any given set of short-term goals and their learning targets, and they can select (and adjust) or design projects based on the student's interests. Teachers can determine whether students should have teammates and who those teammates should be. They can also decide on the nature and amount of self-direction for each student.

- **Personalize scaffolding:** Teachers can personalize scaffolding, or instructional support (in the form of both coaching and tutoring), in two ways—the quantity provided and the nature (or features) of the help.

- **Personalize assessment:** Teachers can personalize assessment by customizing who assesses (teacher, self, peer, computer system, external expert) and the format for demonstrating competence.

- **Personalize reflection:** Reflection on a project experience is one of the most powerful and often overlooked instructional strategies (Schön, 1995). Students can reflect in different ways on both the conduct of the project and the learning that occurred.

One aspect of personalized learning is the personal learning plan. According to the Glossary of Education Reform (Great Schools Partnership, 2014):

> A *personal learning plan (or PLP)* is developed by students—typically in collaboration with teachers, counselors, and parents—as a way to help them achieve short- and long-term learning goals, most commonly at the middle school and high school levels.

The terms *individual learning plan* and *individual student learning plan* are sometimes used as synonyms. PCBE is impossible without personal learning plans; they help teachers manage the learning process when students are learning different content at different rates (Ferguson et al., 2001; Yonezawa, McClure, & Jones, 2012). This level of personalizing is much easier with multi-year mentoring (principle R, page 91), whereby teachers know students well and don't have to get to know a whole new group of students every year.

Principle H: Collaborative Learning

Collaboration is increasingly important in work environments. Collaborating in the school environment will help prepare students for that. It also has many advantages in the classroom setting. First, one of the best ways to learn something is to teach it. Collaborative learning gives students that opportunity. Second, it builds community and interpersonal skills. Collaboration is particularly powerful when used with multi-age grouping (principle R, page 91), wherein younger students learn from older ones, and older students of all abilities can be role models. Third, collaboration enhances motivation by meeting the need for affiliation, discussed in the introduction (page 4). Fourth, collaborative learning enhances critical thinking (Gokhale, 1995). Finally, it frees up time for the teacher to work on cultivating other aspects of the students' learning and development, such as their social-emotional learning and metacognitive skills.

Learner-Centered Instruction

In the workplace, collaborative teams are typically highly diverse, because multiple perspectives strengthen a team's problem-solving ability. Thus, it is helpful for students to work with others who differ greatly from themselves.

Collaboration can take the form of team-based projects or peer assistance. Most project-based learning should be team-based to promote deeper collaboration. However, students may complete some projects individually, and in those cases peer assistance should be the norm. Students who have the same teacher and therefore work in the same physical area (classroom, studio, or learning environment) turn to each other first when they need help in their learning process and view the teacher as a resource of last resort.

Detailed Guidance for Learner-Centered Instruction

We recommend that you read all the sections titled Principles in chapters 1 through 6 before reading the Detailed Guidance section in any of those chapters, because the principles are so interrelated and interdependent that it is crucial to understand the big picture before getting into specific details. Any effort to move to PCBE that focuses on one core idea without making changes in other core ideas is likely to fail.

Classroom-Level Considerations

To implement learner-centered instruction at the classroom level, you need to make decisions about projects, which should be the means by which each student masters content. First think in the ideal for a long-term vision (step 2.1 in chapter 10, page 196), and then compromise as necessary for your first implementation (step 2.3 in chapter 10, page 200).

Principle E: Learning by Doing

Ideally, projects should serve as the way the curriculum is organized, instead of subject-area courses. At Minnesota New Country School and others that take this approach, there are no courses, and students design their own projects based on the state standards that they need to meet and other interests they may have (Aslan, Reigeluth, & Thomas, 2014; Thomas et al., 2005). Student records should still list subject-area competencies mastered, as well as other competencies (social-emotional learning, higher-order thinking skills, and so on).

Thus, your team will ideally decide to replace courses with projects now. However, your team may decide to take a more gradual approach by using projects extensively within existing courses. Either way, you should decide how to support planning, conducting, and ending and displaying projects (addressed in the following sections). For more guidance on project-based learning, see *Project Excellence: A Case Study of a Student-Centred Secondary School* (Anderson, 1990); Transforming Education With Self-Directed

Project-Based Learning: The Minnesota New Country School (Aslan et al., 2014); *Project Based Teaching: How to Create Rigorous and Engaging Learning Experiences* (Boss & Larmer, 2018); *PBL in the Elementary Grades: Step-by-Step Guidance, Tools and Tips for Standards-Focused K–5 Projects* (Hallermann, Larmer, & Mergendoller, 2011); How Science, Technology, Engineering, and Mathematics (STEM) Project-Based Learning (PBL) Affects High, Middle, and Low Achievers Differently: The Impact of Student Factors on Achievement (Han, Capraro, & Capraro, 2014); *Learning to Solve Problems: A Handbook for Designing Problem-Solving Learning Environments* (Jonassen, 2011); *Project Management: A Systems Approach to Planning, Scheduling, and Controlling* (Kerzner, 2009); *Passion for Learning: How Project-Based Learning Meets the Needs of 21st-Century Students* (Newell, 2003); Problem-Based Approach to Instruction (Savery, 2009); *Project-Based Learning Research Review* (Vega, 2012); and *Project Management for Middle School: How One Middle School Teacher Guides His Students to Managing Their Project-Based Learning Groups Like Pros* (Weyers, 2017).

Planning Projects

Should we have fixed project periods?

Even though student progress should be based on learning rather than time, you should consider having fixed project periods at higher age levels, especially when the projects are team-based. In the real world of work, most projects have deadlines, so it is important for students to learn to meet deadlines. In addition, it is important for students to work with different peers on subsequent projects, so they get to know more students better. This means you need to have a common time to finish with old teams and form new teams.

Some students learn faster than others. You can give them more projects or bigger projects to do during the project period. Avoid combining all the fast learners with each other and all the slow learners with each other. Students might also collaborate with students from other classrooms, particularly at higher age levels as interests become more specialized.

The length of the project period should usually be shorter for younger students, who are likely to work on many of their projects or activities alone, as in Montessori schools—though they do also have collaborative activities (Montessori, 1964). Individual projects can have a flexible timeframe, and students typically want to finish each project as quickly as they can. However, in some cases it is wise to establish a deadline, even if it is not the end of a project period. Some projects could be designed to last for two project periods or more. Help students become self-directed learners (principle N, page 73) by teaching them to gauge their project load and learn what is feasible for them. Each student could have a list of individual mini-projects to work on or books to read if he or she finishes a project early or while waiting for teammates to master competencies before the team can proceed with a project.

At the beginning of a project period, teachers should think about planning time and procedures for students to create their short-term personal learning plans. Teachers may also need an initiation process to get each individual student or team started on each of their projects.

What should the classroom be like for learning by doing?

For learning by doing, the classroom must be a workroom, designed somewhat like an artist's studio or woodworker's shop, where students can work collaboratively on their projects with appropriate tools and workspace. Typically, for older students, knowledge-building tools are digital technologies, like computers and tablets with internet connections, but other supplies and maker tools are also important, from simple art supplies and recycled materials to elaborate resources such as 3-D printers and mechanical or woodworking tools. Students of all ages can learn many concepts in a self-directed manner with the aid of hands-on manipulatives like those used in Montessori schools (Montessori, 1912, 1917, 1964), or with "kitchen science" supplies (supplies that are commonly available in supermarkets or other stores).

Which learning targets (short-term goals) will individual students pursue on their projects? Will the learning targets all be required standards, or will students be able to pursue some of their personal interests and talents?

Given the 21st century testing environment, teachers will probably have to focus on required standards, but all students could be given some latitude to pursue learning targets that reflect their personal interests and talents. Too often this latitude is only given to faster learners, even though the slower learners are usually in greater need of motivation.

Will the learning targets span several subject areas?

We recommend this because it allows a focus on improving the student's world, which makes projects more authentic and motivating.

Who will select the learning targets—the student, teacher, or both?

Even for required standards, you can empower students to decide which of those standards (learning targets) they will address during the next project period. Recognize that making good decisions about this is a skill that teachers need to cultivate in students. Younger students typically need more guidance. Student choice and empowerment motivate learning, so it is worth taking the time to engage students in this process.

Once learning targets have been selected, how will projects be chosen?

There are three major options: teachers select the projects from a project bank, design the projects themselves, or help the students to design or select and adapt their own projects based on state standards or other standards.

There are considerable advantages to helping students design their own projects or at least select and adapt projects from a menu or online project bank—especially for older students. This enhances their motivation and self-direction, as well as their understanding of the standards. When students take it a step further and focus their projects on improving their world as well as themselves, they develop an orientation to activism, agency, and empowerment.

If the teacher selects or designs the projects, he or she should allow students some choice of projects from a menu and some opportunity to modify the projects, rather than just assigning projects as is to students. This enhances motivation and student ownership of their learning.

Each student will likely need several projects to address all the learning targets. Again, faster learners will be able to take on more projects than will slower learners, but it is still important to have faster and slower students partner together on however many projects each undertakes.

Where will each project be conducted?

For each project, the teachers or students will have to decide where to conduct it. Projects may take place in the classroom, elsewhere in the school, elsewhere in the district, or in the community. For older students, place- or community-based learning improves motivation and transfer of knowledge and skills to real life through greater authenticity of the project. One of the most powerful approaches to learning by doing is internships or apprenticeships in community organizations. Think about finding community partners who can help make such learning easier to manage. For more information, see the book *Place- and Community-Based Education in Schools* by Gregory Smith and David Sobel (2010) and find ideas in Community Partners for Student Projects.

Learner-Centered Instruction

Community Partners for Student Projects

In **Switzerland**, students in the last two years of high school typically spend half the school week working in an apprenticeship with a company (Singmaster, 2015).

Colorado adopted an apprenticeship program (www.colorado.gov/pacific/cdle /apprenticeships) that entails students working two days a week in a community organization to learn finance, information technology, business operations, or advanced manufacturing. All students learn the twenty-six workplace competencies that Colorado has defined for the program. Individual districts and even schools could adopt a similar program.

The **Give and Take Project** (www.realworldscholars.org/our-programs) from Real World Scholars supports students in partnering with local businesses and community organizations to build meaningful relationships that help communities thrive.

continued →

Iowa BIG (education-reimagined.org/pioneers/iowa-big) is a competency-based program in Cedar Rapids, Iowa. In addition to their regular classes, high school students work on projects with local companies and organizations. This allows them to develop collaborative skills, gain real-world experience, and expand learning beyond the classroom.

Imblaze (www.imblaze.org) is a powerful mobile platform that connects learners who are interested in real-world internships with mentors and workforce opportunities in their communities.

CommunityShare (www.communityshare.us) has an online platform that matches educators with local partners—both individuals and organizations—who can serve as project collaborators, mentors, and more.

Will students work on projects individually or in teams?

Any given student may have some team projects and some individual projects regardless of where the projects are conducted. There are many advantages to team-based (collaborative) projects.

- Students help each other learn, saving a lot of the teacher's time while truly personalizing the learning.

- The student who helps another student learn also benefits by learning the content more deeply.

- Students develop collaboration skills.

- Students develop strong and caring relationships (principle Q, page 90) and a better understanding and appreciation of student differences.

- Collaboration enhances student motivation, if managed properly.

There is one potential disadvantage: a teacher cannot judge mastery from the project's final product, because there is no assurance that more than one student was able to perform to mastery on any given learning target. This concern disappears if each student is assessed individually on each learning target during the project, as described in Principle F: Instructional Support (page 29). Also, an individual reflection component at the conclusion of a project not only helps students to become more reflective learners, but also helps a teacher get a sense of the contributions made by individual team members and the quality of the collaboration that took place. Nonetheless, team products do not indicate individual learning.

If in teams, how will teammates be chosen?

Maximize the benefits of team-based projects by assigning teammates carefully and with intention. The first criterion should be the learning targets and projects that have been selected for this project period. The second should be student interests, because many different projects can be used to master the same learning targets, and different students are motivated by different projects. Other criteria include making teams as diverse as possible in terms of student demographics, speed of learning, skill sets, and personality traits. Those with stronger skills can help those with weaker skills, and mixed-ability teams help develop understanding and caring relationships among all members of the classroom. However, do not always match faster with slower learners, because slower learners also need projects in which they can further develop leadership skills. Group dynamics are always important to consider, but with proper coaching, bad group dynamics can be a good learning experience. Avoid having the same students always team up with each other—give students opportunities to interact with a variety of individuals and build a broad community.

If in teams, will students play different roles (focus on different learning targets), or will all students collaborate on all project activities (meet the same learning targets)?

If students who are working on the same project have somewhat different learning targets, give them different roles that are tailored to their targets. If they have the same targets, then collaboration on each activity is necessary, but make sure that all students participate fully so they all get to use the targets during the project.

What number of projects will each student work on during the project period, and how long will each project take?

Picking the right number and size of projects requires knowing how quickly a student learns and how quickly and effectively a team works together. Teachers should try to determine how long it takes a student of average learning speed to do each project, and then adjust that for how fast each student learns. They can divide the total number of hours by the number of weeks in the project period, and then work with each student to determine the total number of hours per week within the range that the student wants to work on the projects. Eventually, a learning management system will be developed to do most of this monitoring and calculation for teachers.

How will we schedule time for working on projects?

PCBE is most successful when large, flexible learning blocks replace small, rigid periods for the school day. At the elementary level, where students spend most of the day in one classroom, we encourage teachers to support lengthy, flexible learning blocks. Project-based learning is hampered when students are required to stop in the middle of their work. A rigid schedule divided into small blocks of time also creates barriers to teacher collaboration and interrupts a student's sense of flow (Csíkszentmihályi, 1990), hindering motivation and self-direction. Constant transitioning can be particularly difficult for students with special needs. Of course, as students move into high school, supporting large, flexible learning blocks becomes a change that needs to take place at the school and district levels.

Conducting Projects

How will a teacher initiate each project?

A hook event to kick off the project work can provide motivation. Make sure each team is thoroughly familiar with the goals of the project, contextual information, resources needed and available, and other relevant information before they begin.

How much responsibility will teachers give individual students to manage their own projects and monitor their own progress?

Younger students may benefit from the teacher providing a structure for when to work on each project during a project period, but teachers can begin to give them some responsibility as early as preschool, as Montessori Schools do effectively (Lillard & Else-Quest, 2006; Montessori, 1964, 1967). Managing projects and progress is a skill. With coaching (Nowack & Wimer, 1997), students can assume ever greater responsibility as they age, but individual students differ in the kinds and amount of responsibility they can handle at any age. Older students need to coordinate with all their teammates. Teachers should monitor and coach this coordination and scheduling process.

How should teachers monitor student project work?

Teachers need some way to monitor what each student and team is doing—even for the most responsible students. This allows teachers to address problems with motivation, interpersonal relationships, personal situations, and project-management, as well as any other problems that may arise. Teachers can ask students to maintain activity logs, time logs, self-evaluation notes, and other kinds of reflections on their activities. Teachers should take time to observe the teams at work. Scheduling regular check-in meetings with teams is also helpful. The teacher's job will be easier if the students use some sort of online tool, either to manage their projects (like Edio) or to take just-in-time tutorials with the ability to certify and document mastery (like Khan Academy). Otherwise, develop ways for the students to report their progress to the teacher.

How will teachers coach students for managing their own projects and monitoring their progress?

Especially when a teacher first switches from teacher-centered instruction to PCBE, most students will not have effective skills for managing their projects and monitoring their progress. Therefore, the teacher must coach them with explanations and demonstrations about specific skills for managing their projects and monitoring their progress (Nowack & Wimer, 1997). Such skills include scheduling work on each project, monitoring or reporting progress to the teacher, identifying and accessing the materials or resources that they might need, deciding whom they should go to first for help, and deciding how they will demonstrate mastery of learning targets as a project proceeds. For some useful tips on these matters, teachers can check online (for example, www.bie.org /resources and www.edutopia.org/project-based-learning) or with their fellow teachers.

What kinds of support should a teacher provide during students' project work?

Coaching (Nowack & Wimer, 1997) and tutoring are a teacher's main activities to support student learning during project work in several areas: learning targets, the project itself, higher-order thinking skills, and social-emotional learning. In the area of learning targets, if teachers have not been able to find or create tutorials, they should encourage teammates to tutor each other on their learning targets, but teachers should always monitor such tutoring and provide coaching to the tutors when needed.

In the project area, if teachers do not have a project-management tool for teams, they should develop some tools (digital or paper-based) for students to use to keep their projects on track and running smoothly. The Project Management Institute (2013) provides guidance about good project management. Again, teachers should encourage the teammates to coach or tutor each other on project management practices, and teachers should monitor project management activities and provide coaching or tutoring when needed.

In the areas of *higher-order thinking skills* and *social-emotional learning*, teachers should encourage the teammates to help each other, and they should monitor the teams to identify difficulties and provide coaching or tutoring when needed. For example, if a student gets very upset, a teammate could encourage him to use such self-control techniques as taking a deep breath, counting to ten, and expressing his feelings in a calm way with words.

In all areas, teacher support should take the form of asking (Socratic dialogue), rather than telling, to develop better thinking and self-direction skills and promote deeper learning.

How will teachers certify mastery of learning targets as students proceed during a project?

Teachers should not wait until the end of a project to certify mastery of learning targets. It is more efficient and more motivating for the student to work on a learning target until it is mastered, rather than having to go back and remediate later. Finally, it prepares the student better for the real world by helping the student to frequently monitor and evaluate his or her own success at learning.

Teachers can save time if they identify online tutorials that entail the student reaching a criterion for mastery and can keep record of competencies mastered. If this is not possible, teachers should teach their students how to certify their teammates' mastery and develop some form or chart for the students to keep track of each teammate's mastery. Of course, the teacher will need to monitor, coach, and likely verify this assessment and record-keeping process, but it will save the teacher time over doing the assessment and record keeping him- or herself, and it will help develop the students' self-direction skills.

Ending and Displaying Projects

Procedures for ending projects are also necessary, including evaluating, revising, displaying, celebrating, and reflecting. Issues to consider include not finishing by the deadline, substandard project performance, and the roles of students and teachers in the various concluding activities.

Q **What should be evaluated?**

Both learning and project performance should be evaluated. To clarify the difference, a project performance could be writing an article for the school newspaper, while one of the learning targets might have to do with capitalization and punctuation. However, new competencies are best assessed while they are being learned, rather than at the end of the project (see Principle B: Competency-Based Student Assessment, page 16).

Q **Who should do the evaluating?**

As with managing their projects and monitoring their own progress, students need to develop appropriate skills and mindsets for self-evaluation, which includes self-reflection. Teachers must help students develop these skills to become effective lifelong learners.

Q **How should students evaluate their own learning and performance?**

It is helpful for students to have a rubric for self-evaluating their mastery of each learning target and another for their performance on the project—perhaps different rubrics for different parts or aspects of the project. The more often students are involved in developing their own rubrics, the better for developing their self-evaluation and self-direction skills. The less experienced a student is in self-evaluation, the more frequently the student needs to self-evaluate—evaluating smaller episodes of learning and performing.

Q **What role should teachers play in evaluating both student learning and performance?**

Teachers should have a rubric for each learning target and another for each major performance on the project. If it is a team project, they should not rely on team performance on the project to evaluate each student's mastery of the learning targets. Such mastery should be evaluated for each student separately. Teachers typically observe individual student performances, either formally or informally, during and at the end of a project. More importantly, teachers observe and coach student self-evaluation activities. More guidance for doing this is offered in Principle F: Instructional Support (page 29).

Q **How should teachers help their students to self-evaluate?**

Teachers should begin by explicitly teaching students how to self-evaluate, which includes demonstrating how to do it and explaining during the demonstration. In addition, continual coaching is important. Good coaching involves providing guidance during student attempts to self-evaluate. Even younger students can learn to assume much responsibility for self-evaluation.

What should a teacher do if a student or team has not finished their project by the deadline or the final project or performance does not meet standards?

This is a learning process for teachers as well as for students. Missing a deadline is an opportunity for teachers to reflect on their own practices—how they can improve the support related to project deadlines. Also, meeting deadlines is important in the real world, so consequences may be appropriate. It is important that the students continue the project until it is done and they have mastered all the related competencies. There should be a process for asking for and approving extensions. It should go into the student's record that the project was not completed on time or that some competencies were not mastered on time, for that alone could provide considerable incentive to some students, and it will be helpful for potential employers or higher education admissions. Different students will likely benefit from different consequences, and some students may need more severe consequences than others.

Teachers also need a policy about revising a product or redoing a presentation. This may include debriefing (Raemer et al., 2011), self-reflection (Schön, 1995), or a plan of action for addressing project deficits.

For students who work mostly on individual projects or tasks, it makes more sense to end each project whenever the student has finished or mastered it and begin a new project whenever an old one is finished, but there should still be consequences for missed deadlines.

How will teachers help students reflect on their project and learning experiences?

It is also beneficial to have a process for students to reflect on each project. Reflection can be one of the most powerful learning experiences. Help students reflect on the things that went well and what they might do differently in future projects. Also think about ways to have students reflect on other students' (or teams') projects. Debriefing (Raemer et al., 2011) is one tool for encouraging reflection. This could be built into a teacher's process for evaluating student learning and project performances.

Learner-Centered Instruction

Debriefing

During a debriefing, team members reflect upon a recent experience, discuss what went well, and identify opportunities for improvement. Five powerful questions to address during a debriefing are (Stanier, 2017):

1. What were we trying to do?

2. What happened?

3. What can we learn from this?

4. What should we do differently next time?

5. Now what?

How should the results of projects be displayed and celebrated?

Teachers should also think about how their students should display or otherwise share the results of their projects and celebrate their accomplishments. A culminating event can take the form of performances or product showcases. Various kinds of performances include presentations, demonstrations, contests, discussion panels, community events, and other events. Various kinds of products include reports, artifacts (objects), and multimedia programs. Ways to showcase products include performances and displays. Think about who should be invited to the performances or showcases, and where and for how long any products should be displayed. Also, think about each student's portfolio (real or virtual)—what should go into it for each project? In all cases, think about ways to celebrate and honor the students' accomplishments. Celebrations enhance motivation and create a sense of community.

Principle F: Instructional Support

Scaffolding should be used to support learning within a project. Teachers can support both student performance and learning on a project by adjusting the complexity of the project to the level of the student and coaching and tutoring the student just in time during the project.

Once a project has been chosen, how can a teacher adjust the complexity or difficulty of the project to fit the level of the student?

There are at least two ways to decrease the difficulty or complexity of a project. One is to simplify the real-world conditions under which the project takes place. Think of a project as a single version of a broad task. To use a familiar example, imagine the task is for someone with no driving experience to drive a car. A version of this project with simplified conditions could be to successfully drive a car with an automatic transmission roundtrip from your rural home to a store parking lot ten minutes away, in the middle of the day, during clear, dry weather. This entails driving with relatively low speed limits in light traffic with few intersections, no wet or icy roads, and no gear shifting, so much less learning is required to perform successfully under these conditions. The Simplifying Conditions Method (Reigeluth, 1999; Reigeluth & Rodgers, 1980), which is described in chapter 3 (Principle L: Sound Progressions in Content, page 62), can be used to adjust the complexity or difficulty of a project.

Another, less preferable, way to decrease the difficulty is to create *artificial supports* for performance of the task, such as having some parts already completed for the student or not requiring that a certain part of the task be performed. The problem with this kind of adjusting is that it makes the task less realistic, which can reduce both student motivation and ability to transfer the competency to real-world situations (unless it is followed with a project that has no such artificial supports).

While a student or team is working on the project, how can a teacher decide when to provide coaching and what that coaching should be like?

The teacher should look for situations where a team is having difficulty in its project and a hint or a few words of guidance might be sufficient to help the students overcome the difficulty (as opposed to tutoring being needed). But teachers should keep in mind that we naturally tend to rush in when we see a student or team struggling, and we typically want to tell the students how to do it right. Sometimes, it is better to hold off and observe for a while to see if students can overcome challenges on their own. When help is truly needed, it should be in the form of questions or hints.

When should the scaffolding go beyond coaching to actually tutoring the student?

Tutoring is needed whenever a learning target is difficult for the student to master. It is particularly important for the following.

- **Skills** that vary in the way they are done in different situations (because the tutoring includes practice in the full range of real-world situations, whereas the project only provides one situation), including higher-order thinking skills.

- **Understandings** that require the formation of complex mental models (Perkins & Unger, 1999; Wiske, 1998), such as understanding the water cycle with all its interrelated principles—evaporation and all the factors that increase or decrease it, condensation and all the factors that influence it, and transportation of the water and all the factors that influence it (rivers, ground water, reservoirs, and so forth).

- **Memorizing** information that is truly important (such as memorizing the names of all bones in the human body in medical school).

- **Dispositions** that reflect attitudes and values very different from those the student currently holds.

- **Social-emotional learning**, such as developing empathy.

In most cases, tutoring should be provided just in time before the content or competency is needed in a project. Waiting until it is needed greatly enhances student motivation to learn it. However, there are some cases in which a skill cannot be mastered in one sitting. Some require sustained development over weeks, months, or even years, in which case they should be practiced before, during, and after they are needed for a project. Merrill (2013) provides powerful research-based guidance for designing tutorials.

Should tutoring be used to certify mastery for each student?

In a word, yes. The products of a team project do not provide information about individual student mastery of the content (as discussed earlier), for three main reasons: (1) it is possible only one teammate mastered any given learning target, (2) it is possible the student was able to do what needed to be done in this one case but has not learned to generalize to other cases, and (3) assessing mastery with a final product would require, in the case of "not yet mastered," that the student go back and remediate, which is demotivating and costs extra time. Therefore, teachers should use tutoring to certify mastery for each student during a project. Teachers can assess mastery during tutoring by having the student practice a competency on different kinds of cases until mastery is reached. Integrating teaching and testing is more effective, efficient, and motivating.

 What should the tutoring be like for skills?

The nature of tutoring is different for different kinds of learning. It will look different depending on whether the learning targets entail skills, understandings, memorizing, dispositions, or social-emotional learning. For skills, including higher-order thinking skills, a tutorial should demonstrate the skill with an explanation of how to do it, and it should create an opportunity for authentic performance of the skill with immediate feedback that confirms correct performance and helps the student correct inadequate performance (usually with hints or questions, though sometimes explanations or demonstrations are needed). The practice, and often the demonstrations, should include the full range of ways the performance differs for different situations. Demonstrations and performances for higher-order thinking skills should often occur over months or even years and across a variety of subject areas and project types.

 What should the tutoring be like for understandings?

Tutorials are different for the three major kinds of understanding: (1) causal, such as understanding the law of supply and demand; (2) natural process, such as understanding the life cycle of a flowering plant; and (3) conceptual, such as understanding what a civil war is.

For *causal understanding*, a tutorial should have two phases: acquisition and application. Whereas skills are developed gradually through practice, causal understanding is more like a light bulb that goes suddenly from dark to light. *Acquisition* is promoted by observing the effects of causal events. Teachers can present concrete events (examples of the causes and their effects) to the student, or the teacher can enable the student to manipulate a causal factor (or set of factors) and observe its effects. For example, a simple computer simulation could allow the student to use the arrow keys to change the thickness of a convex lens and observe the effects on the focal distance and image. *Application* is promoted by providing opportunities for the student to use that understanding in new situations to (a) make predictions (given a causal event, predict what its effects will be), (b) provide explanations (given an event, explain what caused it), or (c) solve problems (given a desired effect, often called the goal, identify and implement the causal events that will result in the desired effect, often called the solution).

For *understanding a natural process*, a tutorial should demonstrate the phases in the natural process (example) along with a description of the natural process (generality). It should provide opportunities for the student to apply the natural process (practice), like predicting what will happen next in a particular situation. Finally, the tutorial should provide immediate feedback.

For *conceptual understanding*, there are many dimensions, each of which is based on a different kind of relationship between two or more concepts. The most common kinds of relationships include superordinate (a civil war is a kind of war), coordinate (a civil war is not a revolutionary war), and subordinate (one type of civil war is a religious civil war). In these kinds of conceptual relationships, one concept can be either a type or a part of another. Other conceptual relationships include analogical, experiential, and functional. A tutorial should portray the relationship (description) and provide opportunities for the student to use the relationship (application) with immediate feedback. Common instructional strategies include context (for superordinate relationships), comparison and contrast (for coordinate relationships), analysis (for subordinate relationships), analogy (for analogical relationships), case study (for experiential relationships), and purpose (for functional relationships).

For more about tutoring these kinds of understanding, see Causal Understanding as a Developmental Primitive (Corrigan & Denton, 1996); Designing Games for Learning (Myers & Reigeluth, 2017); Dimensions of Causal Understanding: The Role of Complex Causal Models in Students' Understanding of Science (Perkins & Grotzer, 2005); Meaningfulness and Instruction: Relating What Is Being Learned to What a Student Knows (Reigeluth, 1983); and An Instructional Theory for the Design of Computer-Based Simulations (Reigeluth & Schwartz, 1989).

What should the tutoring be like for memorizing information?

For information that is truly important to memorize (such as memorizing the names of all bones in the human body in medical school), drill-and-practice has two major parts: presenting what is to be memorized and practicing recalling or recognizing it. Other strategies include repetition; chunking (presenting no more than 7±2 items until mastered); spacing practice sessions across days, weeks, or months; prompting; and mnemonics (songs, rhymes, acronyms, and so on, like ROY G BIV to remember the colors in the rainbow; Myers & Reigeluth, 2017).

What should the tutoring be like for dispositions?

Tutoring for dispositions must address the three major components of dispositions: cognitive, affective, and psychomotor. All three components must be developed (for a new disposition) or changed (for an existing bad disposition) simultaneously (Kamradt & Kamradt, 1999). The cognitive component requires persuasion through cognitive reasoning. The affective component requires the use of strategies that condition the student to have a positive feeling when demonstrating the disposition. An effective method is social modeling (Bandura, 1977, 1986), such as observing a person with whom the student can easily empathize in a film. Finally, the psychomotor component requires demonstrations and practice with feedback to develop the appropriate behaviors.

What should the tutoring be like for social-emotional learning?

Like dispositions, social-emotional learning has multiple components, including information, understandings, skills, and dispositions. This makes guidance for it more complex than other kinds of learning and beyond the scope of this book. Here we can say that, while much of this kind of learning occurs through normal human interactions (especially collaborative activities on projects), there are many situations in which students need or can benefit from direct tutoring. For guidance on methods for enhancing social and emotional development, see *Promoting Social and Emotional Learning: Guidelines for Educators* (Elias et al., 1997); *Social and Emotional Learning in Action: Experiential Activities to Positively Impact School Climate* (Flippo, 2016); *Social and Emotional Learning in the Classroom: Promoting Mental Health and Academic Success* (Merrell & Gueldner, 2010); Transforming Education's SEL Integration Approach for Classroom Educators (Transforming Education, 2019), and *Building Academic Success on Social and Emotional Learning: What Does the Research Say?* (Zins, Weissberg, Wang, & Walberg, 2004).

How should the tutoring be done?

If your whole school or district is not transforming to PCBE, then teachers will need to implement project-based learning and just-in-time tutorials within the course structure. They may not be able to offer students much choice of projects. One option for tutoring is to have students in a team provide it to each other, with the teacher observing and coaching such tutoring. It is often said that the best way to learn something is to teach it, so this benefits the tutor as well as the recipient (and the teacher). A variation of this is for students to create *instructional tutorials* for specific learning targets. Another option is to provide links to *online tutorials* like those from Khan Academy (Thompson, 2011). If students are working independently on projects that address similar skills, Marzano and colleagues (2017) offer helpful advice about creating a *data wall* with proficiency scales, so any student can easily find out which other students might be able to help him or her learn a particular topic or skill. Eventually, there will be electronic tools to serve the function of the data wall.

Principle G: Personalized Learning

To implement personalized learning, your team needs to make decisions about learning targets, projects, scaffolding, assessments, and reflections.

Personalized Learning Targets

Your team must decide the extent to which you can personalize what each student learns, despite any constraints you are under (like high-stakes tests). All students should learn some universal content (see Principle K: Balance of Universal Content and Individual Strengths, page 61), and it is likely that your state requires all students to learn certain content. Still, there are valuable opportunities for personalizing content. To the extent that teachers can let each student choose her or his targets, it will enhance motivation and allow students to cultivate their individual talents. Here are a few questions you might consider.

Roughly what percentage of the learning targets for a given period do we think should be personalized (selected by the student)?

For universal content and content on which students undergo high-stakes testing, you may not be willing or able to allow student choice. When deciding what portion of learning targets you'll allow students to choose in any given project period, begin with the ideal and compromise as necessary for your first implementation. Your ideal may be as high as 50 percent, depending on the developmental level of the students, but you may need to initially compromise to around 10–20 percent.

Which targets should be selected by students?

To the extent that teachers can let each student choose her or his targets, the better—both to enhance motivation and to allow students to cultivate their individual talents. Thinking in the ideal, your team first needs to use your professional judgment to decide which targets are *not* so important that all students should be required to master them (which we call *universal targets*—see principle K, page 61), even if they are presently required by your state standards or district guidelines. Second, for the universal targets, teachers can still give students some choice as to which of them to work on when. Third, beyond the universal targets, for whatever percent of content students are allowed to choose, teachers should give students great latitude for the selection of targets of personal interest.

How should those targets be personalized?

Students typically need guidance to choose their own learning targets appropriately. It usually helps to start by having each student think about possible career goals (long-term goals—which will not be easy, given that most students haven't thought much about that), and then to think about intermediate-term goals (stepping stones) that will help them to achieve those goals (Schutz & Lanehart, 1994). In that process, have each student think about civic responsibilities and other nonwork responsibilities and set intermediate-term goals that will help them meet those responsibilities. With this context, students may make better choices about learning targets for the next project period.

> States around the country have approved new laws requiring schools to encourage career planning among high school students. This is promoting the development of online tools like Naviance, Kuder, and Career Cruising. It is likely that such tools will change significantly over the next few years, so we encourage your team to do a thorough search.

Career-Planning Tools

Personalized Projects

Various students can achieve the same learning targets through many kinds of projects. Different topics for the same content, different groupings (individual or team), and different kinds of products or presentation formats are a few ways the projects can be personalized. Some students may be more motivated to learn math in a project related to sports, while others may prefer one related to feeding the hungry in their community, and others. The more that teachers can personalize the projects through which students learn, the better.

Q **Should a teacher help students to design their own projects, offer students a menu of projects to choose from, or adapt a project from such a menu?**

In some schools, like the Minnesota New Country School (see chapter 7, page 121), teachers show students the state standards they must master, and then support students as they design their own projects to develop and demonstrate mastery of those standards. When students are accustomed to doing this throughout their schooling years, it works quite well. This student-led approach creates a higher level of motivation that results in deeper learning and better long-term retention, as well as the development of higher-order thinking and self-direction skills. Your team should discuss the supports necessary for teachers to help students design their own projects, compared to offering students a menu of projects to choose from and adapt or just selecting projects for students. Considerations include the logistics of each teacher monitoring, supporting, and assessing a number of different projects (for example, ten to twelve different projects compared to three to five projects or a single project), the tools available to support this work, and the capacity of individual teachers.

Q **If a teacher decides to offer a menu of projects, how should she or he create that menu?**

Teachers can also offer students a menu of projects to choose from or adapt. There are many online *project banks* that offer projects designed by teachers or other experts. If the teacher can't find good projects on the internet, then he or she will need to design them. There are resources to help in this task. See Project Libraries and Project Design Guidance for resources related to both project banks and project design.

Project Libraries and Project Design Guidance

New England Board of Higher Education (www.pblprojects.org) has, with National Science Foundation funding, produced a clearinghouse of teachers' resources for project-based learning.

Mrs. O's House (www.mrsoshouse.com/pbl/pblin.html) provides a variety of problem-based learning projects.

PBLWorks (pblworks.org) offers free projects that it has curated from online project libraries. It also helps teachers use project-based learning (PBL) in all grade levels and subject areas. It creates, gathers, and shares high-quality PBL instructional practices and products, and provides services to teachers (professional development), schools (schoolwide processes and structures to support PBL), and districts (creating and sustaining districtwide PBL initiatives).

TeachThought (www.teachthought.com/project-based-learning/a-better-list-of-ideas-for-project-based-learning) provides a list of ideas for project-based learning for kindergarten through precalculus.

Lesson Planet (www.lessonplanet.com/) offers project-based learning lessons from 200,000 reviewed lesson plans.

Edutopia (www.edutopia.org) offers free materials and downloads for building rigorous projects for all grade levels.

Personalized Scaffolding

To maximize learning in a project-based learning environment, teachers must provide coaching and just-in-time tutorials during the projects. It is difficult to know how to personalize the quantity and quality of each, but we provide some guidance here.

How can a teacher personalize the quantity of coaching and tutoring?

Some students need more support for learning than others—more coaching, more demonstrations, more practice with feedback. A teacher has three options. First, if your school has an LMS with tutorials on all the new content, the teacher can cue students as to when to use them, and the tutorials provide the quantity of demonstrations and practice needed by each student to reach mastery. Alternatively, teachers can try to provide all the coaching and tutoring themselves, which is obviously a large burden. Finally, the students can provide each other with the amount of support they need. If a teacher uses team-based projects and develops a collaborative culture (which is enhanced by multiyear mentoring—see principle R, page 91), the students will provide each other with more coaching and tutoring within their teams as needed and can go to the teacher if they need more help. If the students have individual projects, the teacher can have students work on them in a common area, and encourage the students to go to each other first when they need to learn something new and ask the teacher as a last resort. Research shows that such peer assistance benefits the student giving help as well as the one receiving it (Goodlad & Hirst, 1989; Gordon, 2005; Topping & Ehly, 1998).

How can a teacher personalize the quality of coaching and tutoring?

Students differ in many ways: their interests, how loud or quiet they prefer the learning environment, how much motivational support they need, whether they are more comfortable with abstract or concrete thinking, whether they prefer working with someone else or alone, and much more. To the extent that coaching and tutoring take such individual differences into account, their quality will improve. Doing so requires the teacher to know each student well. But with self-directed learning, it is also important for the teacher to help individual students know their own preferences well. This teaches students to understand how they learn best and to advocate for the support they need. It is difficult but helpful to relate the demonstrations and practice to the student's interests and tailor them to the student's preferences. Eventually, intelligent tutoring systems will be developed to learn such things about each student and personalize the coaching and tutoring effectively.

Personalized Assessment

Personalizing assessment empowers and motivates students. Here are a few questions your team should consider.

Who should assess the student?

In most cases, the teacher will assess each student. But there are considerable benefits to having students assess themselves as well. It develops an important life skill, empowers the student, and often provides a deeper understanding of the content. Similarly, there are benefits to peer assessment. It typically enhances the learning of both students, and the feedback provided is usually more thorough (and personalized) than the teacher can afford to give to every student. If your school has an LMS with good tutorials, it can be designed to provide assessment with highly personalized feedback. Finally, teachers might consider using outside experts to assess final products or presentations for projects. This provides a level of authenticity that can be motivating for students.

What format should the assessment take?

Different students can benefit from different formats for assessment. Options include live performances, written reports, video reports, material products, software, and much more. Helping students to choose their formats empowers students and enhances their motivation.

Personalized Reflection

Having students reflect on their project experiences is one of the most powerful and underused instructional strategies. Here are a few questions for your team to consider.

How can teachers personalize reflection on the way the project was conducted?

Teachers can personalize the timing of the reflection by doing it during the project, at the end of the project, or both. They can personalize the format of the reflection by having it done in writing or through discussion, or a combination of the two. And they can personalize the participants by having it done individually, as a team, or in a large group with several teams. Of course, the points of reflection—often guided by a rubric—can also be personalized.

How can teachers personalize reflection on the learning that occurred?

Teachers can similarly personalize the timing, format, participants, and points of reflection on learning. The points of reflection could address the questions, What were the most important things you learned? How good was the learning process? How could it have been better?

Personal Learning Plans

When conceptualizing your approach to personalized learning plans, there are several questions your team should consider.

What should a PLP be like?

We encourage teachers to help students develop two kinds of personal learning plans: long-term and short-term. *Long-term PLPs* should identify one or more career or life goals in which the student is interested and the major categories of competencies that will help the student achieve those goals. Such a PLP greatly enhances the student's motivation to learn and encourages self-direction and feelings of purpose in life (see Motivational Benefits of Long-Term Planning). A long-term plan can be started at a younger age than you might expect, but students should be expected and encouraged to change their long-term plans as they mature.

> According to the KnowledgeWorks Foundation (2019), for Kelly Culpepper, "a second-grade teacher at Douglas Elementary in Trenton, South Carolina, [the act of] encouraging her students to think about why they come to school each day was about encouraging them to make connections with what they're learning and what they hope for their futures. . . . 'It was like a light bulb came on,' said Culpepper. 'Their eyes began to open. They began to brainstorm what they wanted their lives to look like.'"

Motivational Benefits of Long-Term Planning

Learner-Centered Instruction

Short-term PLPs should identify the state standards and learning targets that each student is to work on next, based on requirements, his or her long-term PLP, and other interests. Short-term PLPs should also specify the projects that each student will use to achieve those standards and learning targets. These plans should identify any teammates they will have for each project, as well as any differences in roles the students may have in a project. Finally, short-term PLPs should specify such project features as milestones, timeline, resources, deliverables, evaluation processes, and reflection processes for each project. The short-term PLP is often called a *learning contract* (Anderson, Boud, & Sampson, 1996). A similar tool is called a *playlist*, which is a series of activities focused on specific content matched to student needs and interests (Herold, 2017a; Putman, 2018).

> PLPs are a central aspect of the Innovation Zone (iZone) supported by the New York City Department of Education and of the Metropolitan School District of Warren Township in Indianapolis.

PLPs in Public Schools

How should teachers help each student to develop a PLP?

Typically, each teacher should meet one-on-one with all his or her students to help them develop their PLPs. For the long-term PLP, it would be wise to check in with each student once a year to see if anything has changed and possibly to encourage the student to think about a different career or long-term goal, based on teacher knowledge of the student's interests and talents. Try to get students to "dream big" in this process. Guide them to think about and list broad categories of competencies that will help them achieve their goals. Also, help the student reflect on his or her progress toward continuing goals.

For the short-term PLP, the teacher should meet with each student just prior to the beginning of the projects. Timing will vary depending on the developmental level (age) of the student. Younger students will have shorter projects and may not have any restrictions on start or end dates, whereas older students will have longer projects that may be constrained to start at the beginning of a new project period. The teacher should give the student as much responsibility as he or she can handle for studying and choosing the state standards and learning targets, choosing or designing the projects, and planning the projects (milestones, timelines, resources, and so on). The teacher will need to offer more guidance to younger students, with the goal that they gradually need less and less guidance. It is likely that technological tools will eventually be developed to make this process quicker and easier for the teacher and students.

You can find more information about personalized learning in various other resources (see, for example, DiMartino, Clarke, & Wolk, 2003; Jenkins & Keefe, 2002; Keefe, 2000, 2007, 2008; Wolf, 2010; Yonezawa et al., 2012).

Principle H: Collaborative Learning

The two most common kinds of collaborative learning are team-based learning and peer assistance.

Team-Based Learning

The following are a few questions to consider related to team-based learning.

 When should team-based learning be used?

Because team-based learning should be the norm, it may be more helpful to talk about when it should not be used. The reasons are mostly logistical, as demonstrated in the following scenarios.

- The teacher has no choice but to use the outcome of the project (a final product or performance) to evaluate mastery of the learning targets—this is not a good situation, so try hard to avoid it.

- There are no other students interested in the same project at the same time.

- There is good reason not to team the eligible students with each other.

- The nature of the project does not lend itself well to a team (as with many Montessori activities; Montessori, 1964).

- The student prefers working alone. However, if that student needs to develop social and emotional skills, keep individual projects to a minimum.

Teachers may think of other reasons.

How should teammate selection be done?

The selection of teammates should be done carefully. Most importantly, the students should be interested in the same project at the same time. This enhances motivation. Other criteria for selection include the following.

- Students have not worked a lot with each other already.

- Students are different from each other in many ways (race, ethnicity, gender, socioeconomic status, speed of learning, and so on).

- Students have complementary working styles.

- Students do not have strong personality conflicts.

- One student does not tend to dominate the others.

How should team-based learning be monitored?

Teachers must monitor the conduct of the teams often to ensure teammates are working well together. When appropriate, teachers should provide feedback, coaching, or even tutoring on how to work well together as a team. It helps for students to establish team norms at the outset. Among these should be the commitment of every team member to be responsible for their teammates' learning as well as their own learning. It also helps to have all teammates periodically reflect together on their performance as a team. Team self-reflection and self-evaluation are important team behaviors. Reflection is a key opportunity for teachers to foster social and emotional skills.

Peer Assistance

Your team can consider a similar set of questions regarding peer assistance.

When should teachers use peer assistance?

Peer assistance is defined as any help one student provides to another outside of a teaming situation. Thus, it is distinct from team-based learning, and it should be used when students are not working in teams, which is mostly for individual projects. The general rule is that the classroom and school culture should encourage all students to assist peers whenever requested or needed. Mostly, students should provide peer assistance when a peer seeks it out, but occasionally it is good for a student to offer help when not solicited, if it seems like help would be appreciated.

How should teachers use peer assistance?

Teachers can cultivate an environment that promotes peer assistance. First, teachers should help students set *norms* for peer assistance. This should include the expectation that a student who needs assistance goes to the internet or another student first and only asks the teacher as a last resort. Second, teachers should observe peer assistance whenever possible to provide feedback, coaching, or even tutoring on how to provide good assistance. Third, teachers can encourage students to periodically *self-reflect* and *self-evaluate* on the ways they have assisted their peers. Finally, teachers can establish routines around peer assistance, such as teaching students how to ask for help, how to recognize who is available or a good choice for help, when and how to say no to a request for help (if in the middle of an activity that requires concentration), and so forth.

Learner-Centered Instruction

School-Level and District-Level Considerations

In an individual school within a district or even in an individual classroom within a school, a teacher can implement some aspects of learner-centered instruction (Anderson, 1990). However, in many ways, a teacher and students will be much better off if you implement both learning by doing and instructional support on the school or even district level.

Q&A

Q   **What changes should be made on the school level or district level for learner-centered instruction?**

Some school-level changes include the following.

- **Replace courses with projects** and just-in-time tutorials as the vehicles for learning and instruction. This could be done for the whole school building if it is small, or for a school-within-the-building for a large school (see Principle U: Small School Size, page 104).

- **Decide whether to have project periods**, and if so, whether they should be determined by each classroom (which gives more flexibility) or by each developmental level or even for the whole school (which allows students to partner on projects across classrooms, among other advantages).

- **Establish some schoolwide structures** and procedures for planning, conducting, ending, and displaying projects. Students particularly like to have the products of their projects displayed outside their classroom.

- **Create multi-age classrooms** (studios) for multi-year mentoring (see principle R, page 91).

- **Develop schoolwide instruction** for students on how to manage projects, collaborate with teammates, and support their teammates' learning.

- **Form collaborative teams for teachers** on the same developmental level to improve their performance in their new roles for learner-centered instruction (see Principle M: Teacher as Guide, page 72).

- **Only implement PLPs schoolwide or districtwide.** PLPs are only useful if you personalize learning through learning-by-doing and self-directed learning, an approach best done schoolwide and even districtwide. It is helpful to have a standard format and use a standard tool to create and update the PLPs. That should be decided by the school or district based on teacher input.

- **Procure or develop an LMS** to assist students and teachers with record keeping, planning, instruction, and assessment (see principle P, page 75). This is most cost-effective if it can be done on the district level.

The preceding list of changes can also be made at the district level by implementing them across other schools in the district. This could be done for the whole district if it is small, or for a few schools (preferably a feeder system) within a large district—perhaps using a one-grade-level-at-a-time approach (see chapter 9, step 3.2, page 174). This requires changes in many district policies, such as grading, record keeping, and much more.

What advantages are there to making these changes on the school level or district level?

There are significant advantages to implementing personalized, collaborative, project-based learning schoolwide and districtwide. Advantages of schoolwide implementation include the following.

- It will be easier for all teachers, because other teachers at each developmental level can help find, adapt, or design projects, tutorials, personalized-learning resources, collaborative-learning resources, special needs resources, and guidelines for students to develop their own projects.

- It will be easier for teachers because the students who enter their classrooms will already have experience managing projects, collaborating with teammates, and supporting their teammates' learning, which reduces the need for the teacher to teach or coach them in how to do those things.

- It will be easier for students because they will have already gone through the difficult process of transitioning from teacher-centered to learner-centered instruction, complete with its demands for more project-management skills, collaboration skills, and peer tutoring skills, as well as a different mindset about education, including a more active learning orientation.

- If your school changes from a course structure to a project structure for organizing the learning process, it will be easier for each teacher to implement project-based learning.

Advantages of districtwide implementation include:

- Teachers will have even more teachers at their level to collaborate on finding, adapting, or designing projects, tutorials, and such.

- Students will have less difficulty adjusting to whichever school they attend next in the district. This is important, because it is frustrating for students to go back to teacher-centered education after they have adjusted to PCBE.

- Districtwide adoption of PBL can eliminate the barriers to replacing courses with projects, making the new system all that more effective and sustainable.

Summary

This chapter described four principles for learner-centered instruction that are universally helpful for maximizing student learning.

Principle E: Learning by doing

Principle F: Instructional support

Principle G: Personalized learning

Principle H: Collaborative learning

It then offered detailed guidelines to help your team develop part of your shared ideal vision for your classrooms, school, and district.

Restructured Curriculum

CHAPTER 3

Core Ideas
1. Competency-Based Education
2. Learner-Centered Instruction
3. Restructured Curriculum
4. New Roles
5. A Nurturing Culture
6. New Organizational Structures

Principles
I. Relevance to students' current and future lives
J. Whole-child education
K. Balance of universal content and individual strengths
L. Sound progressions in content

This chapter discusses four principles for PCBE related to a restructured curriculum, as shown in the preceding map. It then offers detailed guidance to help your team develop more of your shared vision for your classrooms, school, and district. We do not offer these principles and guidelines as a blueprint for what you should do. Rather, we offer them to assist your team as you engage in rich discussions and collaborations to design an ideal PCBE system in your unique context.

Principles for Restructured Curriculum

Your team needs to decide what content to offer to best meet your students' needs in the post-industrial, digital age (see step 2.3 in chapter 10, page 200). We use the term *content* to refer to everything that students should learn, including knowledge, understandings, skills, higher-order thinking skills, dispositions, social-emotional learning, self-direction skills, character development, and so forth. What students need to learn has been changing dramatically as we evolve deeper into the digital age, for reasons noted in the introduction (page 1).

Your team will need to make decisions about two major aspects of content: (1) what content should be selected to offer to students and (2) what progressions in that content will best promote learning. These are often called *scope and sequence*. Three of the four principles for restructured curriculum relate to selection of content, while the fourth addresses progressions in that content.

Principle I: Relevance to students' current and future lives

Principle J: Whole-child education

Principle K: Balance of universal content and individual strengths

Principle L: Sound progressions in content

These principles are highly interrelated and interdependent with each other and with the principles for competency-based education and learner-centered instruction. The following is an introduction to each of these principles.

Principle I: Relevance to Students' Current and Future Lives

We suggest that the most important criterion for deciding what students learn should be relevance to students' current and future lives—what they need to learn to become happy, healthy, caring, successful adults who contribute to their communities in an unpredictable, increasingly high-tech future. Much of what is currently taught is not relevant or useful for most students' lives. Researchers and thought leaders have done important work over the past thirty years to redefine what is important, including the Alan Collins (2017), Next Generation Learning Challenges' MyWays Framework (Lash & Belfiore, 2017), the Partnership for 21st Century Skills (n.d.), David Perkins (2014), and Marc Prensky (2016), U.S. Department of Labor's SCANS Report (Secretary's Commission on Achieving Necessary Skills, 1991), Tony Wagner (2012), and the William and Flora Hewlett Foundation (Watkins, Peterson, & Mehta, 2018). Summaries of their work appear in appendix A (page 209).

In effect, these and other educational experts are proposing that content selection should focus on helping each student find his or her passion and cultivate the individual talents to pursue that passion (Fried, 2001) and to make the world a better place. Other common themes include authentic tasks, interdisciplinary content, metacognitive skills, and social-emotional learning. These require more than piecemeal changes to the content—more than just adding some new courses. They require a fundamental change—a restructuring of the curriculum.

At present, it would be difficult for most classrooms, schools, and even districts to completely transform to the kind of content described by Collins (2017) or Prensky (2016), especially given the current climate of state standards and high-stakes testing. For now, we recommend your team consider a step toward that goal that is still centered on using significant projects as the vehicle for acquiring all content, including community-based or service-learning projects.

Principle J: Whole-Child Education

There is strong evidence that students benefit greatly from education that addresses all aspects of human development: social, emotional, identity, physical, psychological, and ethical, as well as cognitive. Social and emotional development have been shown to improve student outcomes (Durlak, Weissberg, Dymnicki, Taylor, & Schellinger, 2011; Mahoney, Durlak, & Weissberg, 2018; Mahoney & Weissberg, 2018; Rebora, 2018; Stone-McCown & McCormick, 1999). Also, social development is important for the knowledge-work economy in which teamwork is crucial, as well as success in one's family and social life. Daniel Goleman (1995, 1998) presented convincing evidence that emotional intelligence is more important to a person's success in life than intellectual intelligence. *Identity development*, a stage of child development (Erikson, 1968), is crucial for forming a shared identity with others, which is important to stability in many areas as an adult.

Physical health is important to prevent obesity and reduce sickness, which enhances quality of life and workplace productivity. Psychological health is important for reducing suicide and crime rates, child and spousal abuse, drug use, and teen pregnancies, not to mention for improving one's quality of life. Ethical development is important for reducing corruption and crime and generally improving the quality of life. And character development (see Example of a Character Development Program), which overlaps with several of the other categories, is important for both the individual's happiness and success in life and the community's health and well-being (Lickona, 1991).

While some argue that schools should not be responsible for all these aspects of child development, there are many children for whom family, community, or religion do not fulfill these needs, which results in suffering for individuals and degradation of their communities. Schools like the Milton Hershey School show that it is possible to provide whole-child education with current school resources (see Milton Hershey School, page 61). Also, McPartland and Nettles (1991) describe how community adults can serve as advocates or mentors for middle school students.

Example of a Character Development Program

According to Chris Sturgis and Tom Vander Ark (2018), the best character development program in the United States is Valor Compass. They characterize it as a "comprehensive approach to helping students building their capacity to know and manage their social and emotional lives in a community and in relationship to their learning" (Sturgis & Vander Ark, 2018). The compass (see figure 3.1, page 60) has four directions, corresponding to growth in body, mind, heart, and spirit.

- **Body:** Aligned actions (based on determination and integrity)
- **Mind:** Sharp minds (based on curiosity and diversity)
- **Heart:** Big heart (based on courage and kindness)
- **Spirit:** Noble purpose (based on joy and identity)

continued

These culminate in a fifth, **True North** (personal agency).

Sturgis and Vander Ark state, "For people trying to understand personalized and competency-based learning, Valor is a wonderful example of student agency in its fullest sense rather than the narrow focus on choice that we see in most schools." They continue, "At the heart of the Valor model is an advisory system that starts with a morning meeting of students in a circle of support as everyone works the Compass" (Sturgis & Vander Ark, 2018). Students spend ninety minutes per week in Circle, which is facilitated to create a safe place with carefully designed processes and protocols used by students and adults to check in, build trust, and allow people to fully be themselves. Circle is designed to:

- identify early warning indicators and check community "vital signs"

- reinforce and recognize community commitments

- create a safe, intentional space for individual, relational, and communal growth

- develop high trust via hierarchy flattening

Badges are organized around the Compass habits with a developmental progression from fifth to twelfth grade.

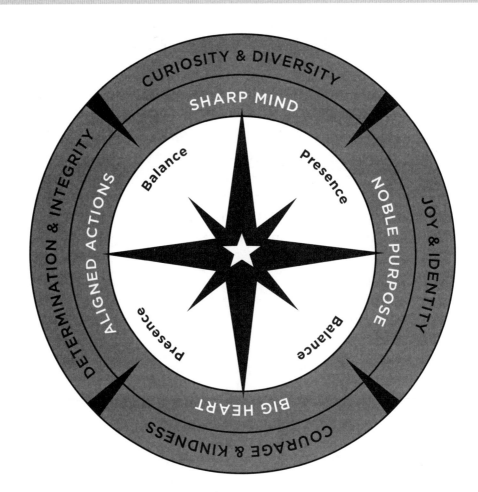

Source: © 2019 by Valor Collegiate Academy. Used with permission.

Figure 3.1: The Valor Compass.

> "Our whole-child approach to education aims to help our students break the cycle of poverty. With more than 100 years of experience . . . we have evolved and grown to help students overcome poverty's impact, including by introducing social-emotional-learning curriculum and providing physical and behavioral health services on our campus." (P. Gurt, personal communication, January 20, 2019).
>
> —*Pete Gurt, president of Milton Hershey School, a tuition-free private boarding school serving low-income students*

Milton Hershey School

Principle K: Balance of Universal Content and Individual Strengths

There is some content that all students should learn: some basic skills, many higher-order thinking skills, self-direction skills, interpersonal skills, emotional development, civic skills and understandings, parenting skills, some character traits, and more. We call this *universal content* or *universal learning targets*, and people have differing opinions on what content should be universal (mastered by all students). There are several ideas we would like to highlight as you consider what all your students should learn.

- Much of what is currently mandated for all children to learn (the Common Core or your state's standards) may not actually be important for *all* your students to learn.

- Content that is truly important for all children will change over time and even from one community to another at any given time.

- Students' future lives will be significantly improved to the extent that you are able to cultivate their individual strengths and talents, including those which are not part of the universal content, because increasing diversity of careers in the economy requires that different students be prepared differently—all students should not be learning all the same things.

Among all the content that is relevant to students' current and future lives, some will be universally relevant to all students, and some will not. Relevance is not an all-or-nothing issue; there are degrees of relevance. Perhaps some lower-relevance universal content should be replaced by higher-relevance individual content. We recommend that your team considers state and national core curricula as an imperfect suggestion for what is truly important for *all* your students to learn. Your content may be restricted by state standards now, but only if you and other educators think in the ideal about universal content will there be any hope of eventually changing the requirements to better meet your students' needs.

We also suggest that, in the ideal, the universal content you decide upon ideally takes up only about half the average student's learning time each day—more than half for younger students but less than half for older students—and that the remainder of their learning time is devoted to cultivating each student's individual strengths, interests, and talents. Much of what is involved in cultivating individual talents lies in exposing students to different endeavors (music, art, sports, writing, mathematical thinking, and so forth). Howard Gardner's (2011) different kinds of intelligence might be a useful frame for thinking about kinds of talents to explore.

Principle L: Sound Progressions in Content

Whatever content you select, your team should organize it around sound progressions, so that learning is neither too difficult nor too easy for each student. For example, if you use Prensky's (2016) suggestions, you would design progressions within each of the four major pillars: effective accomplishing, thinking, relating, and action. The Global Future Education Foundation provides support for designing such a curriculum. Or if you use the MyWays suggestions for content, you would design progressions within each of the twenty subcategories. The MyWays framework is being used by a growing number of schools and school districts across the country to redefine student success and transform learning to better prepare students for the demands of 21st century life and careers. Next Gen Learning Challenges (MyWays' nonprofit developer) has created a set of tools and services to support educators and communities in the use of that framework.

To design sound progressions, we recommend using the *simplifying conditions method* (Reigeluth, 2007). It entails taking a complex task, such as critical thinking, and identifying versions of that task that are simpler than other versions, such as thinking critically about a list of recommendations to improve one's school, which is simpler than thinking critically about recommendations to improve one's community. This helps teachers to identify conditions that make some versions of the task or competency (for example, critical thinking) simpler than others (such as the number of issues to take into consideration for a given version of critical thinking). Note that a given version of a task (in this case, thinking critically about recommendations to improve one's school) may be used in many diverse individual cases (such as making it safer, making the food healthier, or offering more learning options), which can be chosen based on the student's interests and needs. You then design progressions of the various versions, ranging from simple to complex versions. For more guidance about how to do this, see Reigeluth (1999).

On a more micro level, Marzano (2010; Marzano et al., 2017) offers guidance for designing a proficiency scale for each essential topic (also called a *measurement topic*). More detailed guidance on selecting and sequencing the content is provided in the corresponding Detailed Guidance sections (I, J, K, and L) in the remainder of this chapter.

Detailed Guidance for Restructured Curriculum

We recommend that you read all the sections titled Principles in chapters 1 through 6 before reading the Detailed Guidance section in any of those chapters, because the principles are so interrelated and interdependent that it is crucial to understand the big picture before getting into specific details. Any effort to move to PCBE that focuses on one core idea without making changes in other core ideas is likely to fail. Please keep in mind that we use the term *content* to refer to everything that students should learn, including knowledge, understandings, competencies, higher-order thinking skills, dispositions, emotional development, and so forth.

Classroom-Level Considerations

To design a restructured curriculum at the classroom level, your team should work on two scopes: the ideal (long-term) and the currently feasible (short-term). Deciding on the ideal (see step 2.1 in chapter 10, page 196) guides you in strategically deciding among options that are currently feasible. Make decisions about curriculum for the whole system, because the curriculum should fit seamlessly as students move from one level to another. However, your change team only needs to make broad decisions about curriculum. Task forces can later work out the details for each level (as described in step 2.3 in chapter 10, page 200).

Principle I: Relevance to Students' Current and Future Lives

This principle is one of the factors your team should consider when restructuring curriculum. The first three questions in the following set will help you envision your ideal content, while the final question acknowledges you may encounter constraints that limit what is currently feasible.

How will we decide what content students should learn?

We suggest that what is best for the student is most important—and best for the student is relevance to their current and future lives. But also important is what is best for the family, the community, the country, and the world. State standards may or may not be what's best for students or the larger groups to which they belong. Don't feel constrained by such standards. Think in the ideal for now.

Which of the content categories referenced in the overview of principle I (page 58) would best serve the needs of our students, their families, community, country, and the world?

Those content categories include the 21st Century Learning Framework, Wagner's seven survival skills, the topics addressed by Perkins, the six competencies identified by the Deeper Learning Initiative, elements of Collins's passion-based curriculum, and the competencies outlined by MyWays. Please refer to the descriptions of these content categories in appendix A (page 209). You may find others that would be even more helpful.

Educators increasingly recognize that the academic disciplines (mainly math, English, science, and social studies) should not be the sole guides for content selection (Collins, 2017; Prensky, 2016; Wagner, 2012; Wagner & Dintersmith, 2015). Try to think in the ideal again. If there was no school system and you were starting from scratch with your own child, what categories of content would you choose?

How much choice should teachers give to individual students to select their content (learning targets)?

Recognize that as students grow, they should be given increasingly greater choice, and some students may be ready for more choice sooner than others. Although choice empowers and motivates students, some students of any age may make poor decisions. Teachers can actively improve student thinking about where they are and what they need to learn by maintaining involvement in the student choice process (for example, allowing choice while providing feedback on the process).

Now that we've envisioned the ideal, what constraints is our system under?

As part of step 2.3 in chapter 10 (page 200), your team should make a list of all the major constraints that affect your decisions about what to teach, such as high-stakes tests or other curriculum requirements. Then think about what would be needed to eliminate each constraint. Could any of those things be done in the short run? If so, make note of that and remove the constraint from your list. Next, make decisions about what universal content to teach that take the remaining constraints into account. You may find the Common Core, your state's standards, the Marzano Resources Critical Concepts (Simms, 2016), MyWays, or other lists of content helpful in this process. Finally, make a list of constraints that you could work on to remove over time and think about actions you could eventually take for each.

Principle J: Whole-Child Education

What areas are important to teach besides academics?

Consider some of the following areas:

- Three additional areas described by Prensky (2016)—relating effectively, acting effectively, and accomplishing effectively

- Fifteen additional competencies described by MyWays—five in the area of habits of success, five in creative know-how, and five in wayfinding abilities

- Alan Collins's (2017) additional areas of finance, health, economics, the environment, law, strategic thinking, creative thinking, social-emotional learning, and much more

- Additional areas described earlier in this chapter or proposed by others

Your team should devote considerable time to making this decision, and your subsequent task forces (see step 2.3, chapter 10, page 200) should devote considerable time to working out the details.

What curricula or resources are available for each of these areas?

Fortunately, the growing awareness of the importance of social and emotional skills has led to the development of a host of curriculum resources. Look for tools that are research-based. For example, Linda Darling-Hammond and Channa Cook-Harvey (2018) wrote a report for the Learning Policy Institute that examined how schools can use effective, research-based practices to create settings in which students' healthy growth and development are central to the design of classrooms and the school as a whole. They describe key findings from the sciences of learning and development, the school conditions and practices that should derive from these sciences, and the policies that could support those conditions and practices on a wide scale. They also published a book that offers insights on whole-child education from the Comer School Development Program (Darling-Hammond, Cook-Harvey, Flook, Gardner, & Melnick, 2018).

Association for Supervision and Curriculum Development (ASCD) has a whole-child initiative that includes tools for assessing and improving your school's efforts at addressing the needs of the whole child (ascd.org/whole-child.aspx). Also, the Collaborative for Academic, Social, and Emotional Learning (CASEL) helps in many ways to make evidence-based social and emotional learning an integral part of education from preschool through high school. It has created a guide (casel.org/guide) that provides a systematic framework for identifying and evaluating well-designed, evidence-based social-emotional learning (SEL) programs with potential for broad dissemination to schools across the United States. The guide also shares best-practice guidelines for district and school teams on how to select and implement SEL programs. Other resources include *All Learning Is Social and Emotional: Helping Students Develop Essential Skills for the Classroom and Beyond* (Frey, Fisher, & Smith, 2019), *Motivating and Inspiring Students: Strategies to Awaken the Learner* (Marzano, Scott, Boogren, & Newcomb, 2017), and resources from Transforming Education (www.transformingeducation.org/resources/for-educators). It would benefit your team to consult these and similar resources as you consider whole-child education.

How can one help the whole child to develop?

It is not easy to help every child develop socially, emotionally, physically (including health), psychologically, and ethically, in addition to cognitively. A group called Educate the Whole Child (n.d.) recommends five kinds of learning that students should experience each day, if possible.

1. Cognitive-intellectual activity, associated with the left brain

2. Creative-intuitive activity (the arts), associated with the right brain

3. Structured physical movement and unstructured, self-directed play

4. Handwork and making things that can be useful

5. Engagement with nature and community

Educate the Whole Child advocates place-based education that uses real-world projects as the vehicles for learning. Their website (www.educatethewholechild.org) contains links to schools that are doing whole-child education.

The Association for Supervision and Curriculum Development also offers a Whole Child approach which they describe as "an effort to transition from a focus on narrowly defined academic achievement to one that promotes the long-term development and success of all children." They offer advice about what to teach in five categories: healthy, safe, engaged, supported, and challenged (see www .ascd.org/whole-child.aspx).

Choice Schools Associates offers a list of 14 Easy Ways to Create the Whole Child Approach in Your Classroom (choiceschools.com/14-easy-ways-create -whole-child-approach-classroom/).

Nine Competencies for Teaching Empathy (Borba, 2018) is one of several useful articles in a special issue of *Educational Leadership* titled "The Promise of Social-Emotional Learning."

The Devereux Center for Resilient Children (centerforresilientchildren.org) has developed a "student-strengths assessment," a version of which is used by the Urban Assembly charter school network.

CASEL (Collaborative for Academic, Social, and Emotional Learning; schoolguide .casel.org) offers some guidance about how to start an SEL program.

Principle K: Balance of Universal Content and Individual Strengths

Q How much of a student's time should be devoted to mastering universal content versus cultivating their individual strengths and talents?

In most schools today, far too little time is devoted to cultivating students' individual strengths and talents. To address this, start by thinking about the ideal amount of time for students at each developmental level to spend on mastering universal content and the percentage of the students' time that should ideally be reserved for cultivating individual strengths and talents. Don't try to define the universal content yet, just identify a portion of the students' time to devote to their individual strengths and talents—for each developmental level. Then try to decide how close you can feasibly get to that ideal now, again as a percentage of the student's time. Finally, plan what you would have to do to get closer to your ideal over time, make note of those ideas, and set a target date for when you could start to enact each.

Q What content should be universal for each developmental level?

Review your selection of currently feasible content, given state requirements and tests, and compare that to the minimum amount of time your teachers could currently devote to universal content for each developmental level. Try to be creative in finding time for students to work on cultivating their individual strengths and talents. For example, they could be motivated to work on these outside of school (evenings, weekends, and even vacations), and perhaps you could harness technology to give students easy access to the resources they need. Then make a final short-term decision about what content should be universal for each developmental level—stated without much detail for now, more like standards than learning targets.

Principle L: Sound Progressions in Content

Once your team has decided what to teach, teacher task forces (see step 2.3, chapter 10, page 200) need to decide on details and progressions of that content. Competencies and understandings build on each other, so students learn more easily and retain what they have learned longer when the content is sequenced appropriately. So, how can your task forces create effective progressions (sequences of content)? Again, it is helpful to think in the ideal first for a long-term target (see step 2.1, chapter 10, page 196), and then compromise as needed (see step 2.3, page 200) to meet practical constraints for your first implementation.

As experts in their subject areas, teachers have an informed sense of what content needs to come first and what needs to be next. However, it is helpful to understand that different categories of content may have different kinds of progressions. Since skills, understandings, and dispositions are such different kinds of learning, sound progressions are based on different considerations for each. Also, your change team may choose to use integrated, thematic, interdisciplinary categories such as those offered by Prensky (2016; thinking effectively, acting effectively, and relating effectively, all in the service of accomplishing effectively), each of which requires its own sound progressions.

It is beyond the scope of this book to offer much guidance about this, but the following are a few questions and suggestions for you and your task forces to consider when creating sound progressions for competencies, understandings, and dispositions.

What is the basis for sound progressions for skills?

Because skills entail performing tasks, it is important to understand that all tasks have a range of versions from relatively simple to complex. So, a skill like problem solving has a range of versions from simple to complex. A challenge for your task forces is to identify the conditions that distinguish different versions of the task from one another, so they can design a sequence that moves from simpler to more complex versions in steps of appropriate size for their students (to challenge but not overwhelm them). For more about how to do this, see Reigeluth (1999).

What is the basis for sound progressions for understandings (principles and concepts)?

Understandings entail the ability to see relationships (cognitive links), so one must understand how those relationships build on each other. Cause-effect relationships can be broad and inclusive (such as the law of supply and demand in economics), or they can be narrow and specific (such as principles related to marginal costs and marginal revenues in economics). Similarly, concepts can be broad and inclusive (like mammal) and they can be narrow and specific (like polar bear and Siberian tiger). Research has shown that students learn more easily, retain what they have learned longer, and transfer what they have learned better if they learn broader and more inclusive principles and concepts before narrower and more specific ones (Ausubel, 1968).

What is the basis for sound progressions for dispositions?

Because dispositions involve holding attitudes and values that typically lie on a continuum, a sound progression will help a student to move in relatively small steps from their current position on the continuum to the preferable position. It is also helpful to recognize that dispositions are often interrelated, so movement in one disposition may be aided by movement in other dispositions.

For further guidance, we encourage your task forces to consult Marzano's advice for designing a proficiency progression for measurement topics or learning targets (for example, Marzano, 2010; Marzano et al., 2017). Curriculum and standards developers, as well as various professional associations, have created sequences that they believe are good for students. We encourage your task forces to consider those sequences for some general guidance while making these decisions as well.

School-Level and District-Level Considerations

As an individual school within a district or even an individual classroom within a school, you can implement some aspects of a restructured curriculum. However, teachers and their students will be much better off if the entire school or district restructures its curriculum.

What changes should be made on the school level or district level for restructured curriculum?

Some school-level changes include the following.

- **Align curricula across classrooms** (including progressions in the various curricular areas), so that when students move to a new classroom, they can continue with the same curriculum. Whatever changes you make must be made schoolwide, or at least in all classrooms that will share the same students, sometimes called *families, academies, schools-within-the-school,* or *schools-within-the-building.*

- **Create collaborative opportunities for teachers** working with students on the same developmental level to help each other select and sequence (align) their content.

- **Create collaborative opportunities for teachers** working with students of *contiguous* developmental levels to align their scope and sequence.

- **Develop policies and procedures** for outside experts coming into the school and for students getting out into the community for projects.

- **Develop policies for teachers to secure the resources** that students will need for their projects.

For district-level changes, the preceding list also applies—for all schools into which your school's students will go and from which your students will come. This could be done for the whole district if it is small, or for a few schools (preferably a complete feeder system) for a large district—perhaps using a one-grade-level-at-a-time approach (see step 3.2, chapter 10, page 204).

What advantages are there to making these changes on the school level or district level?

While your team can implement the new curriculum in a single classroom, there are advantages to implementing it schoolwide and districtwide. Advantages of schoolwide implementation of a new curriculum include the following.

- It will be easier for teachers to transition because other teachers at each level can help select and sequence the content.

- It will be easier for teachers because the students who enter their classrooms will have experience with the curriculum.

- It will be easier for students because they will already be familiar with curricular areas that are not in the current (Education 2.0) curriculum.

Advantages of districtwide implementation of a new curriculum include the following.

- It will increase the pool of teachers at the same level who can help one another to select and sequence the content.

- Students will have less difficulty adjusting in whatever school they go to next in the district.

What if we cannot make changes on the school or district level for restructured curriculum?

You can still move toward an ideal selection and sequence of content by identifying content you think your students should have access to, if there were enough time. By switching to PCBE, you may find that there is time for faster learners to address some of that content after they have mastered all the content that will be expected of them by subsequent classrooms and schools.

What changes should be made on the school or district level to address the needs of the whole child?

While each educator can and does make a difference, many impactful factors are systemic and thus must be addressed at the school and district levels. A great place to start is with discipline policies. *Lost at School: Why Our Kids With Behavioral Challenges Are Falling Through the Cracks and How We Can Help Them* by Ross Greene (2014) is one resource that can help school and district leaders rethink their approach to school discipline in a manner that uncovers root causes of behavior issues, encourages family involvement, and promotes the development of personal responsibility, empathy, and self-evaluation. A second important step is to look closely at school and district culture to enhance every child's sense of belonging and find ways to ensure alignment with the social, emotional, and developmental needs of students. A third step is for schools and districts to reach out to parents and community partners to help address the physical and emotional health and wellness needs of students.

 What changes should be made on the school level or district level for balancing universal content with cultivating individual strengths and talents?

While you could decide on the best balance of universal content and individual strengths on the classroom level, you should try to reach consensus schoolwide and districtwide, because this will considerably ease student transitions from one developmental level to another and one school to another. It will also make it easier for teachers on the same level to collaborate on their content offerings—especially optional offerings to cultivate individual strengths and talents.

Summary

This chapter described four principles for restructured curriculum that are universally helpful for maximizing student learning and meeting students' needs.

Principle I: Relevance to students' current and future lives

Principle J: Whole-child education

Principle K: Balance of universal content and cultivation of individual strengths

Principle L: Sound progressions in content

It then offered detailed guidelines to help your team develop part of your shared ideal vision for your classrooms, school, and district.

New Roles

CHAPTER 4

Core Ideas
1. Competency-Based Education
2. Learner-Centered Instruction
3. Restructured Curriculum
4. New Roles
5. A Nurturing Culture
6. New Organizational Structures

Principles

M. Teacher as guide

N. Self-directed student

O. Parent as partner

P. Technology as a tool for students

This chapter discusses four principles for PCBE related to new roles, as shown in the preceding map. It then offers detailed guidance to help your team develop more of your shared vision for your classrooms, school, and district. We do not offer these principles and guidelines as a blueprint for what you should do. Rather, we offer them to assist your team as you engage in rich discussions and collaborations to design an ideal PCBE system in your unique context.

Principles for New Roles

To succeed, competency-based education requires learner-centered instruction, which in turn requires changes in roles for it to succeed. Learning by doing and personalized learning require the student to be more active and self-directed, which means the teacher needs to be more of a guide on the side, rather than the sage on the stage. Four principles for new roles have strong research support.

> Principle M: Teacher as guide
>
> Principle N: Self-directed student
>
> Principle O: Parent as partner
>
> Principle P: Technology as a tool for students

These principles are highly interrelated and interdependent with each other and with the principles for competency-based education and learner-centered instruction. The following is an introduction to each of these principles.

Principle M: Teacher as Guide

The teacher's role must change dramatically to effectively implement PCBE. Your team should consider the following five roles for teachers.

1. Mentor

2. Designer (or curator)

3. Facilitator

4. Collaborator and consultor

5. Learner

Mentor

First, the teacher is a mentor for his or her class of perhaps twenty to thirty students—one who genuinely cares about every one of those students and is concerned with all aspects of their development (principle J, whole-child education). Part of the mentor role is helping students prepare a personal learning plan for each project period (principle G, personalized learning), which typically runs for six to twelve weeks but varies with the age of the students. This involves helping the student and parent(s) choose appropriate learning goals (academic and nonacademic, subject to standards set by the community, state, and nation) and identifying and supporting the best means for the student to achieve those goals. This PLP is a powerful tool for addressing both student needs and talents. Another part of the mentor role is to develop a classroom culture that helps each student to become ever more self-directed, responsible, and caring. Ideally, the teacher should stay with a class for several years. Mentoring the same student for several years (see principle R, page 91) allows the teacher to get to know each student well in terms of academic skill, family context, personal goals, personality, and other developmental needs. This deeper knowledge improves the quality of guidance and advice for the student's PLP. It also helps the teacher motivate students and improves the overall climate of the classroom.

Designer (or Curator)

Second, the teacher is a designer of the student learning experience, from the culture of the classroom or studio to the PLP, individual projects, just-in-time tutorials, and other student activities—or curates such resources. Curation entails selecting an array of resources from which students can choose. Teachers who have the same students for several years know them well enough to design or curate—or help them design or select (principle N, self-directed student)—work options that will be interesting to them, help them grow, and improve the culture of community that will enhance learning for all. Much of the burden of the designer role can be alleviated by the many open educational resources that are available to all educators online. Therefore, the teacher can curate a menu of quality options from which students can choose and can modify those options (or help the student modify them) as needed to best suit each student's needs and context.

Facilitator

Third, the teacher is a facilitator of the learning process, which is the notion that the teacher guides learner-centered learning rather than presenting to all students from the front of the classroom. This is a foundational difference between learner-centered and teacher-centered instruction, and at its core it entails helping the student figure out what to do rather than telling the student what to do. The teacher enhances student motivation, monitors student progress, coaches student performance, and provides personalized instruction when necessary (see Principle F: Instructional Support, page 29, and Principle G: Personalized Learning, page 30). The teacher also facilitates relationship-building among students (see Principle Q: Strong and Caring Relationships, page 90).

Collaborator and Consultor

Fourth, the teacher is a collaborator and consultor who knows the strengths and weaknesses of the other teachers in the school and collaborates with them frequently to improve teaching schoolwide. The teacher also consults and even collaborates with experts outside the school—in the district, the community, and beyond. This might range from a one-time consultation with a local electrician for a project, to a multi-year collaboration with an out-of-state ecologist about sources and effects of pollution.

Learner

Finally, the teacher is always learning with the students, about the students, from the students, and for the students. The teacher does not have all the answers, but the teacher helps students find answers and models effective learning practices. And the teacher is always learning more about how to best meet students' needs.

Principle N: Self-Directed Student

Lifelong learning is becoming essential as the pace of change continues to accelerate in the post-industrial era. This requires students to become self-directed learners. Also, while compliance was desired on assembly lines and in bureaucratic structures during the industrial age, initiative is desired today in knowledge-work contexts—and even manufacturing contexts. In the teacher-centered paradigm (Education 2.0), many students develop a passive mindset. They are aimless, at a loss as to what to do with, and how to manage, their lives. In Education 3.0, teachers help students to develop agency (Poon, 2018) by giving them voice and choice (Marzano et al., 2017; Miliband, 2006), helping them develop goals that better their world, and helping them learn how to self-regulate effectively (Desautels, 2018; Huh & Reigeluth, 2017b; Zimmerman, 2002). This can begin at the start of preschool, as it does in Montessori schools (Montessori, 1917, 1964). Self-directed learning requires development of self-direction skills, student responsibility, and student empowerment (Schunk, 1990).

- **Self-direction skills** include students' abilities to (1) plan their learning—before the learning process—including what to learn, how to learn it, and how to monitor one's own learning; (2) perform their learning—during the learning process—which requires ongoing self-assessment; and (3) reflect on their learning—after the learning process—to determine what worked well and what ought to have been done differently (Desautels, 2018; Huh & Reigeluth, 2017a, 2017b, 2017c; Zimmerman, 2002). To be successful doing this, students also need to develop important social and emotional skills to manage their own behaviors and recognize when they are having difficulty. These critical skills must be taught, coached, and scaffolded.

- **Student responsibility** must be cultivated. This entails giving students responsibility in amounts that they can handle and helping them to recognize the benefits and rewards of responsible actions. Likewise, students learn through experiencing the consequences that result from not making responsible choices. Mistakes and failures are important learning experiences, but teacher oversight and guidance are essential to make sure students' skills in this area continually improve.

- **Student empowerment** is also critical. Students must be empowered to manage their own learning, and to manage their classroom and school. Democratic participation helps prepare students for involvement in their community, state, and nation. As one example, assigned chores (such as cleaning and caring for animals in the classroom) give students a greater sense of belonging and ownership.

Acton Academy

"At Acton Academy in Austin, Texas . . . students set their own agenda, learn to access online resources, and manage their own progress. The school has no formal teaching, just adult 'guides' who aren't expected to be subject-matter experts or allowed to answer questions" (Dintersmith, 2018, p. 24).

Principle O: Parent as Partner

Parents and other primary guardians are children's first and most important teachers. Students will be better off to the extent that parents are effective partners in their child's learning and development, especially at lower age levels. Many parents want to be more involved but don't really know how to help. To remedy this, the teacher offers advice to parents (in a diplomatic, empathetic, and collaborative way), ranging from when, where, and how to support their children with homework, to how parents can help their students connect what they are learning at school to their lives at home. This includes providing guidance for specific activities and questions that will support the continued development of emerging skills at home, as well as ways to make the most of special family experiences, such as a trip to the zoo, museum, or vacation site. The teacher also encourages parents to reinforce behaviors that are being cultivated in school and supports parents dealing with child-related challenges at home.

To facilitate this partnership, parents are encouraged to visit the classroom, volunteer in the classroom, and communicate regularly with the teacher to help their child learn and develop into a successful, happy, caring adult. The multi-year model of student-teacher relationships (see principle R, page 91) also helps to build strong parent-teacher relationships (Hampton, Mumford, & Bond, 1998).

Principle P: Technology as a Tool for Students

Technology is an indispensable tool for easing the burdens of PCBE on teachers (Underwood et al., 2007). There is no way technology can replace teachers in a quality educational system, and for now it cannot even increase the number of students a teacher can reasonably handle. Accountants did not lose their jobs when the computer spreadsheet was developed; rather, technology improved accountants' quality of life and work. Perhaps in the long run, as technological tools become a lot more powerful, their use in Education 3.0 could eventually allow the number of students per teacher to increase some, which would help schools adopting this paradigm to address the problem of teacher shortages. But already technology eases some tasks for teachers and helps them to better meet their students' needs (Office of Educational Technology, 2010, 2017). In Education 2.0, technology is used primarily to support teaching, whereas in PCBE, technology is used primarily to support learning. There are four major functions that technology can serve to support student learning and make the teacher's life easier in PCBE: (1) record keeping, (2) planning, (3) instruction, and (4) assessment (Reigeluth et al., 2015).

Record Keeping

Competency-based student progress (principle A) is not possible without keeping track of what each student has learned. In Education 2.0 report cards or transcripts do not tell you specifically what each student has learned—only how well the student has done compared to other students in the class. Technology's record-keeping function for PCBE replaces traditional report cards and provides detailed information about student learning. This function could include three types of records.

1. A list of **standards** that includes all the learning targets that students must or could master, including required and optional, as well as academic and nonacademic targets

2. A list of **personal attainments** that identifies all the learning targets that each student has already mastered, and includes useful learning analytics for each target

3. A list of **personal characteristics** that contains each student's personal characteristics that are pertinent to student learning, such as interests and learning styles or preferences

Planning

While planning is one of the major responsibilities of teachers in Education 2.0 (teacher lesson plans), PCBE encourages students and even parents to be actively involved in the planning process with guidance from the teacher. Planning for student learning in Education 3.0 needs to take place on three different levels: (1) school, (2) classroom or studio, and (3) individual student.

At the school level, technology could aggregate individual student data across a developmental level to identify areas in which student learning is not advancing as well as desired, thereby helping schools to address the issue through such things as professional development or curation of better learning resources.

At the classroom level, each teacher should plan ways in which all of his or her students can learn together in a collaborative environment. Technology's planning function could include guidance for the teacher to do the following.

- **Identify an issue in the classroom**, whether it be curriculum-related or behavior-related, and seek out resources or guidance to address the issue. For example, the technology system could help teachers to identify groups of students who are struggling with mastering the same competency (academic or social-emotional) and could suggest resources that help the teacher to develop solutions. Another example is developing teacher skill in recognizing and taking advantage of teachable moments that address emotional, social, and character development issues. Here a technological tool could help prepare the teacher in advance for issues that commonly arise and how to deal with them. Also, after an academic or social-emotional issue has arisen, technology could help the teacher to reflect on the issue to diagnose potential causes, and could recommend alternative actions. This tool could use both a keyword search and a menu-driven decision tree to accomplish this. While these functions could be performed without technology (for example, with printed materials), they could be done more easily and quickly with technology.

- **Help teachers "debug" student misconceptions or performance errors** (Brown & Burton, 1978) by breaking apart larger understandings or skills to identify the specific causes of problems for struggling students. One example is a student who keeps getting math problems wrong (Jong et al., 2017). After breaking the required skills apart, the teacher learns that the student struggles with multiplying and dividing decimals. Further analysis reveals that she thinks that when you multiply 8 by 0.4, the answer has to be larger than 8, because you are multiplying.

- **Identify the students in a classroom (or studio) who are ready to advance** to the next level in a particular competency, and plan for a small-group lesson or other activity for them.

At the individual student level, each student needs a personal learning plan (see principle G, page 30) that sets out learning goals and ways to meet them. Technology's planning function could help each student's advisory committee (the student, his or her parents, and mentor teacher) to collaboratively decide on career goals, long- and short-term learning goals, projects, teammates, supporting roles, timelines, deliverables, and evaluation methods in the form of a learning contract.

Instruction

When it comes to instruction, technology can enable learning by doing (principle E) and instructional support (principle F) in a personalized manner (principle G). A project database that teachers and students can access helps students organize and manage their projects, and helps teachers monitor the projects. Such a database might introduce projects to the student and provide an authentic virtual environment within which to conduct the project (using a virtual reality tool) or provide project elements that enhance real-life project environments (using an augmented reality tool). It could also help students collaborate with peers using various documentation and communication tools and guide students to resolve conflicts that arise during teamwork.

A coaching database for teachers, which offers advice for coaching tied to each project, would also support learning by doing. An instructional support database for students, with instructional modules linked to specific points in projects when the instruction is needed is also useful for learning by doing. Students can access them anytime and anywhere as they work on their projects. Instruction could be tailored to each student's learning style, kind of intelligence (Gardner, 2011), interests, preferences, knowledge, and background based on the student's personal characteristics inventory (see page 75).

Assessment

Technology's fourth major function is assessment for and of student learning. This could entail assessing team performance outcomes on a project and assessing individual learning outcomes in instructional modules to certify each student's mastery of the learning targets. Furthermore, assessment might include not only academic outcomes, but also metacognitive skills, collaboration and communication skills, work ethic, and other kinds of emotional, social, and character development. In doing so, this function could enable assessment by people other than teachers, including peers, community members, and parents. Student assessment data collected through the technology-based assessment tools could automatically enter into the record-keeping function. Although we describe instruction and assessment as two separate functions here, they should be seamlessly integrated and take place simultaneously. Practice opportunities in tutorials (instructional modules) provide for formative assessment (feedback) and summative assessment (mastery certification) through "practice until perfect."

These four functions (record keeping, planning, instruction, and assessment) should be seamlessly and systemically integrated with each other. In brief, the record-keeping function should automatically provide necessary information to the planning function.

The planning function should identify instructional functions (mainly projects) for the student to use. The assessment function should be fully integrated with instruction. And the assessment function should feed information into the record-keeping function (Reigeluth et al., 2015). Technology should also serve such supporting functions as communication and collaboration. These secondary functions support users in ways less directly related to the learning process.

Detailed Guidance for New Roles

We recommend that you read all the sections titled Principles in chapters 1 through 6 before reading the Detailed Guidance section in any of those chapters, because the principles are so interrelated and interdependent that it is crucial to understand the big picture before getting into specific details. Any effort to move to PCBE that focuses on one core idea without making changes in other core ideas is likely to fail.

Classroom-Level Considerations

To implement new roles at the classroom level, your team needs to consider the new needs for teachers, students, parents, and technology. First think in the ideal for a long-term vision (step 2.1, chapter 10, page 196), and then compromise as necessary for your first implementation (step 2.3, chapter 10, page 200).

Principle M: Teacher as Guide

The teacher as guide fulfills many roles: mentor, designer (or selector), facilitator, collaborator and consultor, and learner. The following sections provide detailed guidance for each of these roles.

Mentor

What should a teacher do to mentor students?

As a team, you should brainstorm what you think a good mentor should do, and then engage your fellow teachers in similar discussions. We suggest that an effective mentor should take on the following four tasks.

1. Develop a caring relationship with each student. Talk to each about his or her dreams, challenges, worries, interests, and so forth. Show you care. Provide guidance, but usually in the form of asking questions that help students to find their passion in life and see the way to pursuing it.

2. Cultivate each student's emotional, social, and ethical development, self-directed learning skills, critical thinking skills, compassion, and ability to find his or her own way in the world (see Principle J: Whole-Child Education, page 59).

3. Work with the student's parents in pursuit of these two goals, because they can either undo or reinforce what the teacher does.

4. Develop a classroom culture that helps each student to become ever more self-directed, reflective, responsible, and caring.

Designer (or Curator)

What should a designer do?

The teacher should carefully consider designing the following.

- **The culture of the classroom or studio** so that it is caring, collaborative, respectful, and empowering

- **A process for students to decide what to learn next** (learning targets), based on both their long-term goals and any required standards

- **Projects for students to select from** (or project ideas for designing their own projects) to pursue their learning targets

- **Instructional support**, preferably in the form of just-in-time tutorials, peer tutoring, mini-workshops, or teacher tutoring

- **A process for certifying mastery** and a system for keeping track of each student's mastered competencies

Redesigning after selecting (see the next question) is also an important part of this role. Note that many of these tasks should be done in collaboration with other teachers.

What should a curator do?

The role of curator entails selection of projects or other activities and tutorials or other instructional support to make available to students, usually offering each student some choice among them. Whenever teachers can curate options for their students from what other teachers have done, it will save them time. They should always think about adapting, not just adopting, what others have done—in other words, redesign it. When appropriate, teachers should consider curating several options to create a menu from which the students can choose, rather than having a single requirement. The first challenge is finding what others have done. See appendix B (page 211) for some helpful resources. The second challenge is adapting it, or helping the student to adapt it, to the student's needs and interests. The guidelines under Principle E: Learning by Doing (page 28) and Principle F: Instructional Support (page 29) should be helpful for this.

Facilitator

What should a facilitator do?

A facilitator provides intentional and active support for student discovery and learning. We suggest that your team discuss ways that teachers can monitor student progress, enhance student motivation, coach student performance, provide instruction when necessary, and help students form caring relationships with each other—keeping in mind

New Roles

the guidance offered under Principle F: Instructional Support (page 29). In all of these ways, the teacher is a facilitator.

For monitoring student progress, look for tools that can provide progress reports, like Khan Academy and many others. If you are unable to find tools that fit your situation, you will need to design your own. While paper-based tools have been used successfully, it will save teachers significant time if you can find digital tools.

For enhancing student motivation, keep in mind the three needs described earlier: need for achievement, affiliation, and power. Need for achievement is most powerfully addressed when the achievement is related to the student's interests. Need for affiliation is powerfully addressed both when one student helps another and when there is positive interdependence (both students rely on the other to achieve their goals). Need for power is addressed when students feel in charge of their learning.

For coaching student performance, the best low-tech approach is usually peer coaching, either by a teammate or by a peer who has recently mastered the learning target. Such coaching is almost as beneficial for the coach as it is for the student. Then, the teacher's task is to monitor peer coaching, make sure it is done effectively, and coach the coach when it is not. Alternatively, computer-based project environments (simulations or virtual worlds) often have coaching built in.

Similarly, for providing instruction, peer tutoring is typically the best low-tech approach, with the teacher monitoring and occasionally coaching that instruction. Alternatively, resources like Khan Academy can be used for just-in-time instruction if the teacher proactively determines which tutorials are best for the student to use during a given project.

Finally, for building relationships, expand on the strategies you developed for collaborative learning (principle H) and strong and caring relationships (principle Q).

Collaborator and Consultor

With whom should teachers collaborate and consult?

Teachers should collaborate and consult with each other and with other experts. First, your team should design into your school some mechanisms for faculty members who teach the same developmental level to collaborate with each other. For these to be successful, you must schedule time for them to meet, observe each other, and work together. These changes must be made on the school level, and there are benefits to making them on the district level (discussed in School-Level and District-Level Considerations, page 86).

Second, design some mechanisms for teachers to find and collaborate with experts within and outside the school—in the district, the community, and beyond. While this is something you could do on the classroom-level, it will be easier on teachers and more effective if implemented throughout a school (or district). Some mechanisms are discussed under School-Level and District-Level Considerations (page 86).

Learner

What should teachers learn?

Being a learner themselves is an extremely important role for learner-centered teachers. Teachers should constantly be learning *about* the student, *with* the student, *from* the student, and *for* the student. They should not pretend they know everything. They should model curiosity and learning strategies. And they should let students teach them some things. It will make students feel good and help develop their teaching skills.

Professional development means constantly learning for the student. Your team should develop structures, resources, and regular times to enhance teacher learning. Because different kinds of students thrive with different kinds of teachers, your school should also encourage teachers to develop the teaching styles with which they are most comfortable and adept, and develop a process to assign each student to a teacher who is well suited to her or him. Casey (2018) provides much guidance about what teachers should learn to be most effective in supporting PCBE.

Principle N: Self-Directed Student

Again, you should first think in the ideal for a long-term vision (step 2.1, chapter 10, page 196), and then compromise as necessary for your first implementation (step 2.3, chapter 10, page 200). We offer guidance for developing self-direction skills, responsibility, and empowerment.

Self-Direction Skills

Marzano and colleagues (2017), Huh and Reigeluth (2017b), and Desautels (2018) offer some research-based guidance on how to help students develop self-direction skills.

Which self-direction skills are important to develop for learning?

Appropriate self-direction skills will vary with the age or developmental level of each student, but it may be helpful to think in terms of progressions within each of the three phases of the self-direction process for learning: planning, performing, and reflecting. Students need skills for the following.

- **Setting learning targets and project goals**, and identifying criteria for mastery of targets and achievement of goals. This includes identifying a project of considerable student interest that encompasses multiple standards across several content domains.

- **Managing performance** of the project and managing their learning process.

- **Recalling relevant prior knowledge and experience** (often called *case-based reasoning*).

- **Self-assessing continually** by asking themselves if their strategies are working during the learning process.

New Roles

- **Conducting summative self-assessment** to determine when they have mastered the learning targets and when they have achieved the project goals.
- **Monitoring and recording their individual learning progress**—for example, with a personal tracking matrix (Marzano et al., 2017).

When should teachers help a student develop self-direction skills?

Just-in-time instruction (right before it will be used) is typically best because it tends to be more motivational (the student understands it will be useful right away). It provides an immediate opportunity to practice the skill, the teacher is right there to give feedback on that practice, and the practice is more authentic.

How should teachers help a student develop self-direction skills?

As with all skills, it is helpful to explain how to do it, demonstrate how to do it (preferably together with the explanation), have the student do it, and give the student immediate feedback on his or her attempt to do it. In terms of feedback, teachers should avoid the instinct to rush in when they see a student struggling, and to tell or show the student how to do it right. Usually, it is better to hold off and observe for a while, and to offer help in the form of questions or hints. This results in deeper cognitive processing and the development of greater self-direction skills by modeling the problem-solving process.

What about supporting self-direction skills for students with behavior challenges?

The development of self-direction skills can be particularly important for students with behavior challenges. *Goal setting* is an important first step towards self-direction. Goals for overcoming behavior challenges might include anticipating the effects of one's actions, self-control, self-monitoring, empathy, courtesy, and self-reflection or self-evaluation. Regarding when and how to teach them, begin by helping the student to set behavior goals. Then look for *teachable moments* wherein an inappropriate behavior occurs, and ask questions that help the student understand the behavior's effects and identify alternative behaviors that would have been more appropriate. When a teachable moment occurs, the teacher can decide whether to interrupt all the students in the classroom for this impromptu lesson or just talk to one student privately. In some cases, more direct, explicit instruction with guided practice will be important. Often behavior challenges are a result of lagging skills or can be linked to some other root cause, such as insufficient sleep. By working collaboratively with the student and family, teachers can identify underlying issues and develop a plan to build student skill or address root causes. Ross Greene (2014) and the organization Lives in the Balance (livesinthebalance .org) provide resources to support the collaborative problem-solving process.

Responsibility

How should teachers help a student develop responsibility as a part of student agency?

Another element of self-direction is responsibility. Being responsible is complex. Teachers need to help students understand the criteria for responsible behavior, and they need to help students *want* to be responsible. Encourage students to recognize the positive feelings that come from getting work done on time and being prepared for a given situation (for example, remembering materials or accomplishing tasks in advance). Teacher recognition of responsible actions can also help, and can be as simple as thanking a student for putting away materials.

Students can learn responsibility at a young age through classroom jobs, and teachers can support this learning through classroom structures such as time for students to organize themselves, note their responsibilities, and check in with others regarding what still needs to be done. It is also important to allow students to experience the natural consequences of not being responsible, when appropriate, such as having to struggle through a practice presentation without note cards if the note cards weren't completed on time.

Empowerment

How can teachers empower students to manage their own learning?

First, teachers need to let students manage their own learning as much as possible given the child's age and disposition. Recognize that there will likely be some aspects of that management that students cannot handle well yet, so provide structure for those aspects in a way that helps students learn how they should manage them. Second, teachers should coach students' management of those aspects. For example, a teacher might support a young child in developing a daily or weekly to-do list. As the child improves this skill, he or she will be able to develop that list independently, and the teacher's role will be to check in occasionally, providing suggestions as needed. Observe, give guidance, and give feedback—again, usually by asking questions that help students to figure out how to manage their learning well.

How can teachers empower students to manage their classroom?

First, we suggest that, at the beginning of each year, the teacher helps the class develop rules for the classroom along with consequences for breaking the rules. These should be posted prominently in the classroom. Second, the teacher guides students to commit to enforcing the rules themselves rather than relying on the teacher to enforce them. Third, the teacher asks students to identify classroom chores (such as cleaning and watering plants in the classroom) and come up with a plan for rotating chore assignments. Strong and consistent classroom routines will help students manage their learning environment, giving students a greater sense of belonging and ownership of the community.

Classroom Culture, Operating Procedures, and Environment

How can teachers cultivate an appropriate culture?

Self-direction, responsibility, growth mindset, and empowerment can and should be promoted through classroom culture, standard operating procedures, and classroom environment. In *A Handbook for Personalized Competency-Based Education*, Marzano and colleagues (2017) offer powerful guidance and tools for cultivating an appropriate culture that values student agency. A class can unpack the school's shared vision, set class goals aligned with that vision, identify behavioral traits for meeting the goals, create tools for measuring progress toward the goals, and establish processes for monitoring and reflecting on progress.

What standard operating procedures might be helpful?

Marzano and colleagues (2017) also offer powerful guidance and tools for standard operating procedures (SOPs) that promote student agency by scaffolding students in a classroom to develop self-direction skills. The guidance includes what kinds of SOPs might be helpful, how to create them, formats they may take (procedural lists and flowcharts), and how to integrate them into the teaching and learning process to enhance choice and voice.

What classroom physical environment might best promote student self-direction, responsibility, and empowerment?

Finally, Marzano and colleagues (2017) offer powerful guidance and tools for teachers to collaborate with students for redesigning the physical classroom environment to provide flexibility and promote student agency.

Principle O: Parent as Partner

How can teachers foster partnerships with parents?

In PCBE, teachers foster partnerships with parents. This takes time, but it can greatly enhance student learning. In general, parents want to be involved and will cooperate if the teacher reaches out to them. Parenting is hard, and most parents welcome the support that comes from a strong parent-teacher relationship. Teachers should contact parents early and often to communicate positive experiences by any and all methods that work for them and the parents, including email, texts, phone, and meetings. Communication could include the following.

- Share what their child is working on (skills and projects) and give them suggestions about how they can help.

- Ask them if there are things they would like you (the teacher) to work on with their child.

- When there is an aspect of the child's behavior that you are working on in school, let the parents know, and ask them to encourage and reinforce those behaviors. Share strategies for addressing or working through specific behaviors.

- Let the parents know that you are there as a resource and partner if they are having any difficulties with their child, so you can not only give them helpful advice, but also work with the student on overcoming those difficulties at school.

- Share information with families about how they can support continued learning at home and during school vacations, keeping in mind family resources. All teachers in your school should share these ideas and activities with each other, so developing them is less of a burden on any one of you.

Your team may find it helpful to consult the Center for Parenting Education (www .centerforparentingeducation.org), which provides support to parents to raise their children in emotionally healthy ways so that their children can thrive personally, socially, and academically. Supports include live online educational workshops, an online library of parenting articles, recommended parenting books, and an online resource directory.

Principle P: Technology as a Tool for Students

It is likely beyond the scope of your change effort to build your own technology system that serves the four major functions previously described (record keeping, planning, instruction, and assessment). This means your task is to find a system that serves these four functions in as seamlessly integrated a way as possible.

What criteria should you use to select a technology system?

First, your team should decide what functions you want your technology system to serve: Do you want all four major functions? Other supporting functions? Once you have decided this, you can use those functions as criteria for rank-ordering technology systems and compare their benefits with their costs. In a 2018 survey of educators (Lee, Huh, Lin, & Reigeluth, 2018), only 12 percent of respondents reported that their technology system integrates all four of the functions.

Some systems you might want to consider include the following. However, this is not an exhaustive list, it is likely to be outdated quickly, and we recommend you do a search yourselves.

- ActivateInstruction
- AIMS
- ALEKS Math
- Alt School's Alt School Open
- Brooklyn Lab's Cortex
- Buzz
- DreamBox
- EdElements
- Edio
- Edmodo
- Empower (formerly Educate)
- Education 2020
- Education City
- Genesis

- Google Classroom
- Infinite Campus
- In-Service
- JumpRope
- K12
- Leadership Public Schools
- Gooru Learning Navigator
- Lexia
- LightSail
- Matchbook School's Spark
- My Access
- Project Foundry
- Read Live
- Reading A–Z
- Study Island
- Summit Public Schools' Personalized Learning Platform
- TI-inspire Navigator
- Water

School-Level and District-Level Considerations

Changing a teacher's role from presenter to mentor and facilitator could be done in a single classroom, but it is very closely linked to learning by doing and self-directed students, both of which are difficult to implement in a single classroom, as they require developing a different mindset and skillset in students. Also, the longer a student has been in teacher-centered classrooms, the harder it is for them to develop that mindset and those skills. Following is some guidance for changes on the school and district levels that will make implementation of new roles considerably easier.

What changes should be made on the school level or district level for teacher as guide and self-directed student?

Schoolwide adoption of self-directed learning will make the process easier for both teachers and students. For teachers, it will be easier because the students who enter their classrooms will already have experience directing their own learning, reducing the need to teach or coach them in how to do so and to develop their attitude to do so. For students, it will be easier because they will have less difficulty transitioning from teacher-directed to student-directed instruction. Also, districtwide adoption of self-directed learning will make the process even easier for students, because they will have less difficulty adjusting in whatever school they go to next in the district. Self-directed learning requires the teacher's role to change from director to guide, and conversely this change in teacher role requires the student's role to change from teacher-directed to self-directed. Hence, we strongly encourage you to implement the change in teachers' and students' roles schoolwide, and preferably districtwide.

A school- or districtwide approach also works best for teachers as collaborators and consultants. The best approach would be to structure the school as a professional learning community (DuFour, DuFour, Eaker, Many, & Mattos, 2016). Teams for each developmental level (or grade level if you can't switch to developmental levels in multi-age classrooms) would provide opportunities for teachers to collaborate. It would also be beneficial for teachers in different schools to communicate with each other about what they are doing and even collaborate.

Similarly, mechanisms for teachers to find and collaborate with experts outside the school will be more efficient if they are implemented districtwide. Such mechanisms might include (a) district records of teachers in different schools who volunteer to be an occasional resource for teachers in other schools, (b) district records of community experts who volunteer some time to helping students, (c) district records of experts outside the local community who have been willing to provide some help to students on projects, including area of expertise, contact information, and history of help provided.

What changes should be made on the school level or district level for parent as partner?

To some extent, this move to parent as partner can be done solely on the classroom level, but it will also be far more efficient and effective if enacted school- or districtwide. Forming partnerships with parents requires time, which teachers will have more of if they take on a guiding role, which in turn requires that students self-direct and learn by doing. All these roles are interconnected and will be far more effective when an entire school or district implements them.

What changes should be made on the school level or district level for technology as a tool for students?

Finally, technology needs to move to a new role as a tool for students. It is confusing for students to move from one technology system to another for different courses (or projects), different grades (or developmental levels), or different schools. It is also generally less expensive to gain access to a technology system if you have more users. For both these reasons, it is preferable to select and use your technology system districtwide. Due to any existing contracts for technology systems, you may need to wait a year or more before you can switch to one more suitable for PCBE, so the decision to switch should be made as soon as possible.

Summary

This chapter described four principles for new roles that are universally helpful for maximizing student learning.

Principle M: Teacher as guide

Principle N: Self-directed student

Principle O: Parent as partner

Principle P: Technology as a tool for students

It then offered detailed guidelines to help your team develop part of your shared ideal vision for your classrooms, school, and district.

New Roles

A Nurturing Culture

Core Ideas
1. Competency-Based Education
2. Learner-Centered Instruction
3. Restructured Curriculum
4. New Roles
5. A Nurturing Culture
6. New Organizational Structures

Principles

Q. Strong and caring relationships

R. Multi-year mentoring and multi-age grouping

S. Motivational learning

T. Family services

This chapter discusses four principles for PCBE related to a nurturing culture, as shown in the preceding map. It then offers detailed guidance to help your team develop more of your shared vision for your classrooms, school, and district. We do not offer these principles and guidelines as a blueprint for what you should do. Rather, we offer them to assist your team as you engage in rich discussions and collaborations to design an ideal PCBE system in your unique context.

Principles for a Nurturing Culture

People learn best when they feel safe and supported. This requires a culture and climate that are more like a healthy home—a small community with strong relationships, multi-year mentoring with multi-age grouping, motivational learning, and family services. Therefore, we offer four principles for creating a nurturing culture that have strong research support.

> Principle Q: Strong and caring relationships
>
> Principle R: Multi-year mentoring and multi-age grouping
>
> Principle S: Motivational learning
>
> Principle T: Family services

These principles are highly interrelated and interdependent with each other and with the principles for competency-based education, learner-centered instruction, restructured curriculum, and new roles. The following is an introduction to each of these principles.

Principle Q: Strong and Caring Relationships

Caring relationships and a sense of belonging are important to healthy child development (Battistich, Solomon, Watson, & Schaps, 1997; Darling-Hammond & Cook-Harvey, 2018; Kohn, 1990; Osher, Cantor, Berg, Steyer, & Rose, 2018). Such relationships promote social, emotional, ethical, and character development, as well as cognitive development. Therefore, development of strong and caring relationships between teachers and their students and among their students is a high priority of Education 3.0.

Caring relationships are promoted by small school size (see principle U, page 104), where anonymity is not an option, all faces quickly become familiar, and a sense of community and belonging is built more easily. If you have a large school building, you can create multiple small schools within it, sometimes referred to as academies, houses, or schools-within-a-school (see principle U, page 104).

Second, they are promoted by classroom culture, climate, and procedures, which are strongly influenced by student ownership of class norms and rules (Lewis, Schaps, & Watson, 1995; Lewis, Watson, & Schaps, 1999; Solomon, Watson, Battistich, Schaps, & Delucchi, 1992). Whole-class sharing and celebration of student accomplishments also promote a sense of community and strengthen relationships. According to Mark Van Ryzin and Cary Roseth (2018), to create strong and caring relationships,

> teachers must establish a social context that promotes the breakdown of biases and prejudices among students who belong to different social groups (Pettigrew, 1998; Pettigrew & Tropp, 2008). A key ingredient of such a social context is "positive interdependence," which occurs when individuals can attain their goals if (and only if) others in their group also reach their goals. (p. 64)

Benefits of such a social context include the following.

- More positive relationships among students

- Greater social acceptance (of people who are in a different social group)

- Greater academic motivation

- Greater academic achievement (Johnson & Johnson, 1989, 2005; Roseth, Johnson, & Johnson, 2008)

Third, caring relationships are developed through the nature and frequency of interactions. For example, they are promoted by a relatively small number of students working together on a wide range of activities, such as projects (see Principle E: Learning by Doing, page 28)—with the teacher in a supportive role—for most of the school day, every day of the week. Behavior problems become rare and relationships improve when students are engaged in work that is meaningful to them and are empowered to make choices about where, when, and how to accomplish their work. Some behavior problems will inevitably occur, but they are valuable opportunities for student learning and development. Finally, caring relationships are promoted by multi-year mentoring (described next).

Principle R: Multi-Year Mentoring and Multi-Age Grouping

In a PCBE system, students learn different things and at different rates. Students move through the content at a pace that suits their learning needs. Therefore, grade levels become arbitrary labels (see Districts Eliminating Grade Levels). It makes more sense to organize the students into developmental levels, which include consideration of social, emotional, and cognitive development (Montessori, 1964). Therefore, in an Education 3.0 system, students stay with the same mentor teacher for a developmental stage of their lives (which typically last three to five years), so they get to know each other well and develop caring, trust, and strong relationships. If the match between a student and teacher is not a good one, the teacher or student requests a change. Since students stay with the same mentor teacher for a developmental stage, students vary in age for any given teacher. We recommend that students are assigned to teachers so that there are roughly equal numbers of students in each age group within the developmental level.

Districts Eliminating Grade Levels

Kankakee Public Schools is one of ten high school districts in Illinois that have started to move to competency-based learning. According to an *EdSurge* article (Hybert, 2018), the district says, "We're continuing to work on improving our mastery-based learning and new grading system, and ridding ourselves of traditional grade levels. . . . Since we implemented our PBL model, data shows that in one year (2016 to 2017), reading comprehension scores increased 8 percent, math application increased 9 percent. We have also seen an increase in student engagement in all of our K–6 classes, and have built partnerships with local businesses and industries that support students' exploration and curiosity about future career options."

Multi-age grouping and multi-year mentoring have been proven beneficial for building strong relationships and improving student learning and development (Aslan et al., 2014; Edwards, 2006; Hampton et al., 1998; Lillard, 2006, 2016; Montessori, 1973). They promote a natural enculturation into the classroom community, and that culture endures year to year rather than having to be created anew each year. They also encourage healthy development as older students serve as important role models for younger ones. Working with younger students engenders a sense of responsibility and self-confidence in the older ones. Multi-age grouping and multi-year mentoring also reduce unhealthy comparisons and competition between students through the understanding that different people are at different levels of development in different areas.

Principle S: Motivational Learning

Self-directed learning (principle N) within motivating curriculum and instruction (core ideas 2 and 3) accelerates learning and contributes to a positive school culture (Pane et al., 2017). When students are engaged and excited by their learning tasks, there are fewer discipline problems in the classroom (Hanover Research, 2015), and the relationship between student and teacher is strengthened (Pane et al., 2017). A love of the learning experience is important for a positive attitude toward lifelong learning, which greatly enhances success later in life.

Powerful tools for motivational learning include passion-based learning (Newell, 2003), purpose-based learning or goal orientation (Damon, Menon, & Bronk, 2003), and strategies related to McClelland's (1987) needs for achievement (competency-based education), affiliation (cooperative learning), and power (self-directed learning; Deci & Ryan, 1985). In addition, John Keller (1983, 2010) offers four major types of instructional strategies to enhance student motivation: (1) gain and maintain student attention, (2) show how content is relevant to student interests, (3) build student confidence in their ability to learn, and (4) promote student satisfaction with their learning.

Principle T: Family Services

As society becomes ever more complex, raising children becomes more difficult, and family services become more important. Parents increasingly need a reliable source of information and advice, someone to turn to with questions about parenting, health services, specific social challenges, and much more. As one example, the Education Week Research Center analyzed federal data and concluded that a third of K–12 students need eye exams (Sparks & Harwin, 2018); schools that provide basic health services such as vision and hearing exams contribute greatly to students' health, wellness, and learning. Also, an important part of the school culture is that families are valued and supported—they can help the teacher, and the teacher can help them. Some home environments are detrimental to students, but virtually all families can use some help in fostering their children's development. Schools have a vested interest in helping families, for without such help, most students cannot reach their potential. For example, the Independence School District in Independence, Missouri, has implemented a collaboration that provides school-based family support to children from birth to twelve years old (Finn-Stevenson, Desimone, & Chung, 1998).

Fortunately, a number of schools are becoming *community schools*, which "assume responsibility for coordinating services that address the many nonacademic needs of students and their families" (Jacobson, Villarreal, Muñoz, & Mahaffey, 2018, p. 8). There is a movement to create *school community centers*, also known as full-service schools, community service centers, human resource centers, and family resource centers (Ringers & Decker, 1995). Schools can create such a center to partner with many community agencies that need teachers' help to know whom, when, and even how to assist. In addition to partnering with a variety of community agencies, teachers can provide direct help to parents on their own. Technological tools (see Principle P: Technology as a Tool for Students, page 75) can free up some teacher time to engage in this crucial activity for the students.

Detailed Guidance for a Nurturing Culture

We recommend that you read all the sections titled Principles in chapters 1 through 6 before reading the Detailed Guidance section in any of those chapters, because the principles are so interrelated and interdependent that it is crucial to understand the big picture before getting into specific details. Any effort to move to PCBE that focuses on one core idea without making changes in other core ideas is likely to fail.

Classroom-Level Considerations

To create a nurturing culture at the classroom level, your team must make decisions about how to foster caring relationships, group students, motivate students, and support students' families. First think in the ideal for a long-term vision (step 2.1, chapter 10, page 196), and then compromise as necessary for your first implementation (step 2.3, chapter 10, page 200).

Principle Q: Strong and Caring Relationships

Strong caring relationships are fostered through several key principles: student collaboration on projects (principle H), a small school (principle U), and multi-year mentoring (principle R). In this section, we will suggest some other ideas your team might consider: creating an appropriate classroom and culture, addressing unacceptable behaviors, communicating with students, and building a sense of community—all of which contribute to strong and caring relationships.

How can teachers foster strong, caring relationships—among students and between a teacher and students—through classroom culture and climate?

As mentioned previously, positive interdependence is a key aspect of positive culture and relationships. The teacher should use collaborative projects to promote positive interdependence. Kinds of interdependence include the following.

- **Resource interdependence:** Teammates are given different materials that the group must share to complete the project.

- **Role interdependence:** Teammates are assigned different roles in a project. (Consider that different roles may entail mastering different content.)

- **Task interdependence:** Each teammate must complete a different step in the process. (Consider that different steps may entail mastering different content.)

- **Identity interdependence:** Each team has its own name, for example.

The teacher should also show that he or she values students supporting and empowering one another. One way to do this is to convene all students in the classroom at the beginning of every school year to adopt a set of norms and rules that they agree on (such as helping each other, valuing differences, and dealing with conflicts through civil communication), building on those of the previous year. They should also reach consensus on how to deal with infractions. Commitment by every student is important, and this should include students agreeing that they are responsible for dealing with such infractions, with the teacher as a resource of last resort. The teacher should ask if any students have any reservations about any of the norms and rules, and if so, encourage discussion about them until they reach consensus about any changes. *Edutopia* (Minero, 2019) offers ten powerful ideas for building community.

How can teachers address unacceptable behaviors?

Collaborative development of norms and rules gives students a clear understanding of which behaviors are unacceptable. When a student strays from the norms and rules, the teacher should decide whether to address it publicly or privately. Most of the time, a private conversation with the student is most appropriate. Understand that negative behavior is a form of communication, and the role of the person receiving the behavior is to identify what the offender is attempting to communicate. It may be a lack of understanding of the expectations, an expression of frustration, or an inappropriate attempt to accomplish a goal (among other things). The teacher should treat each transgression as a teachable moment for the offender, the affected students, and sometimes the entire class. Explore the following questions as appropriate.

- What led to this behavior?

- What was the impact of this behavior on the student, on another student, and on the learning environment of the classroom?

- How might it have made others feel?

- What other choices could the student have made to achieve the desired outcome?

It is also helpful to talk privately to any students who witnessed the infraction and praise them if they spoke up about it or encourage them to speak up next time if they did not. Furthermore, the teacher should partner with the offender's parents to deal with unacceptable behaviors in a consistent way.

The teacher should only address the behavior publicly if there was an immediate impact on the entire learning environment. Avoid publicly shaming students, as this works against self-direction and the development of a nurturing culture. If the teacher thinks the entire learning community would benefit from a discussion about the behavior and its consequences, then he or she should plan a discussion that focuses on the behavior—not the individual student—guiding the group toward problem solving for a classroom-oriented remedy, such as adjusting routines or established norms.

There are many valuable resources on behavior management, but given the needs and goals of PCBE, teachers should consider the following when choosing behavior management practices.

- **Provide instruction** or information about alternative courses of action the transgressor could have taken.

- **Include a consequence** that is clearly linked to the transgression (for example, if a student has an altercation with another student, the teacher might help to guide a conversation between the two students where the transgressor takes on the role of listener and the two students determine how to rectify the situation).

- **Provide an opportunity for discussion** between the transgressor and teacher when everyone is calm, and engage in collaborative problem solving to develop a plan that will increase the probability of positive behavior in the future.

- **Follow up with teacher self-reflection** regarding classroom layout, procedures, routines, and the student's work plan to determine whether any changes to these might help the student behave more appropriately in the future.

How can teachers foster strong, caring relationships through one-on-one communication with students?

In addition to behavior management, communicating one-on-one with students in positive and neutral situations also fosters strong, caring relationships. The teacher should take time to talk privately with each student at least once every week or two to see how she or he is doing inside and outside of school and find ways of supporting any student dealing with in-school or out-of-school challenges. Not only does this show that the teacher cares, but the resolution of such problems can substantially increase learning. This communication is key to effective mentoring.

How can teachers foster strong, caring relationships through building a sense of community with students?

Finally, a sense of community promotes strong, caring relationships. Develop classroom structures and processes that support community building and allow time for one-on-one interactions between the teacher and students, and among students of different ages, abilities, and interests. Some ideas include the following.

- **A regular whole-class sharing time** when students have a chance to talk about important things (good or bad) going on in their lives and engage in age-appropriate conversations about current events and community issues

- **Routines and procedures** for how to begin the school day and how to end the school day, including cleaning up workspaces and tidying shared spaces

- **An expectation for peer assistance**—for example, that students seek the help of up to three peers before asking for teacher help

- **A structure for peer feedback** on writing, presentations, and products

- **Classroom rituals for celebrating student milestones**, such as birthdays, accomplishments, and important community dates or events

- **Guidelines for group activities**, such as working with teammates on projects and participating in whole-class events like collaborative performances of various kinds

- **A consistent mentoring meeting schedule** (biweekly, perhaps) for the teacher to check in with each student

- **Explicit instruction for new students** around expected behavior and procedures (how to ask for help, how to get needed materials, how to track their work, how to put away materials)

- **Regular demonstrations** or role-playing of healthy communication practices

- **Classroom and schoolwide chores** for all students, including some janitorial, cafeteria, and grounds responsibilities. This builds in the student a deeper commitment to the school and a deeper sense of ownership of, and responsibility for, the school as a community.

Principle R: Multi-Year Mentoring and Multi-Age Grouping

Obviously, multi-year mentoring and multi-age grouping impact the classroom level, but they must be implemented on the school level (see School-Level and District-Level Considerations, page 98).

 How can these be implemented?

We recommend that a student stays with the same teacher for a developmental stage of the student's life, which is typically three to five years (Piaget, 1952, 1977). Montessori levels, for example, are infant (ages 0–3), preschool (ages 3–6), lower elementary (ages 6–9), upper elementary (ages 9–12), middle school (ages 12–14), and high school (ages 14–18; Montessori, 1973). As students age and develop, a roughly equal number of students enter and leave the classroom (or studio) each year. In such an arrangement, diversity is an important consideration in classroom composition. Diversity in aptitude allows for a range of heterogeneous groupings and peer mentoring arrangements. Diversity in gender, race, ethnicity, socio-economic status, religion, and so forth fosters understanding of people who are different from oneself, as well as better student learning and team performance through exposure to different perspectives.

What if the teacher is not well suited for the student?

If a strong relationship does not develop between the teacher and the student, then the student should be matched with a different mentor and studio. The change could be initiated by the student or the teacher, but the teacher typically takes the initiative to make the change, which can be made any time during the school year. Typically, the current mentor will talk with other teachers to find a better match, and that prospective mentor will review the student's records and meet with the student so that both the student and the prospective mentor can decide if they are a good match. Final approval could be delegated to the school leader or a teacher committee assigned that task.

Principle S: Motivational Learning

How can teachers foster greater motivation for learning?

Perhaps the most important thing teachers can do to enhance motivation for older students (and even for many younger ones) is to help them discover and develop their passion in life. Expose them to many different problems and opportunities in their community. Help them discover their talents and develop their interests. Take note of student responses to different experiences and situations, and encourage self-reflection activities. Use those notes to help design future learning experiences that tap into student interests. For younger students and those who have not yet developed a passion, we earlier mentioned three great human motives or needs—achievement, affiliation, and power—that can be used to enhance student motivation.

Need for achievement is fostered by competency-based student assessment and is particularly powerful when the achievement is related to the student's interests. Allow students to pursue their interests, relate other important content to those interests, and provide students with a visual representation of what they have mastered. *Need for affiliation* is fostered by collaborative learning, peer tutoring, and mentoring. As with all interpersonal relationships, the nature of the relationship is key—it should, in all cases, be caring and supportive. The teacher's relationship with the student is the most important one. *Need for power* is fostered by self-directed learning. The teacher should give students choice about both what to learn and how to learn it, to the extent your school and district will allow, as well as responsibility, to the extent the learner can handle.

Principle T: Family Services

There are two kinds of help for families that schools can provide: (1) partnering with community agencies and (2) teachers providing direct support to families on their own.

How can you partner with community agencies?

While you can partner with community agencies on the classroom level, it is far more efficient to do it on the school or district level. Therefore, guidance for this is provided under School-Level and District-Level Considerations (page 98).

How can teachers can provide direct support to families on their own?

In our discussion of parents as partners (principle O, page 74), we recommended frequent communication with every student's parents about how they can reinforce what their child is learning in school and how the teacher can support parents in dealing with problems they encounter with their child at home. Experience in Montessori schools shows that teachers can do much to develop behaviors and attitudes that benefit home life (Lillard & Else-Quest, 2006). The teacher may simply ask the parents periodically if there is anything he or she can do to help with their child. Inviting families to share concerns or problems can open the door to conversations about ways the teacher can help parents and aspects of development the teacher can work on with the student. It also gives the teacher insights and information for soliciting help from community agencies and improving the efficacy of their work with the family.

Teachers should ask questions, be good listeners, and build trust. They must show that they care. In doing so, teachers will find out if the student is experiencing challenges at home. When appropriate, teachers can explore possible reasons with the family, propose possible remedies, and help the family decide what would be the best course of action—what the family can do and what the teacher can do to support them.

While this activity is largely done on the classroom level, teachers will learn about some families' concerns or problems that are beyond their capability or time to deal with. In such cases, the teacher should ask for help from community or social service agencies, and the teacher can share information to help the agency be more effective in their work with the family. However, it is important to respect the privacy and confidentiality of the family. Typically, the teacher would ask the family's permission before making any requests or sharing any information with social service agencies.

School-Level and District-Level Considerations

The majority of the principles in this chapter require school- or districtwide implementation for maximum effectiveness. In the following sections, we provide detailed guidance for enacting these principles on the school or district level.

Principle Q: Strong and Caring Relationships

Should unacceptable behaviors be dealt with on the school or district level?

In Classroom-Level Considerations (page 93), we discussed how to promote strong, caring relationships in the classroom culture by involving students in setting norms and appropriately addressing unacceptable behaviors. While unacceptable behaviors can and must be addressed within the classroom, inconsistencies in rules and procedures among classrooms can create ill will. One solution is to have students develop both classroom and school rules—classroom rules at the beginning of each year and schoolwide rules every couple of years.

How can we build a sense of community?

Similarly, a sense of community can certainly be built in a single classroom, but it is important to develop a sense of community for a whole school and even a whole district. Consider schoolwide events, such as science fairs, field trips, community service projects, school beautification events, theatrical and musical performances, and sporting events. A sense of school community is often built by competing against other schools in the district. Similar events can be held to build a sense of districtwide community by competing against other districts, as is currently often done in sports.

Principle R: Multi-Year Mentoring and Multi-Age Grouping

Multi-age classrooms cannot be implemented solely on the classroom level. It requires a shift from the "one teacher for one year" aspect of Education 2.0 to an arrangement wherein students stay with the same teacher for three to five years (one developmental stage of the student's life). Such a multi-age classroom would include roughly an equal number of students in each age category. This must be done schoolwide but can be done in a single school in a district.

How can this be implemented?

First, your team should decide which ages should make up each developmental level. You will initially be constrained by the school's current grade levels, but this can be changed over time. If possible, you should allocate a minimum of three years to each developmental level, so that the teacher has time to get to know each student well. If your school only spans four or five grades, we recommend that each student stays with the same teacher throughout his or her time at the school. Also, keep in mind that age should not be the only, or even most important, criterion. Some children develop faster than others and are ready to move on to the next developmental level at a younger age.

Your team should also decide how each school will decide which students to assign to each teacher. One criterion should be compatibility. Personality, attitude, interests, and learning and teaching styles are some criteria for you to consider. For example, some students need more structure, while others thrive with more flexibility. Some students need a lot of emotional support, while others are more independent. A second criterion for allocating students to teachers is diversity. It is preferable for each classroom (or studio) to reflect the diversity of the school regarding race, gender, ethnicity, socioeconomic status, religion, and so forth. A third possible criterion is student choice. Principle W (Student Choice, Teacher Incentives, and Accountability, page 107) offers guidance for deciding whether to allow students to choose their teacher or just their school.

Principle S: Motivational Learning

To some extent, teachers can apply motivational learning principles on the classroom level. However, full implementation requires competency-based education (core idea 1, page 15) and learning by doing (principle E, page 28) to address the need for achievement; collaborative learning and strong and caring relationships (principle H, page 31, and principle Q, page 90) to address the need for affiliation; and self-directed learning (principle N, page 73) to address the need for power. All of these require changes on the school and district levels to maximize their impact, although competency-based education is most dependent on district-level changes, as the grading and record-keeping systems must change from norm-referenced to criterion-referenced. Therefore, your team should either be a district-level team designing changes for district-level policies and

A Nurturing Culture

practices, or it should be a school-level team under the auspices of such a district-level team. See part II for guidance on forming such teams.

Principle T: Family Services

Family services are far more efficient when an entire school or district provides them, because the same arrangements made with local service agencies can be used with all the classrooms in a school and all the schools in a district.

How can our school or district be a community school that partners with community agencies?

Generally, the school or even the district should be the unit that enters into partnerships with community agencies, typically in the form of a school community center. *School Community Centers: Guidelines for Interagency Planners* (Ringers & Decker, 1995) offers guidelines for creating such a center, which they characterize as follows.

- It is planned and operated through participative planning processes that involve a representative cross section of the community.

- It is jointly operated by several agencies; the lead agency is usually the public schools.

- It is funded by a separate budget that is subject to regular review by all participating agencies.

- Programming is determined by a council of participating agencies and representative community advisory groups.

- It is administered by a unit manager with the advice of program managers from participating agencies.

You might consider partnering with agencies related to the following areas.

- **Physical development** (such as health clubs, youth sports leagues, and recreational sports clubs)

- **Health** (such as those that provide dental exams, eye exams, vaccinations, speech therapy, autism services, and other health services)

- **Mental health** (including services for depression, anxiety, juvenile delinquency, drug addiction, and trauma)

- **Cognitive, social, and emotional development** (such as mentoring programs, computer clubs, book clubs, and other hobby clubs)

- **Support for parents** (such as those offering childcare or development of parenting skills)

- **The arts** (such as drama clubs, graphic arts, and music)

- Any **other areas** your team thinks are important

The partnerships might entail the school providing some facilities in the school building for these agencies to provide their services to students, either during or after the school day. Other tools of partnership might include coordinating schedules and providing transportation. For more guidance, see It Takes a Community (Jacobson et al., 2018); *School Community Centers: Guidelines for Interagency Planners* (Ringers and Decker, 1995); Moving From Survival to Fulfillment: A Planning Framework for Community Schools (Shaia and Finigan-Carr, 2018); School-Based Coordinators Link Students to Community Resources (Walter, 2018); Districts Embrace the Community to Benefit All Students (Weinzapfel, 2018); and the Coalition for Community Schools (www.communityschools.org). Also, Union Public Schools, south of Tulsa, Oklahoma, has a strong community schools initiative (see www.unionps.org/CommunitySchools) you might want to look at.

Some organizations are exploring new ways of measuring community impact. Harvard's Transparency for Development project (Ash Center for Democratic Governance and Innovation, 2017) has explored whether a community-led transparency and accountability program could improve health outcomes and community empowerment. *Metrics for Healthy Communities* (www.metricsforhealthycommunities.org) is a site to get you started in planning for and measuring the impact of initiatives to improve community health and well-being.

How can our school or district provide direct support to families?

Schools and districts can also provide direct support to families. An ideal option is to form a parent education center in your school or district. For ideas about how to do this, consult the following resources and examples.

- Center for Effective Parenting (parenting-ed.org)
- The Alabama Parent Education Center (alabamaparentcenter.com)
- The 2017 special issue of *Educational Leadership* titled "In Sync with Families," which provides useful articles on building partnerships with parents.

> The **CAP Tulsa network** combines early childhood education with innovative family services and resources. Their two-generation approach "aims not only to prepare young children for future success in school, but also to help their parents succeed through programs designed to increase parenting skills, employability and earning potential" (https://captulsa.org/who-we-are/mission-vision-method /2gen-approach/).
>
> **Pasco School District's Parent Education Center** (www.psd1.org/domain/64) provides an example of services available in one district.
>
> **Weld County Family Services Visitation Center** (www.weldgov.com/departments /human_services/child_welfare/family_services_visitation_center/), while not a part of a school district, is an example of an effective parent education center.
>
> **The Center for Parent Information and Resources** (www.parentcenterhub.org /find-your-center/) provides a list of parent education centers across the U.S., so your team can see what services they offer and how they are organized.

Examples of Parent Education Centers

A Nurturing Culture

Summary

This chapter described four principles for a nurturing culture that are universally helpful for maximizing student learning.

Principle Q: Strong and caring relationships

Principle R: Multi-year mentoring and multi-age grouping

Principle S: Motivational learning

Principle T: Family services

It then offered detailed guidelines to help your team develop part of your shared ideal vision for your classrooms, school, and district.

New Organizational Structures

CHAPTER 6

Core Ideas
1. Competency-Based Education
2. Learner-Centered Instruction
3. Restructured Curriculum
4. New Roles
5. A Nurturing Culture
6. New Organizational Structures

Principles

U. Small school size

V. Professional organizational structure

W. Student choice, teacher incentives, and accountability

X. Administrative structures

Y. Governance structures

This chapter discusses five principles for PCBE related to organizational structures, choice, incentives, and decision-making systems, as shown in the preceding map. It then offers detailed guidance to help your team develop more of your shared vision for your classrooms, school, and district. Finally, it will present common problems that teams encounter when envisioning Education 3.0. We do not offer these principles and guidelines as a blueprint for what you should do. Rather, we offer them to assist your team as you engage in rich discussions and collaborations to design an ideal PCBE system in your unique context.

Principles for New Organizational Structures

Education 2.0 is dominated by top-down, bureaucratic decision-making structures, a focus on compliance (that is, disempowerment of both teachers and students), rigidity, seniority, political influence, and little to no choice for students or teachers. But there are already effective non-bureaucratic alternatives (Pinchot & Pinchot, 1993) for Education 3.0, PCBE. We offer five principles for organizational structures.

Principle U: Small school size

Principle V: Professional organizational structure

Principle W: Student choice, teacher incentives, and accountability

Principle X: Administrative structures

Principle Y: Governance structures

These principles are interrelated and interdependent with each other and with the principles for competency-based education, learner-centered instruction, restructured curriculum, new roles, and a nurturing culture. The following is an introduction to each of these principles.

Principle U: Small School Size

Small school size has many advantages, including the following.

- **It mitigates the alienation** that a large school engenders, with its side effects of adversarial cliques and bullying.

- **It promotes understanding** across race, gender, ethnicity, religion, and other differences among people, because students have more opportunities to interact with and know those students in the school who are different from themselves.

- **It tends to be less bureaucratic**, have lower administrative expenses, and be more adaptive to students' needs.

- **It amplifies teachers' collective voice** in running their school.

In a word, small schools empower students and teachers. They promote the development of strong, caring relationships (principle Q, page 90), including social, emotional, and character development.

On the other hand, some disadvantages of small schools include the following.

- **Difficulty affording facilities** such as libraries, media centers, cafeterias, auditoriums, gymnasiums, and other athletic facilities

- **Difficulty affording to offer specialized services**, like special education and gifted and talented education

- **Difficulty affording to offer a large variety of courses**

All three of these disadvantages can be overcome by housing several small schools in a single building in which such facilities, services, and courses can be shared by all the schools. We describe this further in Principle V: Professional Organizational Structure (page 105).

Micro Schools

Micro schools are one model of a small school. They "have no more than 150 students in grades K–12; multiple ages learn together in a single classroom; teachers act more as guides than lecturers; there's a heavy emphasis on digital and project-based learning; and small class sizes, combined with those other factors, make for a highly personalized education" (Prothero, 2016). AltSchool is a well-known micro school network (Horn, 2015).

Principle V: Professional Organizational Structure

We call teaching a profession, but we do not treat teachers as professionals. Other professionals, like architects, accountants, and lawyers, can if they wish work in partnerships in which they control their work. In the partnerships, the professionals run their firms, including all managerial decisions. Those firms tend to be small, avoiding the need for expensive bureaucracy. The professionals are not only responsible for serving the best interests of their clients, but are empowered to do so. Could such an organizational structure work in public education?

In fact, this arrangement is already appearing in public education (American Institutes for Research, 1999; Dirkswager, 2002; Farris-Berg & Dirkswager, 2013; Kolderie, Dirkswager, Farris-Berg, & Schroeder, 2003). The Minnesota New Country School was established in Henderson, Minnesota, in 1994 by about ten teachers who wanted to collectively run their own school. They were able to do so as a public charter school, but such a school could become the norm within public school districts, with some restructuring of the district. This school (and many others in the EdVisions network; see edvisions.org) is a *professional model* of teaching, rather than a *factory model* (or supervisory or labor-management model). This school was recognized as one of the top eight charter schools in the country by the U.S. Department of Education Office of Innovation and Improvement in 2006.

In 2014, Education Evolving, jointly with the Center for Teaching Quality, created the Teacher-Powered School Initiative to build awareness of, interest in, support for, and use of the idea of teachers controlling professional issues, as other professionals do (see www.teacherpowered.org). This initiative helps schools to form or transform into ones that are collaboratively designed and run by teachers. As of April 2019, there were over one hundred teacher-powered schools in seventeen states (listed at www.teacherpowered .org/inventory/list), and many more were under development. More than half of these schools are in public school districts. Furthermore, research conducted by Richard Ingersoll at the University of Pennsylvania found that "students who go to schools where their teachers have a leadership role in decision making perform significantly better on state tests" (Will, 2017).

The Teacher-Powered Schools Initiative has identified fifteen dimensions of teacher power (https://www.teacherpowered.org/inventory/autonomies):

1. Selecting colleagues
2. Transferring and terminating colleagues
3. Evaluating colleagues
4. Setting staff pattern (size and allocation of staff)
5. Selecting leaders
6. Determining budget

Teacher-Powered Schools Initiative

New Organizational Structures

continued →

7. Determining compensation, including leaders

8. Determining learning program and materials (teaching methods, curriculum, technology)

9. Setting the schedule (including school hours and length of school year)

10. Setting school-level policies

11. Determining tenure policy

12. Determining professional development

13. Determining whether to take, when to take, and how much to count assessments

14. Assessing school performance according to multiple measures

15. Determining work hours

For more details, see *Trusting Teachers with School Success: What Happens When Teachers Call the Shots* (Farris-Berg & Dirkswager, 2013).

Some of the major features that we recommend for this professional kind of organizational structure include the following.

- Teachers have the authority as well as responsibility to best meet each of their students' individual needs. Their authority includes the power to set the mission of their school, build a structure that supports their mission, choose their fellow teachers, choose their leader, and allocate resources as needed to fulfill the mission.

- Because the school's survival depends on retaining students, teachers are accountable directly to their individual students and students' parents (see Principle W: Student Choice, Teacher Incentives, and Accountability), rather than being indirectly accountable to students and parents through a bureaucracy and elected officials (bureaucracy-based accountability).

- Flexibility and innovation are not impeded by an expensive, slow bureaucracy.

- Students and parents choose not only a school, but also possibly a teacher.

- They are public schools, so they cannot charge any tuition or decide who to admit, and they have other processes in place to support equal access for all students.

- To be run by teachers and avoid expensive bureaucracy, the schools must be small—we advocate up to about ten teachers and 150 students, which allows several schools to be housed in a single school building. This, in turn, allows parents to choose their child's school without leaving their local school building.

Such a professional organizational structure is an option your team may wish to explore. It would provide true freedom with responsibility for teachers that could do much to attract more teachers to the profession and improve teacher retention. The fact that so many schools have already been converted to teacher-led schools proves that this organizational structure need not just be part of your long-term ideal vision—that it is viable today.

Principle W: Student Choice, Teacher Incentives, and Accountability

There is a great deal of contention about accountability systems that emphasize high-stakes testing. It is an expensive bureaucratic accountability system that severely constrains flexibility and innovation. But there is an alternative—the same kind of system that holds other professionals accountable, like accountants, architects, and lawyers. Here we propose one way it can be designed with the following components in mind: student choice, student admissions, funding, accountability, and leadership.

- **Student choice:** Each student (or the student's family) rank-orders his or her choice of teachers, who could be in the same or different small schools. An alternative would be for them to choose among schools, with the school assigning students to teachers, preferably using criteria that result in the best match for each student (see Principle R: Multi-Year Mentoring and Multi-Age Grouping, page 91). Choices are made with the understanding that different kinds of teachers (and schools) are better for different kinds of students, and unbiased, easily understandable information about the options would be available to help families (or teachers) make good choices. Such information about different kinds of teachers might include the kinds of structures, routines, and behavior supports they provide in their studio, any kinds of student disabilities or challenges they are particularly adept at dealing with, and any kinds of student interests they are particularly adept with. This information could be made available through online profiles created by each teacher and reviews by parents and students, similar to the product reviews you see on websites like Amazon. With several small schools in a single building, families and students have choice without needing to leave their neighborhood school. It is crucial that this process include safeguards to prevent families from choosing teachers or schools based solely on popularity or recommendations from friends. See Detailed Guidance for New Organizational Structures (Principle W: Student Choice, Teacher Incentives, and Accountability, page 112, and Principle X: Administrative Structures, page 113) for suggestions.

- **Student admissions:** Each teacher (or school) decides how many students to accept each year, but does not decide which ones to admit. This is decided by a stratified lottery that maximizes the number of first choices filled districtwide, within the constraints of diversity guidelines. This admissions process is handled by the district, not by each school (Anderson, 2016). This policy equalizes access to the best schools for students, while promoting understanding among students who are different from each other.

- **Funding:** We propose that public funds (local, state, and federal) follow individual students to whatever public school they attend in the district, and this is already the case in some places (see Public Funds Follow Students to Public Schools). The funds that follow each child are the same across all schools for a given developmental level, except for supplements for children with special needs and those of disadvantaged socioeconomic status. The funds per child are higher at higher developmental levels. No school can charge more than the public funds that follow the student, to ensure that all students have equal access to the best schools for them. This policy provides schools with power: schools control their budgets, and in one variation of this policy, each school hires services from the central administration (or outside vendors), making the central administration a servant of the schools, rather than the other way around (see Principle X: Administrative Structures, page 109).

Public Funds Follow Students to Public Schools

According to *Education Week* (Klein, 2018a):

"The U.S. Department of Education is officially opening up the Weighted Student Funding Pilot in the Every Student Succeeds Act. . . . Under the funding pilot, participating districts can combine federal, state, and local dollars into a single funding stream tied to individual students. English-language learners, poor children, and students in special education—who cost more to educate—would carry with them more money than other students." (p. 4)

- **Accountability:** Organizational structures must address accountability. In a system such as we propose, low demand for a teacher (or school) reduces their enrollment and revenue, thereby forcing it to reduce the number of teachers or teacher incomes, much like an architectural or law firm would do. Ineffective teachers, therefore, do not receive a full salary and might decide that teaching is not the best career for them. This decision is made by the teacher and his or her fellow teachers in the school, precipitated by the choices of students and parents, rather than through a contentious process between the administration and the teachers' union. Conversely, the teachers in a school would likely decide to pay higher salaries to their teachers who are in high demand to discourage them from leaving. Of course, this kind of accountability system will only work well if students and parents have good information to make good choices. Organizational structures to address this problem are described in Principle X: Administrative Structures (page 109). This non-bureaucratic decision-making system (Pinchot & Pinchot, 1993) combines the benefits of competition among schools (which incentivizes excellence and responsiveness to the community's diverse and changing needs) and cooperation among teachers within each school (providing support and encouragement among teachers) to make better and quicker decisions at a significantly lower cost. It also provides greater incentives for the best teachers to remain in teaching.

- **Leadership:** Finally, the teachers choose their own head of school, who typically also teaches part-time. Teachers also serve on committees that handle such matters as personnel, finance, curriculum and standards, operations, public relations (and a few others), sometimes with the help of an administrative assistant whom the teachers hire. A teacher's income is no longer based on seniority but on performance as perceived collectively by one's colleagues in the school, constrained only by the school's revenue.

Principle X: Administrative Structures

One feature you might consider for your long-term ideal vision is for the districtwide administrative system to play a servant role rather than a command-and-control role with its schools. The following are some ideas for how this could be designed.

- **Landlord:** If multiple small schools occupy space in a single building and money follows the students to their schools, the district office could serve as landlord for the schools, charging them rent for their facilities.

- **Support services:** The district office could be contracted by each school to provide such support services as student placement, finances and accounting, purchasing, janitorial, transportation, security, special education, technology support, food services, family services, and coordination with community organizations.

- **Incubation:** The district office could support the incubation of new schools, primarily through funds ("seed money") and advice for start-up planning and implementation.

- **Enforcement**: The district office should enforce the few district policies and regulations (adopted by the district school board) for all schools.

Principle Y: Governance Structures

The current governance structure of schools is not working well (Sarason, 1995), partly because school boards often want to micro-manage the system. Fortunately, the choice-driven decision-making and accountability system changes the role of the school board. Its role becomes more like a regulatory agency. It sets and monitors the attainment of community standards (learning outcomes) much like a chartering organization does now, and it establishes a small number of policies and regulations that ensure the choice-driven accountability system promotes equity, diversity, excellence, and other community values. A nonprofit charter school authorizer in Minnesota called Innovative Quality Schools (see iqsmn.org) provides a good example of how this kind of school district could operate. The good news is that as of 2017, at least fifteen states had taken steps to waive regulations, set up innovation zones, or establish task forces to encourage use of PCBE (Burnette, 2017). Vermont passed a law that requires "students in grades 7–12 to have personalized learning plans, more flexible options for earning academic credit, and proficiency assessments to measure their skills" (Bushweller, 2017, p. 19). In this new governance structure, the district board also manages a citizen review board that adjudicates disputes among stakeholders (teachers, parents, students, schools, the district office, and other service providers) and protects the rights of disadvantaged students.

Detailed Guidance for New Organizational Structures

We recommend that you read all sections titled Principles in chapters 1 through 6 before reading the Detailed Guidance section in any of those chapters, because the principles are so interrelated and interdependent that it really helps to understand the big picture before getting into the details. Any effort to move to PCBE that focuses on one core idea without making changes in other core ideas is likely to fail.

School-Level and District-Level Considerations

Organizational structures must be addressed on the school or district level, so there are no classroom-level considerations for these principles. Again, you should first think in the ideal for a long-term vision (step 2.1, chapter 10, page 196), and then compromise as necessary for your first implementation (step 2.3, chapter 10, page 200).

Principle U: Small School Size

Your change team must consider how to form small schools and decide how to handle issues related to facilities, staffing, and connections with the community.

Q How should small schools be formed?

Teachers should decide which other teachers they would like to partner with to form a small school—typically three to twelve teachers each. Their partners do not have to come from the same school building. It is important to partner with others who have similar beliefs and philosophies of education and whose personalities are compatible. Strong relationships among the teachers in a school will foster strong relationships between teachers and students and among students. Complementary areas of expertise are also an important criterion. Some teachers may band together to offer a teacher-centered school (Education 2.0), given the likelihood that some families in the community will prefer the familiar for their children.

Each small school functions like an independent contractor within the school district (with some requirements to ensure equity) and is licensed (or chartered) by the district office. This is similar to the common practice of creating academies or schools-within-a-school, except that each of these smaller schools has much more auton-omy and is run by its teachers rather than by a building principal (see Principle V: Professional Organizational Structure, page 105), with choice-based accountability rather than bureaucracy-based accountability (see Principle W: Student Choice, Teacher Incentives, and Accountability, page 107).

What facilities should small schools have?

In larger traditional school buildings, each school would rent a wing or floor of the building from the district and share some facilities, such as the gym, library, auditorium, and cafeteria. Anywhere from one to twenty schools are located in a single building, depending on its size. New educational buildings have a very different design that places shared facilities in a central area, like the hub of a wheel, surrounded by a small school on each spoke of the wheel.

What staffing should small schools have?

Staffing should be decided collectively by the teachers in the school. Keep in mind that other professions have different levels and kinds of staffing. Perhaps not all teachers are full partners; perhaps there are some assistant teachers. A school may take on interns (teachers in training). It may take on volunteers, especially family members, for some tasks. It may hire an administrative assistant to free the head teacher and other teachers from some administrative tasks, and several small schools might share an administrative assistant. The school may also contract some people from the district office or outside contractors to perform some tasks, usually part-time.

What ties should a small school have with its community?

Finally, we recommend that every school has an advisory board made up primarily of its students' families and a few community members who are committed to education. The board is made up of volunteers who are either appointed by the teachers or elected by the families. The board provides advice and assistance to the school and supports the school's community-based education activities. Individual teachers also have personal ties to all their students' families.

Principle V: Professional Organizational Structure

What power should teachers have?

In Education 3.0, teachers, as professionals, have full responsibility for the success of their school and therefore are given far more power than teachers have in Education 2.0. Teachers have power to decide the following.

- Which other teachers should be partners in their school (as in a small law firm or accounting firm)

- How to spend their school revenue, including salaries and bonuses for their teachers, salaries for any support personnel, amount of space to rent, services to contract, and budgets for technology and other learning resources

- Whom to hire and fire, including which other staff should be part of their school (assistants, interns, volunteers)

- Their hours and days of operation

- Their content, ways to teach it, and ways to assess mastery

The school district (central office and school board) has the responsibility to set certain standards and policies regarding these matters, but they should be kept to a minimum. Ultimately, the state has the responsibility to make sure that districts are living up to state standards and policies, but again they should be kept to a minimum—far less obtrusive than at present—because the bureaucracy-based accountability system is replaced by the choice-based accountability system.

In an Education 3.0 system, teachers, as professionals, also have the ability to move to a different school at any time, with the power to negotiate their seniority status and benefits and keep their retirement accounts, much like most professionals going to a different organization. Similarly, teachers can choose their focus area and the developmental level of their students. The new system removes these decisions from the bureaucracy-based decision-making process. Also, should a teacher want a lighter load, the team could approve such, recognizing that opting for fewer students will likely reduce that teacher's salary and may have other impacts on the school.

Principle W: Student Choice, Teacher Incentives, and Accountability

Q   **How should student choice be implemented?**

Your team needs to carefully implement student choice and consider how to structure teacher incentives and accountability while promoting innovation. In the kind of system we propose, there is an open admissions process each year. When a student is about to enter a new developmental level, the student or his or her family submits their rank-ordered choice of approximately three teachers, which could be in the same or different small schools. Alternatively, the choice could be among schools, with the school assigning the student to a teacher. Also, the teachers decide collaboratively on the maximum number of new students to accept that year (which affects the school's income).

Student admission is then decided by a stratified lottery that maximizes the students' preferences districtwide, within the constraints of balance guidelines regarding race, gender, ethnicity, socioeconomic status, religion, and whatever other diversity factors the community or state values. In this age of increasing divisions within the United States and other countries, these balance guidelines are important. Finally, all educational revenues—local, state, and federal—follow the student to whatever school she or he attends. This system can avoid becoming a popularity contest by having a certain kind of districtwide student placement service, which is described in Principle X: Administrative Structures.

What ways can incentives, innovation, and accountability be implemented?

Incentives and accountability are natural results of the student choice system, depending on how it is designed. Teachers are accountable to their students and their fellow teachers. First, if students choose teachers rather than schools, then those teachers who are in low demand are at risk of being let go by their fellow teachers. There is great incentive not only for them to improve their own teaching, but also for their fellow teachers to help them improve (because their school's revenues will increase if those teachers can get more students). This arrangement also rewards innovation by the teachers individually and collectively in the school, because innovation improves their ratings and demand for their teachers.

Second, if students choose schools rather than teachers, then schools that are in low demand will likely have fewer students and lower revenues. This provides a strong incentive for teachers in a small school to help each other improve, to innovate, and to adapt to the ever-evolving educational needs of their community.

How else can innovation be promoted?

Our current educational system is highly resistant to change—significant change only occurs in response to a crisis. To prevent the new system from being equally resistant to change, it must be a self-adjusting learning organization in which crises are minimized because change is continuous (Senge, 1990, 2000). Teachers are in charge of adapting their practices to the changing educational needs of the community and students, rather than administrators and politicians controlling the changes. Furthermore, an incubation policy could be designed to encourage the formation of new small schools to bring fresh ideas into education. This policy is described in greater detail under principle X next.

Principle X: Administrative Structures

In Education 3.0, the district administrative system is designed to support rather than to control, so it receives most of its budget from the small schools, rather than the other way around. The district's role is that of a service provider, particularly in the areas of facilities and related services, student placement, and school quality assurance.

What might the landlord role be for the district office?

The district would generate some of its budget by being the landlord for small schools. The district office would charge each small school rent for their facilities, including a prorated share of such common facilities as cafeteria, gymnasium, library, technology center, and auditorium. In return, the district office could handle all maintenance, improvements, heating and cooling, water, and electricity. The district office's budget for this role would come solely from rents paid by each school. In a variation of this design,

the schools could rent such facilities from the private sector if they could find a better deal there.

What might the support services role be for the district office?

The district office might fulfill the support services role in many ways, such as the following.

- District personnel provide services.

- A school outsources services to private or nonprofit contractors, including government bodies such as county offices (for transportation, facilities, purchasing, and so on), with the district office serving an oversight role.

- The district office outsources services to private or nonprofit contractors at a group-negotiated rate.

- Services are provided through some combination of these methods.

The budget for this role also would come solely from fees paid by each school (except for the district oversight role—see Principle Y: Governance Structures), which offers more control to the teachers, as well as flexibility.

What might the student placement service role be for the district office?

For the choice system to work well, the district office needs to provide placement services to students and their families. As part of this, it collects and disseminates unbiased information about the performance of all the district's small schools, their teachers, buildings, and support service providers, patterned somewhat after *Consumer Reports*. The district prepares comprehensive measures of performance for each of these and makes them available to families and students (with state auditing), along with information about teaching styles and other factors that influence which teacher will be the best match for each student. The descriptions for a school might include a comprehensive school culture rating, such as the Vibrant School Scale developed at the William & Mary School of Education (tinyurl.com/vibrant-schools).

The placement office also serves as a placement counseling service for matching students with teachers or schools. It conducts diagnostic testing (different from standardized, high-stakes testing) and interviews students to help find the best match for each student—and to make the choices for families who don't participate in this process. This assistance helps break the cycle of poverty by ensuring that all students are well matched with a teacher. It is important for this placement office to have some independence, to avoid inappropriate influences from schools.

Furthermore, education is a public good that benefits the whole community—not just the individual student—through lower crime rate, greater economic development, more taxes received, and much more. Therefore, the placement office should offer a rating mechanism that allows external community members, such as employers and senior citizens, to submit ratings or reviews of individual teachers or schools, to further inform students' or families' selection of teachers (or schools). This could be done with a product rating system similar to that used by Amazon, for rating individual teachers or their small schools, but it is important to have some monitoring of those ratings and reviews to ensure truthfulness. Of course, teachers also have access to this information, so they can make improvements in response to feedback and could even respond to reviews with which they disagree.

What might the incubation and enforcement role be for the district office?

The district also plays a role in making sure it consists of high-quality schools that serve stakeholders' needs. This might involve being like a watchdog agency, making sure that all the small schools and service providers follow the (hopefully few) district policies, regulations, and ethical standards adopted by the district school board. The budget for this role would likely come from local property taxes or (eventually) from state funds based on student enrollment districtwide. If a group of teachers were to solicit enough parent signatures to support creation of a new small school, the district office could support its creation with a grant for start-up funds and expertise to help them plan and start operations.

Principle Y: Governance Structures

Here we will present some ideas for your change team to consider as you make decisions about what local and state governance structures could be like, as well as the educational finance systems for funding them. Even though your team may not be able to influence state governance at all now, we recommend thinking about changes you would like to see there, because that will help you see a more distant horizon for your ideal vision.

What could the local governance structures be like?

The local school board could continue to exist in its current (Education 2.0) form, elected by the community citizens. However, it would have considerably less power over the schools. It would set policies and regulations, much like the legislative branch of a government. It would also make decisions about the local school taxes—rates (subject to voter approval), collection, and allocation (how much would follow each student to his or her school and how much would support the district office in its various roles as described in Principle X: Administrative Structures, page 113)—subject to the funding equity measures addressed in the educational finance system question (page 116).

The superintendent and the district office would carry out and enforce the policies, much like the executive branch of government, with such structures as those described in Principle X: Administrative Structures (page 113). The superintendent could be chosen by the school board or elected by the citizens—there are pros and cons to each arrangement.

The school board could also appoint an arbitration committee, which would arbitrate any disputes about district policies, practices, and regulations, much like the judicial branch of government. Committee members should serve relatively long, fixed terms to avoid undue pressure from the school board in its decisions.

What could the state governance structures be like?

The state governance system should be designed to support and monitor both equity and quality, rather than control the districts, because bureaucratic control is made unnecessary by the choice-based accountability system. The state school board and department of education establish policies and regulations that ensure the choice-driven decision-making system promotes equity, diversity, excellence, and other state values, as a kind of check-and-balance on local variance. It also sets statewide content standards and monitors their attainment—influencing ends rather than means. Most standards are optional, rather than required, giving more discretion to the choice-based decision-making system. The department no longer dictates how or when students must master the required standards. It no longer requires state tests, but assists districts in monitoring student learning.

The department of education ensures that districts receive funds equitably (see next section on educational finance system). It provides consultants and manages networks to help school districts do a better job of supporting schools and families. It supports research and development to help schools and districts improve their practices and to provide them with better educational tools and resources. Finally, the state school board could appoint an arbitration committee to review disputes that district arbitration committees were unable to resolve.

What could the educational finance system be like?

School funding is a difficult and controversial topic. Property taxes—the way most schools are traditionally funded—are the most regressive way to support public education, because lower-income people end up paying a larger proportion of their income to school taxes. Also, communities with fewer businesses are at a disadvantage. However, state income tax revenues fluctuate considerably from economic expansion and recession, and large, periodic budget cutbacks due to economic downturns have a strongly negative effect on schools, as happened during the Great Recession of 2007. Three solutions include an income tax option, a property tax option, and a hybrid option.

- **Income tax option:** One solution is to fund education with a dedicated portion of the state income tax, but this option would require building a funding reserve (a certain percent of the annual education budget) during years of economic expansion, to be used to maintain the education budget during years of recession (reduced tax revenues). The state (perhaps its department of education or an independent committee) could project a ten-year budget for its public schools that builds in an adjustment for student population change and inflation. Then, it could identify a metric for strength of the state economy to automatically determine when the state budget should allocate money to the reserve, and how much, so that the state budget can be planned accordingly.

- **Property tax option:** An alternative solution is to use property taxes to fund education, but to set local school tax rates on a sliding scale, so less expensive single-family dwellings and apartment buildings are charged a lower school tax rate. However, this does not address the inequities inherent in some communities being poorer than others or having fewer businesses that pay local property or income taxes. State income tax could be used to even out such inequities.

- **Hybrid option:** A third solution is a hybrid. The new system must find a revenue stream that is both more stable throughout the economic cycle and more equitable across communities of differing means to support it. Perhaps some combination of the two options just described would be the optimal design. Minnesota has developed an interesting system that entails districts collecting a uniform percentage of their wealth (say, 1.25 percent of property market values) for education and the state paying the balance up to a per-pupil amount deemed appropriate (for a student without special needs in a district without unusual cost-drivers). Thus, districts are equitably funded, with wealthier districts paying a larger share of their education expenses and poorer districts receiving more support from the state. In addition, Minnesota had adopted an innovative tax-base sharing program that "narrowed significantly the disparity in commercial-industrial valuations per capita" (Kolderie, 2018, p. 89).

Another issue is how the revenues are distributed. Several mechanisms are needed. First, the state should fund each school directly (bypassing the district office) through a formula based on the number of its students, the age of each student, any special needs each student may have, and a supplement for socioeconomically disadvantaged students. Second, the state should fund each district for its role in incubating new schools, enforcing regulations, and protecting the interests of schools in their external contracts—through a formula based on the number of students in the district. Money for such support services as transportation, special education, technology support, and others listed under Principle X: Administrative Structures (page 113) comes from the small schools on a fee-for-services basis. Third, some money goes directly to the district for its placement counseling service and school- and teacher-rating services, again through a formula based on the number of students in the district. Fourth, some money goes directly to the district school board to fund the board itself, the superintendent, and perhaps one or two staff members, depending on the size of the district.

Common Problems With Visions

This chapter offered guidance for the last of the six core ideas for your vision of PCBE for Education 3.0. We close our guidance for your vision with a caution about two common problems with visions that teams like yours develop: difficulty thinking in the ideal and lack of systemic compatibility.

Difficulty Thinking in the Ideal

Educators are practical people. It is difficult for us to think in the ideal. It takes constant reminders for your team members to imagine what an ideal educational system would be like. Rest assured that there will be time later in the process (see step 2.3 in chapter 10, page 200) to compromise on that ideal to address current constraints for your new PCBE system. Experience shows that many perceived constraints can be overcome or worked around within a few years, if not right away. Be bold! Create an ideal vision first, then compromise as needed, but continue to work toward the ideal.

Lack of Systemic Compatibility

PCBE represents a fundamental change. Competency-based student progress cannot succeed without competency-based student assessment, targets, and records. It cannot succeed without personalized learning, which requires learning by doing and self-directed learning. And none of these can succeed without changes in the roles of teachers, students, parents, and technology. And they require big changes in the culture and organizational structures of a school. If your team decides to take it slow, one change at a time, you will inevitably find that each change is a failure. It is like trying to change a railroad, one paradigm of transportation, into an airline, a different paradigm, one part at a time. The parts must all be changed in concert, due to their systemic interdependencies. Be comprehensive in your vision! The way you *should* take it slow is by not trying to change all schools in a district at the same time (see step 3.2 in chapter 10, page 204).

Summary

This chapter described five principles for organizational structures that are universally helpful for maximizing student learning.

> Principle U: Small school size
>
> Principle V: Professional organizational structure
>
> Principle W: Student choice, teacher incentives, and accountability
>
> Principle X: Administrative structures
>
> Principle Y: Governance structures

It then offered detailed guidelines to help your team develop part of your shared ideal vision for your classrooms, school, and district. Finally, it offered cautions about two common problems with visions: difficulty thinking in the ideal and lack of systemic compatibility.

This chapter concludes our guidance for what a PCBE classroom, school, and district should be like in Education 3.0. The purpose of these guidelines is to stimulate your team's thinking. We encourage you to think critically about all these principles and suggestions and tailor them to your specific situation.

To help you visualize some of the changes described in chapters 1 through 6, chapter 7 presents two comprehensive case studies that span the classroom, school, and district levels. Part II (page 145) then offers guidance about the change process, to increase the chances you will be successful in bringing about whatever changes you envision.

The Principles in Action

In this chapter, we offer two case studies that demonstrate two of the many ways that the principles of PCBE can be implemented, one in a single school and the other in a school district.

Case 1: The Minnesota New Country School

This case description was prepared with assistance from Paul Jaeger and Layne Sherwood at Minnesota New Country School. We are grateful for their contributions.

The Minnesota New Country School (MNCS) is a public charter school in Henderson, Minnesota, with two buildings, one operating at the elementary level and one at the secondary level. It was founded in 1994 and has 220 students in grades K–12. The mission of MNCS is to guide students toward self-actualization. To achieve that mission, they leverage the power of purposeful relationships, community, student-led project-based learning, and experiential education. MNCS is a teacher-powered school, and teachers work closely with one another, students, and parents to strengthen their learning community. More information is available about MNCS at the following websites.

- www.newcountryschool.com

- www.edvisions.org

- www.education-reimagined.org/pioneers/minnesota-new-country-school

MNCS Evidence of Success

MNCS reported the following effectiveness metrics in its 2016–2017 Annual Report:

- One hundred percent of sophomores, juniors, and seniors completing grade-level projects at MNCS had career and college exploration components that were focused and meaningful.

- Ninety percent (eighteen of twenty) of graduating seniors in 2016–2017 had specific post-secondary plans in place upon graduating from MNCS.

continued →

MNCS reported the following metrics in its Spring 2018 Student Survey:

- Ninety-one percent of students agreed or strongly agreed attending MNCS benefits them.
- Ninety-one percent of students agreed or strongly agreed that MNCS helped them understand how they learn best.
- Ninety-four percent of students agreed or strongly agreed that they possess the project skills to make a great project.
- Ninety-four percent of students agreed or strongly agreed they will graduate from MNCS.
- Ninety-five percent of students agreed or strongly agreed they feel accepted for who they are at MNCS.

MNCS reported the following metrics in its Spring 2018 Parent Survey:

- Ninety-four percent of parents agreed or strongly agreed that they receive feedback on their child's areas of growth and areas for growth from their advisor.
- Ninety-five percent of parents agreed or strongly agreed that their input is utilized to help strengthen their child's learning plan.
- Ninety-six percent of parents agreed or strongly agreed their child has a good working relationship with their advisor.

For life skills, a survey of MNCS graduates in 2009 reported percentages of alumni who graded the school as good or excellent in instilling the following skills:

Skill	Percentage of Alumni Grading MNCS as Good or Excellent
Creativity	100
Problem solving	95
Decision making	91
Time management	87
Finding information	100
Learning to learn	91
Responsibility	92
Self-esteem	84
Social skills	79
Self-direction	92
Leadership	84

MNCS was recognized as one of the top eight charter schools in the country by the U.S. Department of Education's Office of Innovation and Improvement in 2006.

Table 7.1 shows our estimation of how thoroughly MNCS has implemented the six core ideas and related principles described in chapters 1 through 6. A *0* indicates that the principle is apparently not used in the school, and a *5* indicates that the principle is, in our opinion, exhibiting an excellent level of application.

Core Ideas	Principles	Score
Competency-Based Education	A. Competency-based student progress	5
	B. Competency-based student assessment	4
	C. Competency-based learning targets	3
	D. Competency-based student records	5
Learner-Centered Instruction	E. Learning by doing	5
	F. Instructional support	5
	G. Personalized learning	5
	H. Collaborative learning	3
Restructured Curriculum	I. Relevance to students' current and future lives	5
	J. Whole-child education	5
	K. Balance of universal content and individual strengths	4
	L. Sound progressions in content	3
New Roles	M. Teacher as guide	5
	N. Self-directed student	5
	O. Parent as partner	4
	P. Technology as a tool for students	4
A Nurturing Culture	Q. Strong and caring relationships	5
	R. Multi-year mentoring and multi-age grouping	5
	S. Motivational learning	5
	T. Family services	4
New Organizational Structures	U. Small school size	5
	V. Professional organizational structure	5
	W. Student choice, teacher incentives, and accountability	5
	X. Administrative structures	4
	Y. Governance structures	4

Table 7.1:

Implementation of the Twenty-Five Principles in MNCS

The following sections describe how MNCS applies the six core ideas.

1. Competency-Based Education

As described in chapter 1 (page 15), competency-based education includes competency-based student progress, competency-based student assessment, competency-based learning targets, and competency-based student records.

Principle A: Competency-Based Student Progress

Students' progress in this school is based on successful completion of projects. After students complete a project, they must present and defend the project before a team consisting of the students' advisor (the MNCS term for teacher) and another advisor—the same team that approved the proposal for the project—before they can move on to a new project. There are clear expectations and rules, including the expected pace of ten credits per year and sixty credits by graduation in the secondary school. The elementary and secondary schools are in separate buildings, and credits do not become part of the curriculum until students reach the secondary school in seventh grade. A credit is roughly one hundred hours of work, but that is adjusted based on the quality of the student's effort, making it less of a time-based criterion and more of a competency-based one.

Principle B: Competency-Based Student Assessment

Each student develops her or his own detailed self-assessment rubric for his or her projects. The rubric includes three main categories: project skills (for example, task completion), critical thinking skills (for example, self-evaluation), and performance skills (for example, organization).

Principle C: Competency-Based Learning Targets

In order to graduate, each student is responsible for figuring out how he or she wants to go about meeting the learning targets provided by Minnesota's Department of Education. Students may do so through independent project work, participation in Experience Fridays (teacher-led learning experiences), or involvement in seminars led by teachers or Postsecondary Enrollment Options classes.

Principle D: Competency-Based Student Records

Instead of a grade, the student receives credits for their project work. The team decides how many credits the student earned in the project, based on demonstrated achievement through authentic assessment. A student graduates from high school when they have completed all the requisite state standards, as well as sixty project credits, required life skills, and a senior project.

2. Learner-Centered Instruction

As described in chapter 2 (page 27), learner-centered instruction involves learning by doing, instructional support, personalized learning, and collaborative learning.

Principle E: Learning by Doing

At the MNCS secondary school, students create their own academic programs through self-directed, individualized, and occasionally small-group learning projects. Individual students work with an advisor to complete a project proposal form that specifies what they will do, the resources they will use, a timeline for completing project tasks, what state standards will be met, and how much credit they seek for doing the project. The proposal must be approved by an advisor team (the same one that evaluates the project when it's complete) before the student may initiate work on the project. The approved proposal serves as a learning contract. This process allows students to explore topics that interest them in their own way and largely at their own pace. In this manner, students engage in experiential activities, such as service-learning, place-based learning, and internships. Project-based learning is practiced at the elementary school, though in a more teacher-led manner, as described in table 7.2. Elementary teachers begin with projects at the top of the chart and work to increasingly transfer more agency to the learner (moving to the bottom of the chart).

Types of Projects	Description
Curriculum-Controlled Projects	Project is part of curricular unit, text, or similar All students do the same thing No student choice Graded as part of class unit
Teacher-Directed Class Projects	Student inquiry, choice of topic within curriculum Students must frame their own questions All students have the same timeframe Graded as part of class unit
Interdisciplinary Teacher-Directed Projects	Project is inquiry-based, still curriculum-based Project is interdisciplinary and thematic Students may be in cooperative groups Performance, product assessment, and class grade used
Authentic Projects Created With Teacher-Student Interaction	Project is interdisciplinary, inquiry-based, authentic Rubrics assess performances, critical thinking, and problem solving Students work in groups, teams, or as whole class Project includes place-based learning, service learning, and so on
Authentic, Self-Directed Projects	Project is teacher-facilitated The world is the curriculum, guided by standards Rubrics assess learning-to-learn skills, personal development, and so on Performance and products assessed, includes real-world audience May be individual or group projects Could include place-based, service-learning projects Non-graded, timeframe negotiable

Table 7.2:

The MNCS Degrees of Project-Based Learning

Source: Adapted by MNCS from the EdVisions Coop of Henderson, Minnesota. www.edvisions.org

Principle F: Instructional Support

During a project, the student works with different advisors at the school, experts from the local community, and digital resources to learn what they want to learn. Students are encouraged to help each other learn when they are having difficulty learning on their own. The school offers on-demand seminars and how-to workshops to provide direct instruction and practice in support of student projects. Advisors provide basic skills instruction to individuals or small groups when diagnostic assessments reveal the need. Learners with cognitive disabilities have the same self-directed, project-based learning experiences as all other learners. Rather than mainstreaming special needs learners into a standardized classroom, the opposite happens here: all students experience personalized learning with individual learning plans.

Principle G: Personalized Learning

While some goals (the state standards) are required of all students, goals are personalized to the extent that students can add other goals of interest in the design of their projects. Projects themselves are completely personalized as each student designs his or her own projects. Scaffolding is largely personalized to the extent that the student typically decides when he or she needs support, how much, and who will provide it (peers, teachers, or outside experts). Individual students personalize assessment by developing their own criteria for what will make their project successful and by presenting and defending the project before the same team that approved the proposal for the project. That defense is also an opportunity for personalized reflection on the project and learning process.

Principle H: Collaborative Learning

Students do not work in teams on their projects, primarily because that makes it easier to assess individual learning. However, students collaborate on their projects as needed. Students are encouraged to assist each other when they encounter difficulties in understanding what they need to learn, and such peer assistance involves some degree of collaboration.

3. Restructured Curriculum

As described in chapter 3 (page 57), restructured curriculum includes relevance to students' current and future lives, whole-child education, balance of universal content and individual strengths, and sound progressions in content.

Principle I: Relevance to Students' Current and Future Lives

Academic achievement is driven by Minnesota's state standards, but students design their own interdisciplinary projects to meet those standards, so they can make their respective projects relevant to their interests and needs.

Principle J: Whole-Child Education

Recently, MNCS established expectations for three areas: (1) respect and responsibility, (2) academic achievement, and (3) engagement. Each area has four levels of development, and a student's privileges increase with each level. For example, students at level 1 of responsibility have supervised computer and internet use, whereas students who have reached level 4 may use their personal computers with full internet access at any time. In addition to these three core areas, MNCS fosters social, emotional, and other aspects of development (see figure 7.1) through group projects, peace-keeping circles, life skills, a restorative justice program, and other means.

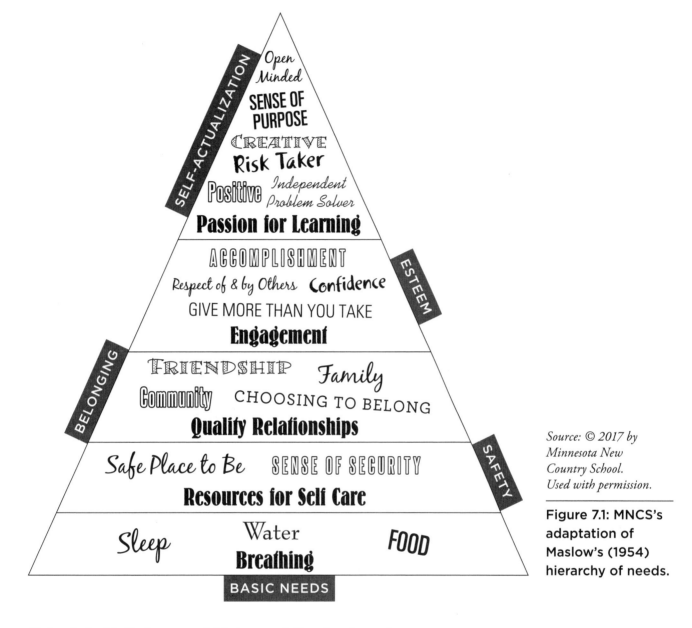

Source: © 2017 by Minnesota New Country School. Used with permission.

Figure 7.1: MNCS's adaptation of Maslow's (1954) hierarchy of needs.

Principle K: Balance of Universal Content and Individual Strengths

The Minnesota Department of Education defines some of what students need to learn in order to graduate from high school, but does not prescribe how to go about learning those things. At MNCS, students decide how they meet state standards as they move toward graduation, and advisors support them in making that happen. This allows students to play to their strengths and construct *producibles* (work products that show what they know) that are meaningful to them as they move through required content that they may or may not enjoy.

Principle L: Sound Progressions in Content

Students figure out how to address their content standards (dictated by the state of Minnesota) in ways that work for them (rather than the teacher deciding for them). Thus, the progression is fundamentally determined by the state standards on the macro level and by the student on the micro level.

4. New Roles

As described in chapter 4 (page 71), the new roles in PCBE are teacher as guide, self-directed student, parent as partner, and technology as a tool for students.

Principle M: Teacher as Guide

Teachers are called *advisors* at MNCS, and they serve two major roles: teaching and administration. For the teaching role, the advisor facilitates learning rather than disseminating knowledge. This means that advisors do not define the course sequence for students, they do not set the syllabus for each course, and they do not pick texts for student reading, assign work, create deadlines, measure progress, or give grades. In fact, there aren't any courses as we know them in Education 2.0. Instead, students have control over these matters, with advisor guidance as described in Learner-Centered Instruction (page 124). Each advisor serves a generalist role as a mentor-advisor for a group of nineteen students, called an *advisory*, but also serves a specialist role for a particular subject area or two. For the administration role, the advisors collectively run the school without a principal (find more on this in New Organizational Structures, page 130).

Principle N: Self-Directed Student

As students design their own projects, the planning phase is self-directed to the extent the student can handle (with guidance from the teacher as needed). The performing phase is also self-directed, with students managing their own work, receiving guidance from the teacher only when needed. The advisor also encourages students to reflect and self-evaluate throughout and at the end of each project. Students play a democratic role in the operation of the school through a weekly town meeting and a student congress made up of elected representatives.

Principle O: Parent as Partner

Advisors contact parents regularly by phone or email to seek input and invite them to engage significantly in their students' learning.

Principle P: Technology as a Tool for Students

MNCS is a high-tech learning environment in which all students have their own personal computer with internet access, and responsible students have unrestricted access to the internet. The school adopted Edio, a project management system, in 2018 to help students navigate their projects and learning progress and to help staff organize and support student progress. Technology plays a central role in MNCS and is used mostly for planning student learning, developing projects, accessing resources, and keeping records of student learning. It is not used much for direct instruction or assessment. Students are encouraged to learn from each other.

5. A Nurturing Culture

As described in chapter 5 (page 89), the components of a nurturing culture include strong and caring relationships, multi-year mentoring and multi-age grouping, motivational learning, and family services.

Principle Q: Strong and Caring Relationships

Quality relationships are the pulse of MNCS. Each advisor takes great care to establish positive, professional relationships with her or his students and students' families. Advisories are made up of nineteen students who meet for thirty minutes each morning before moving into project work. This time is used for team building and community development. For instance, in one advisory the advisor does a check-in every Monday, and in another the advisor does a Go Around where each student shares his or her action plan for the day. Beyond advisories, there is a small student-to-teacher ratio, which allows many students to interact with more staff than their primary advisor. This creates an environment where each student is known and known well.

Principle R: Multi-Year Mentoring and Multi-Age Grouping

Students at the MNCS secondary school are not sorted by age, which means there could be as much as a six-year difference among students sharing an advisory. At the end of each school year, students are able to select their top three advisor preferences for the coming year. A student wishing to remain with their current advisor marks them down as their first option and is guaranteed to be part of that advisory the following year. At the elementary school, students are grouped by the following four developmental levels: kindergarten, grades 1–2, grades 2–3, and grades 4–6. Two teachers share the fourth, fifth, and sixth graders. Each grade level at the elementary school includes no more than eighteen students.

Principle S: Motivational Learning

MNCS places great emphasis on intrinsic motivation, and students are empowered through self-directed, project-based learning, and democratic participation in the operation of the school. When students first arrive to MNCS, rather than giving them an assignment, the advisor asks them to design a project born from their curiosity. From the beginning, the onus is on students to create powerful learning experiences for themselves. In doing so, students discover and deepen their interests, all the while nurturing what motivates them to be at their best.

Principle T: Family Services

MNCS has a school nurse, a social worker, and a behavior interventionist. It also has a partnership with a therapist at Sioux Trails, a mental health center in southern Minnesota. These staff members work closely with families to ensure their students are being served well in the areas of mental, physical, and emotional health. Along with these services, staff at MNCS have at least three forty-five-minute conferences with parents or guardians each year. At these conferences, which include the support staff listed above as necessary, input is gathered to help strengthen the learning plan for each student.

6. New Organizational Structures

As described in chapter 6 (page 103), new organizational structures for PCBE include small school size; professional organizational structure; student choice, teacher incentives, and accountability; administrative structures; and governance structures.

Principle U: Small School Size

MNCS is small; the student body totals 220 pupils, with eighty-seven at the K–6 elementary building and 133 at the 7–12 secondary building. The secondary school has a 2,750-square-foot room called the Atrium in which all students spend most of their time, somewhat like the one-room schoolhouse that characterized education in the agrarian age (Education 1.0). This open room is divvied into seven advisory spaces, as well as a large area to gather for Town Meeting, group project work, and eating lunch (see figure 7.2). The building also has small rooms that serve as specialized learning centers, including the following.

- A science room where students conduct experiments
- An arts studio with a pottery wheel and kiln, a recording studio, and materials for making stained glass and screen-printing fabrics
- A greenhouse
- A woodshop
- A mechanics and metal shop
- A media center

The elementary school is housed in a separate building a few blocks away from the secondary school. It has a more traditional layout, with the lower developmental levels (grades K, 1–2, and 2–3) having their own classrooms and the upper developmental level (grades 4–6) sharing a great room that serves as a common working space.

Principle V: Professional Organizational Structure

MNCS is a small professional organization that's centered on learning. Advisors (teachers) run the elementary and secondary schools without a principal and without supervisory control by a school district office. Therefore, MNCS is a teacher-led school as described in principle V (page 105). Also, all the staff at MNCS chose to work there, and there is little turnover. None were assigned there by an administrator.

**Figure 7.2:
The Atrium.**

Principle W: Student Choice, Teacher Incentives, and Accountability

All students who attend MNCS made a choice to go to this public charter school. The advisors' jobs depend on the school attracting enough students. At the end of each school year, students rank the advisors they want to work with the following year, and they are placed with one of their top choices. This provides great incentive for the advisors to meet their students' needs and listen to their students' parents. This is a choice-driven element of the decision-making and accountability systems. However, because the advisors make all the administrative decisions by consensus, there is also a peer-based decision-making element. Additional incentives for advisors come from performance-based pay, which is influenced by evaluations from students and parents.

Principle X: Administrative Structures

MNCS has no principal. The school is run—both instructionally and administratively— by a cooperative of staff using a consensus model. The staff cooperative has a contract with the school board to provide administrative and other services. Each advisor serves on at least two of the seven management committees that make all the decisions about instruction and administration in their school (including budget and staffing), within the limits of the law.

The school calendar is designed to facilitate organizational learning. Normal operations take place throughout the year in five- to seven-week blocks. Following each block, advisors have a planning week that allows them time to talk and think about their approach to guiding student work. Students and parents complete advisor evaluations, which provide valuable information for advisor and organizational learning.

As a single school, there is no district office, but MNCS does contract some services. Nearly 27 percent of the student body receives special education and related services. The special education department contracts with several qualified professionals to provide required and related services to students. MNCS works with contracted providers such as speech and language pathologists, occupational therapists, physical therapists, school psychologists, developmentally adaptive physical education specialists, specialists who work with physically impaired students, and autism specialists. MNCS also has a special education director and an in-house social worker and behavior interventionist.

Principle Y: Governance Structures

The school is governed by an eight-member school board elected annually. As of August 2019, the school board had four staff members, three parents, and one community member. A finance committee handles the finances and signs checks. A single-purpose authorizer, Innovative Quality Schools, is the current authorizer of MNCS. The authorizer provides oversight to ensure that the school meets academic, budgetary, and administrative standards specified in the school's charter. Figure 7.3 shows the school's organizational chart.

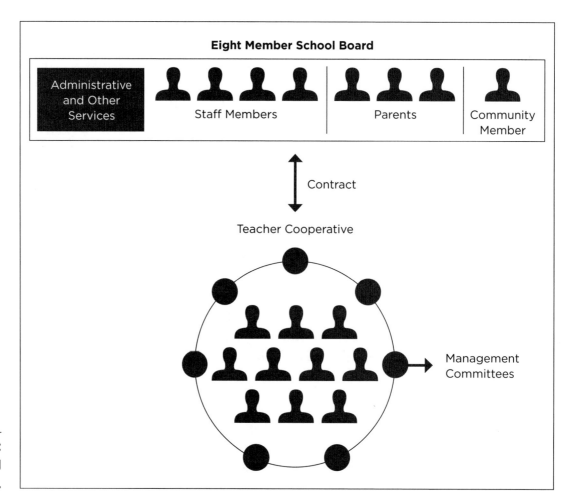

Figure 7.3: Organizational chart for MNCS.

Case 2: Lindsay Unified School District

This case description was written by Barry Sommer and Nikolaus Namba of Lindsay Unified School District.

Lindsay Unified School District (LUSD), which serves over 4,200 learners in preschool through twelfth grade, is a public school district located in California's agriculturally diverse San Joaquin Valley. Lindsay is a small, rural community known for its citrus orchards and olive groves. Home to a large population of immigrant families, Lindsay is 90 percent Hispanic and 50 percent English learners. Lindsay is characterized by a high percentage of families living below the federal poverty level, low levels of literacy in English, and low levels of parental education. Many of the district's learners come from migrant families who work in the surrounding fields and production areas.

Due to Lindsay's geographic, economic, linguistic, and cultural isolation, children face multiple barriers, including the lack of basic needs and command of the English language. Approximately 78 percent of LUSD learners are from low-income families, and 13 percent of learners are considered homeless per state and federal criteria. One hundred percent receive free-or-reduced-price meals. In 2008, graduation rates were in the low 70th percentile.

After many years of low academic performance and implementing various practices, programs, and reforms, the Lindsay Board of Education adopted the strategic design in 2007. This was a crucial turning point for the district as it established the mission, core values, beliefs and guiding principles, vision, and lifelong learning outcomes for the LUSD learning community. The strategic design implementation essentially became the mandate from the Board of Education to develop a performance based system (PBS; Lindsay's term for its PCBE system), which would ensure academic and social success for all learners. The PBS is an innovative, learner-centered approach to education designed to personalize learning to meet learners' academic needs, learning styles, and interests.

To find out more about Lindsay's system and journey, please see the following websites.

- www.lindsay.k12.ca.us
- www.tinyurl.com/y7ekhfku

Table 7.3 (page 134) presents some evidence of success of the PBS. Table 7.4 (page 134) shows our estimation of how thoroughly LUSD has implemented the core ideas and principles described in chapters 1 through 6. A *0* indicates that the principle is not used in the school, and a *5* indicates that the principle is, in our opinion, exhibiting an excellent level of application.

Table 7.3:

Some Pre- and Post-
PBS Comparisons

Category	Metrics	Before PBS	2018
Behavior and Discipline	Suspension and expulsion rate	9.1 percent (2011–12)	3.4 percent
Academic Achievement	Reading: K–2 district reading assessment	46 percent (2013–14)	75 percent
	Reading: 3–12 Scholastic Reading Inventory	25 percent (2013–14)	57 percent
Post-Secondary Trajectory	High school graduation rates	69 percent (2010–11)	95 percent
	College enrollment rates	66 percent (2010–12)	73 percent
College Persistence	Percentage of Lindsay graduates who went to college and obtained a college degree in four years	12 percent	57 percent*
Technology	Availability of computers and internet	A few classroom sets of computers, plus a lab of thirty computers at each school site, little home connectivity	Every learner has a device; 92 percent connected at home
School Climate and Learner Engagement	School Climate Index (SCI)	296/500 (2010–11)	418/500
	SCI state percentile	52 percent (2010–11)	97 percent
	High school dropout rate	6.8 percent (2010–11)	0.5 percent

* Projected (65 percent projected in five years and over 70 percent in six years)

Table 7.4:

Implementation of
the Twenty-Five
Principles in LUSD

Core Ideas	Principles	Score
Competency-Based Education	A. Competency-based student progress	5
	B. Competency-based student assessment	4
	C. Competency-based learning targets	5
	D. Competency-based student records	4
Learner-Centered Instruction	E. Learning by doing	3
	F. Instructional support	4
	G. Personalized learning	5
	H. Collaborative learning	4
Restructured Curriculum	I. Relevance to students' current and future lives	5
	J. Whole-child education	4
	K. Balance of universal content and individual strengths	4
	L. Sound progressions in content	4

Core Ideas	Principles	Score
New Roles	M. Teacher as guide	4
	N. Self-directed student	4
	O. Parent as partner	4
	P. Technology as a tool for students	5
A Nurturing Culture	Q. Strong and caring relationships	5
	R. Multi-year mentoring and multi-age grouping	4
	S. Motivational learning	4
	T. Family services	5
New Organizational Structures	U. Small school size	4
	V. Professional organizational structure	5
	W. Student choice, teacher incentives, and accountability	5
	X. Administrative structures	5
	Y. Governance structures	5

The following sections describe the core ideas as implemented at LUSD.

1. Competency-Based Education

As described in chapter 1 (page 15), competency-based education includes competency-based student progress, competency-based student assessment, competency-based learning targets, and competency-based student records.

Principle A: Competency-Based Student Progress

Learners at LUSD only move to the next level of learning when they have reached proficiency at the prior content level (previously, grade level). This process ensures learners receive the support they need and acquire the prerequisite knowledge to thrive in the next level of learning. All stakeholders can see the progress of student learning using the Empower Learning digital platform. This access enables learners and their parents or guardians to see the granular details of what they have learned, are currently working on, and have not started yet. Learning facilitators (LUSD's term for teachers) and administrators also have access to technology tools that assist in the aggregation and disaggregation of data to speed up the analysis required for effective learner support. Learners then use a personalized learning plan to ensure that conversations take place around understanding their data, appropriate goals, and needed supports.

Principle B: Competency-Based Student Assessment

Assessments in LUSD are learning-target specific. Learners take *3V assessments*, or three-proficiency verifiers, to ensure they have the appropriate knowledge of each learning target and confirm mastery. This system allows for consistent expectations and confidence that all learners are held to the same level of rigor for each learning target, without the concern of subjective opinions influencing the decision. This also allows for the curriculum to be viable, tech-enhanced, and linguistically aligned. Multiple versions of each 3V assessment exist to allow learners who do not meet the expectation on the first attempt to have additional opportunities to meet the same criteria. In some academic content areas, these 3V assessments consist of constructed-response questions with rubric-based scoring. LUSD hopes to move toward a system that allows more experiential learning to take the place of these assessments once the district can ensure that all stakeholders will meet the appropriate rigor expectation per learning target.

Principle C: Competency-Based Learning Targets

All content in LUSD has been defined as learning targets, and several learning targets make up a measurement topic. These measurement topics hold larger conceptual groupings of the content but lack the specificity needed to score learners on a specific skill. It is for that reason each measurement topic is broken into specific learning targets (smaller concepts). Content levels consist of groups of measurement topics.

LUSD takes care to ensure learning is not compartmentalized and has a healthy balance of the more significant measurement topic and the specificity of the skills needed. The district has gone through the process of defining measurement topics and learning targets twice. The first process was with the California State Standards, and then the content was altered when the California Common Core Standards were released. LUSD also continues to iterate the curriculum as state targets and other frameworks change. Regardless of the material, it is always defined to the granularity of the learning target level.

Principle D: Competency-Based Student Records

All learners in LUSD can directly access their comprehensive learning record throughout their entire learning career in the district. Learners can access the evidence they created and the scores they received. The learning management system also presents learners a clear visual representation of every content level in which they have received proficiency across their entire career, called My Learning Path. With only two clicks, learners can see what learning targets they still need to accomplish, those they have completed, and targets they are currently working on, in any content area. This level of clarity and transparency enables all learners to genuinely and authentically articulate where they are in their learning, what they have accomplished, and what is next. In addition, parents or guardians have equal access to this information for all their children. The platform is accessible at any time of the day and any day of the week from any computer. Lindsay still has some work to do around including personalized learning plans in a digital format and including a way to see learner interests and preferences.

2. Learner-Centered Instruction

As described in chapter 2 (page 27), learner-centered instruction involves learning by doing, instructional support, personalized learning, and collaborative learning.

Principle E: Learning by Doing

Many learners apply their learning through projects based on interest. The projects are collaborative and often cover multiple content areas. One example of this would be using block-based coding to show a historical event, and then hold a Socratic seminar on how one subtle change in the decision making of the leader at the time could have produced an alternate outcome. This project allows for a learner to use his or her skills in computer science, history and social science, language arts, and public speaking. LUSD partners with PBLWorks to continue developing the learning facilitators' capacity to support even more of this active learning. In addition to project-based learning, Lindsay's alternative education site also employs the use of internships and project-based learning in the community. Learners apply for specific internships to acquire proficiency in numerous learning targets across multiple disciplines. These real-life learning opportunities allow learners to enact the learning from their current classes.

Principle F: Instructional Support

All aspects of learning in LUSD require adjustments, coaching, and individual support for every learner. One can argue that when appropriately personalizing learning, a learner's needs are not identified retroactively, but are evident at the moment, and allow for accelerated support. It is also essential that learners—not just adults—can identify the supports and adjustments they need. Before overhauling the learning management system, LUSD interviewed older students, asking, "What do you need to see and have access to for you to be fully informed of your level of learning and rate of learning?" Learners' answers allowed the district to design the learner-facing side of the tool to best meet learners' needs. When learners have access to this information, they can seek out instructional support from peers and learning facilitators. Lindsay also uses specific instructional structures to ensure adjustments, coaching, and tutoring can occur. One of the blended learning structures is the station rotation model. This model allows learning facilitators to focus on the different needs of groups of learners while having the time to dig deeper into both conversations about learning and instructional support.

Principle G: Personalized Learning

One of the structures Lindsay uses to personalize learning is called *data chats*. Every day, learners are achieving and acquiring new knowledge. Data chats promote frequent conversations between learners and learning facilitators around any aspect of their learning. In these coaching sessions, learners might discuss a project, internship, or moment in learning and use their data to prove how they are improving. This allows the learner and the learning facilitator to review and make changes to the personalized learning plan that holds the learner's goals. It is from these meetings and these data sets that learners discover, along with their learning facilitators, whether they need more support in certain areas or on specific projects. While the learning facilitators have these conversations with all their learners, administrators have a similar version of the data chat with each learning facilitator. It is in these meetings that learner achievement and support are discussed, ensuring the administration and learning facilitators are setting the conditions for every learner to succeed.

Principle H: Collaborative Learning

In Lindsay's personalized model, collaboration is a key element used to ensure discussion and dialogue among learners around the content. Learners having the opportunity to learn from one another is a critical component of building their lifelong learning and teamwork skills. One way learners do this in Lindsay is through the use of *expert charts*, which list the learners who have mastered specific measurement topics, allowing other learners to ask peers for assistance independently. The identified "expert" then can support the learner in need. Expert support is structured by a standard operating procedure. This structure gives learners a consistent process that ensures appropriate support while taking into consideration that "experts" also have to learn and should not spend all their time supporting others. Many learning communities (that is, individual schools) in LUSD also use Kagan cooperative structures, which create optimal moments of collaboration in creative and engaging ways.

3. Restructured Curriculum

As described in chapter 3 (page 57), restructured curriculum includes relevance to students' current and future lives, whole-child education, balance of universal content and individual strengths, and sound progressions in content.

Principle I: Relevance to Students' Current and Future Lives

In 2007, along with asking the Lindsay community what type of academic knowledge they thought their kids should be experiencing, LUSD also asked what type of person should be graduating from the system. This information was then used to create everything in the strategic design documentation (tinyurl.com/yb8u297o). The document includes Lindsay's Lifelong Learning Standards. These are skills, mindsets, and dispositions that the community wanted learners to have when they graduate. There are components of 21st century skills, the four Cs (critical thinking, communication, collaboration, and creativity; Battelle for Kids, n.d.), technological capabilities, and life and career skills—all relevant to learners' current and future lives—throughout the standards. The seven spheres that encompass the Lifelong Learning Standards are (1) personal, (2) learning, (3) relationships, (4) civic, (5) global, (6) economic, and (7) cultural. They are broken down into learning targets at each content level and have defined rubrics, the same as the academic content. Lindsay believes it is essential to call attention to the community's help in creating this content, therefore making it even more meaningful and relevant to our families.

Principle J: Whole-Child Education

The Lifelong Learning Standards are critical to this principle, but one stands out from the others: the personal sphere. Inside the personal sphere, one would find a well-balanced person who articulates a clear set of values and beliefs that drive decisions; sets and pursues personal goals; uses a variety of interpersonal communication skills; establishes a balanced lifestyle (mental, emotional, physical, spiritual); adapts to changes, stress, adversity, and diversity; and seeks, reflects on, and adjusts to feedback. Lindsay has worked with the Collaborative for Academic, Social, and Emotional Learning (CASEL) to diagnose areas of strength and improvement around this implementation and has increased the effectiveness of content delivery in this area. LUSD not only identified the content in the Lifelong Learning Spheres, but also created many digital playlists within the learning management system that provide curriculum linking personal-sphere content with other core content areas. The personal sphere is integral to learning in Lindsay, not merely an add-on expectation.

Principle K: Balance of Universal Content and Individual Strengths

As mentioned in previous sections, LUSD's Lifelong Learning Standards, in combination with academic content, forms the majority of the universal content, which they call *guaranteed curriculum*. Individual learner strengths come into play in several areas. Consider a learner's personalized learning plan: since a learning facilitator and a learner are meeting consistently to examine areas of strengths, needs, and interests, learning will most often be relevant to learners' interests. Projects, internships, and other varied opportunities to show proficiency allow learners a chance to apply knowledge in any way they choose, including areas they consider strengths.

Principle L: Sound Progressions in Content

Academic content was identified and organized developmentally as a series of competency-based progressions based on the curriculum standards that define the learner's content level. For example, an age-based fifth grader may be in content level 4 in mathematics (fourth grade California math standards), and content level 6 in English language arts (sixth grade California ELA standards). The content levels, or progressions, allow learning facilitators to see what is developmentally appropriate for the groups of learners they serve, as well as the higher and lower levels of each skill, disposition, or mindset. Similarly, developmentally appropriate progressions for the Lifelong Learning Standards were developed. In Lindsay, Lifelong Learning is just as important as academic content; therefore, it must have the same granular level of detail. Many educators feel they have less experience with this material than with academic content, so it was vital to provide learning facilitators with curriculum broken down into discernable progressions. Learners and parents have complete transparency and access to the full expectations and graduation requirements for Lifelong Learning, just as they do in any of the academic content areas.

4. New Roles

As described in chapter 4 (page 71), the new roles in PCBE are teacher as guide, self-directed student, parent as partner, and technology as a tool for students.

Principle M: Teacher as Guide

When LUSD embraced the strategic design in 2007, the district defined a new vernacular to describe the vision and align roles and expectations that are uncompromisingly learner-centered. *Students* was replaced with *learners*, and *teachers* was replaced with *learning facilitators*. Every stakeholder in Lindsay refers to the adult in the *learning environment* (previously the *classroom*) as the *LF* or *learning facilitator*. These adults facilitate learning. They do so by serving as the guide, not the owner and transmitter of knowledge. They understand their learners, build relationships with them, support and guide their goal setting, establish their Personalized Learning Plans, and help them monitor progress. They may deliver group instruction, but rarely to the whole class. They facilitate learning experiences by co-constructing meaning alongside learners. The role of the learning facilitator has three guiding principles identified in the Strategic Plan.

1. Learning facilitators are models of continuous learning and improvement— they inspire, motivate, and empower learners.

2. Learning facilitators set the conditions for a safe, welcoming, and joyful learning environment—they relate to and connect with learners.

3. Learning facilitators are knowledgeable and competent in pedagogy and human development, which enables them to design personalized instruction to meet learners at their developmental level.

Principle N: Self-Directed Student

Because Lindsay's Performance-Based System is driven by the needs and decisions of learners themselves, each learner is an active decision maker in the education process. Adults guide the learning with clear objectives, but learners have legitimate voice and choice. Learners take responsibility for setting goals, identifying their preferred learning paths, completing activities, and demonstrating proficiency. They may accelerate in areas of interest and strength and adopt a more deliberate pace in areas they find more challenging. They can choose relevant and meaningful learning opportunities and demonstrate their learning and proficiency in their preferred modality. Learners are honored as partners in the educational process (setting goals, tracking progress, setting policy, advancing PBS). Learners can share their ideas, concerns, preferences, interests, and personal aspirations. Learners are empowered to own their learning. The learning management system provides constant access to the curriculum for learner and family progress monitoring.

Principle O: Parent as Partner

Parents are leaders and partners in supporting the performance-based system. They receive free internet access to district servers through the community Wi-Fi program, so all parents can connect to the learning management system, where they can monitor their learners' record and progress and view the entire LUSD curriculum. The district works closely with each learning community and various program directors (migrant services, after-school programs, student services, and so on) to coordinate parent engagement and training to ensure that parents are prepared to be involved in their children's education.

Principle P: Technology as a Tool for Students

Lindsay makes maximum use of technology to accelerate learning and to create systems that support LUSD's "Ideal Learning Experience" model. Consistent with the strategic design, which states that every learner must have access to a computer and the internet at school and at home, the district's "One World" initiative ensures that all learners have connected devices, for free, both in and out of school. Each learning community has a blended learning assistant dedicated to supporting learners and learning facilitators by infusing blended learning strategies and integrating technology into the curriculum.

The learning management system, Empower Learning, houses the learning outcomes, learning objects and activities, evidence of learning, curricular playlists, and resources for all learners. Technology enables personalized learning by extending learning opportunities outside the classroom, meeting learner needs, deepening learning experiences through authentic applications of knowledge, and providing customized learning options. Learners have access to academy pathways in engineering and multimedia production, and participate annually in the Slick Rock Film Festival with submissions they have co-constructed with their peers and their blended learning assistant.

5. A Nurturing Culture

As described in chapter 5 (page 89), the components of a nurturing culture include strong and caring relationships, multi-year mentoring and multi-age grouping, motivational learning, and family services.

Principle Q: Strong and Caring Relationships

LUSD continuously communicates the importance of the relationships that learners have as central to the Ideal Learning Experience. Every staff member has been oriented to the behavioral dynamics that provide a culture of caring for learners. Staff members frequently use the word *love* to characterize their bonds with learners. Lindsay has strong evidence from student surveys (California Healthy Kids Survey) that learners feel safe and supported at school.

Principle R: Multi-Year Mentoring and Multi-Age Grouping

There are some structures in place that support multi-year mentoring and multi-age groupings. The Learning Labs at Jefferson Learning Community comprise 150 multi-age learners with six learning facilitators. These, and many learners districtwide, are grouped and regrouped based on need and data. For example, learning facilitators at content levels 3, 4, and 5 (see principle L) share responsibility for a group of learners, but use learning data to group and regroup fluidly to meet learner needs. In the performance-based system, learning is the constant and time the variable, so learners are organized in a sequence of learning with the guaranteed curriculum (universal content).

Principle S: Motivational Learning

One of the eight core components of Lindsay's Ideal Learning Experience model is motivating learning opportunities, which are relevant, engaging, and future-focused, ensuring that learners attain the 21st century skills needed to succeed in the information age. These include content knowledge, problem solving, communication, critical thinking, creativity, and media and technology skills. Learners are intrinsically motivated when the content and activities are interesting, authentic, challenging, and meaningful. Specific strategies to build motivating learning opportunities include allowing learners to work on concepts and skills of interest to them, in various learning opportunities (seminars, labs, flipped lessons, online, mentorships, individual and group projects); co-design their learning opportunities; move through learning outcomes at a flexible pace using their optimal style of learning; and receive immediate, formative, and productive feedback on their progress.

Principle T: Family Services

LUSD is oriented toward a vision of school-community integration. The learning management system contains playlists designed for parent education, in their native language. Parent nights at each learning community provide opportunities for parent and family learning (for example, classes on digital citizenship and family digital literacy, math and literacy nights, and English-as-a-second-language classes). More importantly, since 1994, the district has operated the Lindsay Healthy Start Family Resource Center as the central hub providing all wrap-around services. Any agency that serves Lindsay families provides its service through the Family Resource Center, such that it coordinates all services and minimizes duplication. Families can receive case management support, emergency services, counseling, psychiatry, parent-child interactive therapy, basic need support, and connection with all health and social services through this one-stop hub. Additionally, the community of Lindsay is designated as Migrant Education Region 24, and more than 1,200 families receive services through the California Department of Education's Migrant Education Program. These services include preschool, in-home parenting classes, family literacy, a mobile dental clinic, supplemental academic programs and services, specialized extracurricular activities, and support from the Mexican consulate. The services provided by the Family Resource Center and Migrant Education

Program are designed to level the playing field and ensure that all learners can excel in school and their preferred futures.

6. New Organizational Structures

As described in chapter 6 (page 103), new organizational structures for PCBE include small school size; professional organizational structure; student choice, teacher incentives, and accountability; administrative structures; and governance structures.

Principle U: Small School Size

LUSD operates six preK–8 neighborhood learning communities, a comprehensive high school, and alternative high school programs. Elementary sites range from 390 to 723 learners. They are neighborhood schools, and many learners walk to school.

Principle V: Professional Organizational Structure

Many new structures support a productive, innovative organizational structure. In addition to their role in developing and shaping the organization, they are tightly aligned with the strategic design, including the district's ten core values. Hence, high levels of ownership and leadership at all levels characterize the professional structure. Learning facilitators activate learning and ensure mastery. Site leaders create the conditions that support a personalized system, while support staff provide the supports that empower others to be efficient in their work and focus on continual improvement. Teachers do not choose their leaders, but they are given much authority to best meet each of their students' needs.

Principle W: Student Choice, Teacher Incentives, and Accountability

Learners typically choose their neighborhood schools, but they can choose other learning communities if they perceive a better fit (for example, a dual language immersion site). Learners do not choose their teachers. They are assigned to learning environments based on recommendations for best fit from site leaders, learning facilitators, and other staff, including site counselors and specialists. Learners have voice and choice in what they learn and how they learn it. They can choose to learn about areas of special interest and passion, and they have options regarding demonstrating proficiency with measurement topics (the standards). Data are used for accountability at every level, from site leaders to learning facilitators to learners. District leaders are accountable to ensure alignment with the strategic design.

Principle X: Administrative Structures

Clear standard operating procedures create clarity, alignment, and accountability. Leaders receive personalized coaching and supervision. All senior leaders and their secretaries are formally trained in the Breakthrough Coach program, which teaches school leaders how to build productive front-office environments that then free them up to focus on creating sustainable, schoolwide improvement. Several key structures provide the framework for professional operations.

- District Strategic Leaders (meets monthly and includes all directors, principals, learning directors, and cabinet members)

- Performance-Based System team (leads the essential efforts to realize the strategic design and Ideal Learning Experience model for all Lindsay stakeholders)

- Communications Campaign (strategically advances the alignment, branding, and messaging of LUSD to all stakeholders)

- Organizational Health team (provides training to all internal stakeholders to ensure that the teams are functioning optimally, with minimum politics and maximum impact)

While not an administrative structure for Lindsay itself, the district created Lindsay Leads as a public service. It is a select group of learners, staff, district leaders, board members, and parents who intentionally and strategically support and empower other districts and schools to transform their systems to personalized models. Members of Lindsay Leads are formally trained as trainers, coaches, and ambassadors for Lindsay's Performance-Based System.

Principle Y: Governance Structures

Governance structures are consistent with California public schools. A five-member Board of Trustees is elected by the populace. The board has been remarkably engaged and supportive of the LUSD Performance-Based System, and members have attended thematic conferences. The board hires the superintendent, with the strategic design as his or her job description. Under the superintendent is the deputy superintendent and the cabinet, who develop and supervise all staff. Even with these traditional governance structures, Lindsay's uncompromisingly learner-centered model means that learners come first.

Summary

These two case studies are but two of literally hundreds, if not thousands, of school systems that have already taken great strides to transform from Education 2.0 to PCBE. In our previous book, *Reinventing Schools: It's Time to Break the Mold* (Reigeluth & Karnopp, 2013), we list more than 140 such schools, and the number has grown considerably since then. This is a change you can make!

PART II:
ACTION

The Change Process

The process for transforming your classroom, school, or district to personalized competency-based education is difficult, even treacherous. Deciding what changes to make (described in part I) is only part of the process. Minimizing resistance and accessing information, resources, and other kinds of help are critical.

Chapter 8 helps you to decide on the best scope for your change effort and describes a framework for the change process that applies to all different scopes. Chapter 9 (page 159) offers detailed guidance for a school district. Chapter 10 (page 189) offers such guidance for an independent school (not part of a school district or charter network).

Overview of the Change Process

The change process will be very different depending on whether the scope of your change is for a single classroom, a school, or a whole district. However, there are common elements across these different scopes. Those common elements constitute a framework for the change process. In this chapter, we describe such a framework, followed by guidance for deciding on the best scope for your change effort.

A Framework for Fundamental Change

The guidance we provide in the following chapters is based on a set of values and principles about the change process. Values are more a matter of philosophy, based on preference, whereas principles are more a matter of science, based on evidence, though principles are founded in values, and there is a fuzzy boundary between the two. It also includes guidance in the form of activities that should be done in a sequence (phases and steps, like forming a team) and activities that should be done continuously throughout the process (like building and maintaining motivation for change). Figure 8.1 (page 148) shows that the values are the foundation for the whole change process. The principles are based on the values but are also based on evidence. The principles guide the activities—both sequential and continuous.

Values

The values that underlie this fundamental change process include the following.

- Putting students first in all decisions
- Improving the quality of life for the adults who work in schools
- Creating healthy relationships between a school system and its community
- Building a shared vision among all stakeholder groups and empowering them
- Exemplifying group-action values, such as collaboration, consensus-building, dialogue, team learning, systemic thinking, and social responsibility as tools for change in mental models or mindsets
- Exemplifying personal-action values, such as full disclosure of concerns, trust, respect, responsibility, commitment, self-criticality, and flexibility

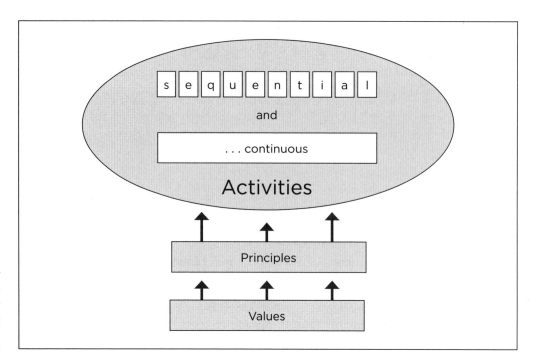

- Understanding societal evolution and the need for co-evolution of educational systems

- Building readiness and capacity for change

Principles

The principles that underlie the change process include the following (Banathy, 1991, 1996; Jenlink, Reigeluth, Carr, & Nelson, 1998; Reigeluth, 1993, 1995).

- **Change in mental models:** Change in mental models is essential to this paradigm change because PCBE represents a different conception of education than does the time-based, teacher-centered paradigm. Stakeholders who do not redefine their own ideas of education will not understand or support the changes well enough for PCBE to succeed. Therefore, the process must be a learning process as well as a decision-making process.

- **Broad stakeholder involvement and ownership:** Resistance is often the first reaction to change. A large number of stakeholders must undergo change in mental models, or there will be more resisters than supporters of the educational changes. Stakeholders will best evolve their thinking and commit to the process if they are involved in and feel ownership over it. Commitment is essential for change that is as complex as paradigm change of a school system.

- **Process over product:** Given the first two principles, the actual decisions made about the new system (the product) are less important than participants' experiences during the change process, for it is the experiences that help people change their mental models about education.

- **Consensus-building process:** Decisions should not be made autocratically, nor even democratically. Majority rule creates winners and losers. Stakeholders should make decisions through a process of learning and consensus building.

- **Participatory leadership:** Stakeholder ownership cannot exist without the participatory paradigm of leadership (sometimes called developmental, transformational, or servant leadership), which contrasts with the top-down, command-and-control paradigm of leadership dominant in most industrial-age schools (Senge, 2000). Participatory leadership generates not only greater commitment to the changes, but also a better PCBE system that is more suited to your school context.

- **Leadership and political support:** Current educational systems are run by elected and appointed leaders. They must support the paradigm change, or it will not happen.

- **Readiness and capacity:** Capacity-building should pervade the entire change process, with each step of the process undertaken only as a sufficient level of readiness is reached. Capacity includes change-process expertise, money to free up participants' time, and various other resources and structures.

Capacity Building

A report from the Carnegie Corporation of New York (Srinivasan & Archer, 2018) calls for a learning agenda on how to build the capacities of organizations to work in ways that produce greater integration of effort and less fragmentation. Part of that agenda includes the Integration Design Consortium, a series of five action-learning projects taking place in states and local communities across the country. Visit www.carnegie.org/edequity to learn more and download the report.

- **Culture:** Paradigm change both (a) requires a healthy culture in order to succeed and (b) results in a new culture (Fullan, 2001, 2003). It is an essential part of the change process. Some of the most important elements of culture include empowerment, inclusion, collaboration, consensus orientation, systems thinking, trust, disclosure, and the norm of not blaming people.

- **Ideal design and invention:** In order to transform their mental models (see, for example, Banathy, 1991, 1996; Senge, 2000), stakeholders must think in the ideal about what their educational system should be like (Ackoff, 1981). Thus, the process is a design and invention process, more than a decision-making process. Human-centered design (IDEO, 2015) is an important tool in this process (see www.teachersguild.org/approach).

- **Emergence and leverage:** A new paradigm of education is far too complex and time-consuming to invent all at once before implementing it. However, if a fundamental change is made in just one part of a system, it will be incompatible with the rest of the system. Therefore, the initial changes need to be able to exert more influence on changing the rest of the system than the rest of the system exerts on changing them back (Senge, 1990, 2000). After the initial high-leverage changes are made, the remaining changes emerge as the system develops (Reigeluth, 2006, 2008).

- **Prioritization of learning experiences:** The design of PCBE must begin with the learning experiences, and then move on to designing the instructional systems that best support those learning experiences, then the administrative systems that best support those instructional systems, and finally the governance systems that best support the rest of the new paradigm (Banathy, 1991).

Sequential Activities

These activities vary depending on whether the scope of the change is a classroom, school, or district, but in all three cases there are four fundamental phases (Duffy, 2002; Duffy & Reigeluth, 2008; Reigeluth & Duffy, 2019).

1. **Prepare:** Initiate the change effort and develop a prelaunch team to build capacity for the change process.

2. **Envision:** Engage in a collection of change activities to develop the capacity for the design, development, and implementation work; decide on a strategy for design, development, and implementation of PCBE; and envision an ideal future.

3. **Transform:** Develop, implement, and incorporate emergent changes, with some changes beginning before all the envisioning is done. Expand the transformation to other classrooms or schools.

4. **Evolve:** Continue to formatively evaluate the new system and make additional changes as needed for continuous improvement of the system.

Detailed guidance for sequential activities is provided in chapters 9 (for a school district; page 159) and 10 (for an independent school; page 189).

Continuous Activities

These activities address ongoing needs that the change team should monitor throughout the change effort and address whenever they fall below a critical threshold (Jenlink, Reigeluth, Carr, & Nelson, 1996; Jenlink et al., 1998).

- **Engage in evaluation and reflection:** Continuously engage participants in individual and collective evaluation and reflection for improvement of the change process and their own skills. This functions as a positive feedback system for learning, self-correction, and formative development of the change process. We recommend establishing formal periods for each team to review their recent process and make suggestions for how it could have been done better.

- **Build and maintain trust:** Continuously build and sustain trust among participants, as well as between the change team and individuals in the school system and community. This requires developing an understanding of what trust is and how trust figures into building successful relationships within and across the change effort.

- **Evolve mental models and culture:** Help participants to continuously evolve their mindsets and culture regarding both education and the change process. This requires developing an appreciation for, and understanding of, the need to continuously evolve both individual and collective mindsets, primarily through readings and dialogue.

- **Sustain motivation:** Continuously monitor and attend to participants' motivation for paradigm change, using a balance of extrinsic and intrinsic motivation that attends to participants' beliefs about and the purpose of paradigm change. This includes developing an understanding and appreciation of team spirit in paradigm change.

- **Develop systems-thinking and design skills:** Continuously develop participants' skills and knowledge for systems thinking and design, which includes an understanding of the interrelatedness of all the various parts of an educational system and between an educational system and its community (Banathy, 1996; Betts, 1992; Cabrera & Cabrera, 2015; Checkland, 1984; Forrester, 1999; Hutchins, 1996; Stroh, 2015). Participants should continuously advance their knowledge of the theory and practice of educational systems design so that they can be effective user-designers of PCBE.

- **Develop and sustain appropriate leadership:** Continuously evolve from top-down, authoritarian leadership to consensus-oriented, supportive leadership (Ruyle, 2018; Senge, 2000; Spillane, 2006; Theobald, 1987). This requires developing an understanding of the need for and nature of this different approach, as well as nurturing the necessary skills and knowledge to effect this evolution.

- **Communicate interactively with stakeholders:** Continuously develop participants' communication skills and knowledge as they apply to paradigm change. This includes the development of open communication systems (transparency), common language, and appropriate conventions of conversation for effecting paradigm change. Share information with and gather information from all stakeholders, including elected officials and other political leaders, to seek feedback and maintain support.

- **Periodically secure and allocate necessary resources:** Continuously identify and secure the types of resources essential to successful paradigm change throughout the change effort. In addition to external resources, a line item should be established in the school's or district's budget for this effort, to demonstrate its commitment to the change process and enhance the sustainability of the process. Allocate resources to the paradigm change effort as needed.

- **Develop group-process and team-building skills:** Continuously develop participants' skills and knowledge in group process and team building, which requires groups and teams to devote time and energy to learning to perform in a healthy and positive manner. This includes conversation skills and knowledge of the various types of conversation important to the change effort, including dialogue, design, and community building. This learning also helps to build and sustain community.

- **Engage in self-disclosure:** Continuously engage participants in self-disclosure as it applies to dialogue, design conversation, and other similar processes. Self-disclosure is an activity that entails sharing personal beliefs, assumptions, and mindsets. It is essential to building and sustaining a paradigm change effort.

- **Build and evolve community:** Continuously develop participants' understanding of what a community is and how it differs from other forms of collectives, such as groups and teams. This includes developing the skills and knowledge for building and sustaining a learning community for working on paradigm change.

- **Foster organizational learning and memory:** Continuously develop participants' skills and knowledge about different types of organizational learning and how they relate to the paradigm change effort. This includes developing an understanding of how individual and team learning contribute to organizational learning. Explore adaptive, generative, and design learning. Also, develop participants' understanding of how schools build and maintain organizational memories over time, how organizational memory contributes to resistance to change, and how this memory may be used to facilitate paradigm change in an education system.

Many of these continuous activities are informed by the concepts of improvement science (for example, see Bryk, Gomez, Grunow, & LeMahieu, 2015, for a description of the key principles of improvement science and their application for continuous improvement in education). With this framework in mind, we now offer some guidance for deciding on the scope of your change effort.

The Scope of Your Change

To undertake the change to PCBE, you should begin by deciding on the scope of your change: one classroom, one school, one school district, or one state.

Classroom

What are the pros and cons of making one classroom the scope of your change? It is certainly far quicker and easier to change one classroom than to change a whole school. However, as described in part I, the change to PCBE is a fundamental change—one that requires changes throughout all parts of an educational system: curriculum, instruction, assessment, record keeping, teacher roles, student roles, organizational structures, and more. Such a fundamental change would make the classroom incompatible with the other classrooms in the school. It would be like swimming upstream. Even if you had the approval of your principal and fellow teachers, the rest of the school as a system would inevitably and continuously work to convert your classroom back to one that is compatible with the rest of the school. You would soon tire of fighting that subtle but relentless cultural and organizational pressure. We have seen this happen in many schools. There are only a few conditions under which a PCBE classroom can work in a traditional school, as follows.

- The changes in that classroom are supported by the principal and at least one-third of the teachers as the first step for the whole school to transform.

- There is a school or district commitment to have other classrooms follow suit, including a plan and schedule for expansion.

- There are arrangements for extra resources to support the change in that classroom and the classrooms that follow.

- There are provisions to waive certain school, district, and even state requirements.

School

What are the pros and cons of making one school in a district the scope of your change? Again, it is easier and quicker to transform one school than to transform a whole district. But many district policies, practices, and structures fundamental to Education 2.0 are incompatible with PCBE. If you do not change them, your school will suffer the same fate of having to swim upstream and will eventually revert in order to be compatible with the rest of the district (Tyack & Cuban, 1995). We have seen this happen in many districts. The Saturn School of Tomorrow, hailed as a school of the future by President George H. W. Bush and many others, finally gave in to the relentless pressure to conform with the Education 2.0 paradigm of the rest of its school district (Walsh, 1993). If your school is not part of a district, as with independent charter schools (ones not controlled by a network) and private schools, this is not a problem, and the school is likely the best scope of change. Within a district or other network, again, there are a few conditions under which a single PCBE school can work, as follows.

- The changes in that school are supported by the superintendent and school board as the first step for the whole district to transform.

- There is a district commitment to have other schools follow suit, including a plan and schedule for expansion and new administrative structures.

- There are arrangements for extra resources to support the change in that school and the schools to follow.

- There are provisions to waive certain district and even state requirements.

District

What are the pros and cons of making a school district the scope of your change? It is certainly more difficult, time consuming, and expensive to transform a whole district, but it has the advantage of sustainability. Nevertheless, the district is part of the larger system of the state educational system, and some aspects of PCBE will be incompatible with the state system. High-stakes tests and many rules and regulations are common roadblocks. However, most states have a process whereby waivers can be obtained, making district transformation a viable and sustainable option.

State

The replacement of No Child Left Behind (NCLB) with the Every Student Succeeds Act (ESSA) is a move away from a compliance-driven system on the national level. This provides a great incentive for states to take the initiative to rethink their education systems and hopefully follow the federal lead by moving away from a compliance-driven, teacher-centered system toward a learner-centered PCBE system.

The only people who can make the state level the scope of change are state leaders. However, changing the paradigm of education to PCBE will take longer than any one political cycle. Therefore, any effort on this level must entail building a shared vision that is owned by public and private stakeholders (Herdman, 2016). Education leaders in Delaware, for example, have created and sustained a collaboration of public and private leaders called the Vision Coalition, which produced an education plan for Delaware called Student Success 2025 (www.visioncoalitionde.org). Herdman (2016) offers five lessons that may be helpful to other states wanting to undertake paradigm change at the state level. Also, the Center for Policy Design offers ten ideas as to what states can do to create a climate for innovation for school districts, schools, and teachers and what a state legislature can do to overcome the pressure for sameness in school districts and redesign a district to be a self-improving organization (Kolderie, 2019).

State leaders in Ohio engaged in an effective process called the Transformational Dialogue for Public Education (Jung, Reigeluth, Kim, & Trepper, 2019; Kim, 2014) that offers further insights for state-level transformation of public education. Iowa created the Iowa CBE Collaborative in 2012 "to investigate, develop, and implement competency-based educational pathways for their students and create a framework to guide the state-wide implementation of CBE" (Iowa Department of Education, n.d.). Ten districts are members of the collaborative. Colorado created the Colorado Education Initiative (www.coloradoedinitiative.org), a statewide nonprofit organization that questions current assumptions about education, conducts research, hosts outside-the-box dialogues, and seeds innovative ideas. It catalyzes bold, comprehensive change by sharing knowledge, creating collaborative partnerships, and building capacity.

Kolderie (2018) documents how Minnesota successfully reinvented its regional governance and is transforming its public education. The report shows that government needs a strong civic sector to push elected officials to think about the causes of problems and to provide radical but implementable strategies for policy action.

There are several resources to help state policymakers facilitate districts' transition to PCBE. *iNACOL 2019 State Policy Priorities* (Patrick, Worthen, & Truong, 2019) recommends seven priorities, including the following.

- Create meaningful qualifications that are based on mastery, rather than seat time.

- Build balanced systems of assessments to certify student mastery of knowledge and skills.

- Build leadership capacity for creating and sustaining change for personalized competency-based education.

- Establish enabling state policies to create and launch innovative new learning designs and multiple pathways in schools and systems through innovation zones, pilots, credit flexibility, mastery-based diplomas, and mastery-based transcripts.

Other helpful reports from the Aurora Institute (formerly iNACOL) include *Moving Toward Mastery: Growing, Developing and Sustaining Educators for Competency-Based Education* (Casey, 2018), *iNACOL Issue Brief: State Policy & K–12 Competency-Based Education* (Frost & Worthen, 2017), *Making Mastery Work: A Close-up View of Competency Education* (Priest et al., 2012), and *It's Not a Matter of Time: Highlights from the 2011 Competency-Based Learning Summit* (Sturgis, Patrick, & Pittenger, 2011).

In addition, the Foundation for Excellence in Education (www.excelined.org) offers customized support for state policymakers, reformers, educators, parents, and communities to cultivate policy conditions that advance student-centered, personalized education systems at the state level and improve education equity and quality—both inside and outside the traditional public education system. It also sponsors a national summit on education reform.

School Quality Reviews

Educators in Vermont "have conducted 'school quality reviews,' in which a team of outside educators works with a nearby district, giving feedback on everything from curriculum to social and emotional learning" (Klein, 2018b, p. 16). This is a good model for states to fund a feedback mechanism for districts transforming to PCBE.

It is beyond the scope of this book to offer guidance for the state level, and we do not recommend changing a single classroom. Thus, we offer guidance for a school district (chapter 9, page 159) and for an independent school (chapter 10, page 189). Once you have decided on the scope of your change, go to the corresponding chapter for guidance on the process.

Common Obstacles in the Transformation Process

Whether in a school or district, a typical PCBE transformation process will encounter some common obstacles. Research by the RAND Corporation (Steiner Hamilton, Stelitano, & Rudwick, 2017) found the following obstacles that a network of ten small high schools faced during transformation to PCBE.

- A lack of clarity on what mastery means and how it should be implemented

- A lack of high-quality curriculum materials

- A need to personalize across multiple student ability levels in a classroom

- A lack of time for teachers to create or find learning materials that are differentiated for each student

- Inadequate staff preparation

- Maintaining universally high expectations for students

- External pressure to advance students at a certain pace whether or not they had mastered the material

- Wide variation in the complexity of tasks used to assess mastery

- Inconsistent application of mastery-based grading systems

- Inconsistent access to high-quality data about what students know and can do.

Another study by the RAND Corporation (Pane et al., 2017) found the following obstacles to implementing PCBE, in order of prevalence.

- Pressure to cover specific material as a result of state or district standards or testing requirements

- Lack of flexibility in the curriculum requirements

- Scheduling constraints

- Lack of support from school administration

- Inadequate data to help the teacher personalize students' instruction

Based on our own eleven years of experience facilitating a paradigm change process, the following are some things that your team should try to avoid in your process of transforming to PCBE.

- Rushing the process

- Trying to change the whole district or school (for large schools) at once

- Failing to build trust, consensus, support, and ownership or to include all stakeholder groups

- Failing to make the process open and transparent

- Ignoring resisters or failing to address their needs and fears

- Failing to constantly build motivation for change, reward sacrifices, and celebrate small successes

- Procuring insufficient funding

- Failing to think systemically, to account for interdependencies among parts of the system

- Neglecting to acquire an experienced, neutral facilitator

- Failing to identify and mitigate state-level and district-level obstacles

An evaluation of the Annenberg Challenge (Annenberg Institute for School Reform, 2002) describes additional obstacles. The transformation processes described in chapters 9 and 10 are designed to overcome these obstacles.

Change Process
for a District

<hr />

CHAPTER

9

All the values, principles, and continuous activities described in chapter 8 (page 147) apply to the change process for a district. Only the sequential activities are significantly different across the two scopes of change addressed in this book. This chapter opens with an overview of the process for changing an entire school district; it then provides more detailed guidance for sequential activities. This guidance is based on a paradigm change process that Charles Reigeluth facilitated over the course of eleven years, with the support of his research team at Indiana University, in a small school district in Indianapolis (Chen & Reigeluth, 2010; Joseph & Reigeluth, 2005; Lee & Reigeluth, 2007; Reigeluth & Stinson, 2007a, 2007b, 2007c, 2007d; Richter, 2007; Richter & Reigeluth, 2006, 2010; Watson, 2008; Watson & Reigeluth, 2008, 2013). It is also based on literature about the transformation process, including a five-phase framework for school change based on the Highlander Institute's experience helping nearly five hundred classrooms to pursue personalized learning (Duffy, 2002, 2003, 2004, 2010; Duffy & Chance, 2007; Duffy, Rogerson, & Blick, 2000; Eckel, Hill, & Green, 1998; Emery & Purser, 1996; Fishman, Marx, Best, & Tal, 2003; Fullan, 2001, 2003; Fullan & Stiegelbauer, 1991; Hall & Hord, 1987, 2001; Lytle, 2002; Miller, George, & Fogt, 2005; Nevis, Lancourt, & Vassallo, 1996; Pasmore, 1988; Rogers, 2003; Rowan & Miller, 2007; Ruyle, 2018; Schlechty, 2001, 2005; Togneri & Anderson, 2003; Wagner, 1994, 2001; Wagner & Kegan, 2006).

However, conditions vary significantly from one school district to another, and this requires variations in the change process (Jenlink et al., 1998; Rubin & Sanford, 2018). We encourage your change team to look for beneficial ways to adapt the process described herein, with the caution that careless adaptations can be detrimental to the change process. Your team must carefully consider adaptations with respect to the framework and common obstacles offered in chapter 8 (page 147). In addition, we encourage you to continually monitor, evaluate, and improve all aspects of your change process as it proceeds.

Recommended Reading

In addition to the excellent *A Handbook for Personalized Competency-Based Education* by Marzano and colleagues (2017), we highly recommend *Leading the Evolution: How to Make Personalized Competency-Based Education a Reality* by Mike Ruyle (2018), which introduces a three-pronged approach to driving substantive change—called the evolutionary triad—that connects transformative educational leadership, student engagement, and teacher optimism around personalized competency-based education. Each chapter includes supporting research and theory, as well as clear direction and strategies for putting the evolutionary triad into practice.

Overview of Sequential Activities for the District Change Process

The following is an overview of eight phases for the sequential activities in a district-level change process.

1. **Prepare for the change process:** A building needs a foundation. So does the change process. Preparing a school district for paradigm change is critical to successful implementation of PCBE. Kotter (2012) identified eight reasons for failed transformational change. Six of those eight reasons are linked to inadequate preparation of the system. It is important to partner with an experienced external process facilitator, marshal political support, form a small prelaunch team (seven or eight people) that includes leaders from the major stakeholder groups, and enhance district capacity for paradigm change.

2. **Create a shared ideal district vision and develop capacity and a strategy for change:** Developing a shared vision of PCBE promotes learning, mindset change, and commitment to change, and it reduces resistance to change (Banathy, 1991; Hammonds, 2018; Jenlink et al., 1998; Senge, 2000; Theobald, 1987). The prelaunch team expands into a district leadership team (roughly thirty people), which includes leaders of all stakeholder groups in the district, to lead the districtwide transformation to PCBE. Each member of the leadership team engages others in their stakeholder group (akin to pyramid groups) in a manner that gives stakeholders an opportunity to give input and helps those stakeholders' thinking to evolve as the leadership team members' thinking evolves. In this way, stakeholders' mindsets shift towards the PCBE paradigm as the district leadership team's vision begins to crystalize. The districtwide vision must be sufficiently general that different schools can implement it in different ways. During this time, the district leadership team also develops the district's capacity for change. This primarily entails cultivating a culture for change, developing the change process skills of participants, and procuring resources for the implementation process. Participants need release time to work on the transformation, and the district

will soon need funding to visit other PCBE districts and schools, provide professional development for teachers, remodel facilities, and procure tools and materials for PCBE. Finally, the district leadership team develops a strategy for implementing the vision, typically involving decisions about the number of schools (one "feeder system" versus all the schools) and the number of teachers in each school (one "school within the school" versus the entire school). These options are explained in step 2 of the Detailed Guidance section, page 169).

3. **Choose a school or schools to pioneer PCBE:** The district leadership team solicits applications for schools to pioneer PCBE and selects the one (or more, if enough resources are available) that demonstrates the highest level of readiness—not the one with the greatest need. This is typically an elementary school for several reasons that are discussed in step 3.2 in the Detailed Guidance section of this chapter (page 174). The district leadership team also helps other schools to improve their readiness for change.

4. **Create a shared ideal school vision:** Leaders of all stakeholder groups in the chosen school or schools form a school leadership team to participate in this phase. Each leader engages others in his or her stakeholder group so that their thinking evolves with their leader's and they can provide input through their leader. The vision must be consistent with the district vision but could do so in different ways from other schools that are transforming in the district.

5. **Create a separate district administrative structure:** The district leadership team designs and implements a separate administrative structure (akin to that described in Principle X: Administrative Structures in chapter 6, page 109) to support the transformed school. A separate administrative structure is essential, because many aspects of the current administrative structure are incompatible with PCBE but remain important for the schools that have not yet transformed. This new administrative structure obtains any needed waivers for the PCBE school or schools from the state education agency.

6. **Implement and evolve the school vision:** The chosen school implements high-leverage changes in its vision and then makes other changes as the need emerges. It is important to allow sufficient time to procure tools (for example, hands-on learning materials, digital tools, online tutorials and assessments), design projects and other activities for students, receive professional development for effective use of tools and design of projects, and possibly remodel facilities (for example, classrooms into studios). If the school is large, there are likely teachers and families who are reluctant to pioneer the changes. One solution is to divide the school into two schools within the same building and allow both teachers and students to choose; however, this must be done with a commitment that the reluctant group will transform in the future. Also, as students advance in grade levels, it becomes progressively harder for them to switch to PCBE, because they become conditioned to be passive learners and

lack the self-direction skills and mindsets necessary for success in a PCBE classroom. It would also be frustrating for PCBE students to go back to the teacher-centered system. Therefore, it is wise to first implement PCBE in the first three to five grades (say, ages five to eight) and convert one grade per year thereafter. This progressive approach also helps prevent spreading resources for change too thinly. Finally, the chosen school makes additional changes as needed or desired in order to make the high-leverage changes work better. Formative evaluation of the PCBE system is key. No summative evaluation should be done for about five years, to give time for the evolution to overcome inevitable problems.

7. **Expand to additional schools:** Repeat phases 3, 4, and 6 for a few more schools that are at the highest levels of readiness, helping each to gradually work up to higher grade levels.

8. **Evolve the ideal visions:** Educational needs and tools change over time. After about ten years of expanding and continuously improving the school and district visions, the district and schools should form new leadership teams to develop new ideal visions toward which they can continue to evolve.

The next section presents detailed guidance for these sequential activities.

Detailed Guidance for the Sequential Activities

The sequential activities for transformation at the district level involve the following eight phases.

Phase 1: Prepare for the change process.

Phase 2: Create a shared ideal district vision and develop capacity and a strategy for change.

Phase 3: Choose a school or schools to pioneer PCBE.

Phase 4: Create a shared ideal school vision.

Phase 5: Create a separate district administrative structure.

Phase 6: Implement and evolve the school vision.

Phase 7: Expand to additional schools.

Phase 8: Evolve the ideal visions.

Phase 1: Prepare for the Change Process

This phase answers the question, Where do we start? There are two major steps in the preparation process: (1) initiating the effort and (2) developing a prelaunch team to build district capacity for the transformation process. However, as with the phases, the steps and the activities that make up each step should not be thought of as a lockstep sequence. Rather, they are a set of activities that converge, diverge, and backflow from time to time, and do so repeatedly throughout the phase. Also, activities often need to be adapted to local conditions. Some activities listed here may not be needed, while some activities not listed here may be needed. We caution that extreme care and thought should precede any changes to these guidelines.

Step 1.1—Initiate the Change Process

Initiating the change process is the first step toward district transformation. It involves several activities related to readiness.

1.1a—Ensure Sufficient District Readiness

The superintendent assesses and, if necessary, enhances the readiness of the school district to embark on the journey. It would be a mistake to initiate the transformation process if the district's readiness is such that success is unlikely. Also, a readiness assessment allows the superintendent to solicit a preliminary contract to improve the district's readiness. The following are the most important criteria.

- **Is the school board supportive of the change to PCBE?** If not, how difficult might it be to win the support of all board members? Without their full support, the change effort is not likely to succeed.

- **Is the superintendent a transformational leader?** If not, does the superintendent have the potential to become one? If not, then the change effort should not be undertaken.

- **What is the quality of the relationships among the teachers, the teachers' union, the district and building administrators, and the school board?** If the quality of any of these relationships is not good, how difficult will it be to build sound, trusting relationships? That will require extra time and money and may make the change effort inadvisable unless preceded by a contract to improve readiness.

- **What is the district's history with change?** Are the teachers exhausted from frequent change efforts? Do they believe that "this too shall pass" and largely ignore change initiatives? If attitudes about change are negative, the change process will be more difficult, and those attitudes must be addressed.

See appendix C (page 217) for a more thorough set of criteria for assessing the district's readiness for paradigm change. If the district is at an insufficient level of readiness, the change effort could still be undertaken. We recommend it be preceded by a separate contract to build readiness, but if the level of readiness is not too bad, readiness can be addressed during the transformation process.

1.1b—Select an External Facilitator

The superintendent makes a tentative selection of an external facilitator. Criteria for selection are indicated in figure 9.1. The facilitator should generally come from outside the district in order to avoid any biases, favoritisms (or perception thereof), or other baggage that could sabotage the essential neutrality of a process facilitator. Often districts have a history of working with consultants in a "solve the problem for us" capacity or "doctor-patient" relationship where a diagnosis is provided and a treatment prescribed. Facilitation differs from consultation in that the facilitator is not the expert but a process guide. Whereas consultation calls for an expert knowledge base on one or a few areas of education, facilitation calls for an expert knowledge base in systems thinking, the language of change, group dynamics, and so on.

Rate each candidate on a scale of 1–10 on each of the following factors.

Knowledge and Skills

_____ Systems thinking

_____ Educational systems design

_____ Language of change

_____ Group psychodynamics

_____ Dialogue and design conversation

_____ Evaluation

Total Score for Knowledge and Skills: _____

Personal Characteristics

_____ Managing transitions

_____ Suspending biases and judgments

_____ Global consciousness

_____ Deep listening

_____ Self-reflection

_____ Self-inquiry

_____ Disclosure

_____ Self-renewal

Total Score for Personal Characteristics: _____

Process Engagement

_____ Individual, team, and organizational learning

_____ Building and sustaining community

_____ Leadership

_____ Managing change

_____ Creating contextual understanding

Total Score for Process Engagement: _____

Total Overall Score: _____

---

*Visit **MarzanoResources.com/reproducibles** to download a reproducible version of this figure.*

Figure 9.1: Criteria for facilitator selection.

External
Facilitator

It is very important to have an external facilitator to guide the transformation process, for several reasons. First, that person, if selected well, has expertise in all the aspects of district change processes that were described in chapter 8: visioning, capacity building, stakeholder engagement, strategic planning, and consensus building. As in any journey into new territory, without a good guide, it is almost certain you will never reach your destination. It is unlikely anyone in your district has the needed expertise. Second, an external facilitator has a neutrality that is essential for engendering trust, and without trust by all stakeholder groups, the process cannot succeed.

The external facilitator does not tell you what changes you should make, but instead helps you decide what changes to make. While your district has likely experienced multiple piecemeal change efforts, paradigm change is a lot more complex and difficult than piecemeal reforms. The process by which you try to transform to PCBE is key to successful transformation. The external facilitator must be an expert in that process, one who can help you avoid the deserts, canyons, and mountains that would cause your team to fail in your difficult journey to PCBE land. The facilitator will likely start by playing a dominant role in helping your team develop the capacity, culture, and norms to guide your own process, but over time the facilitator's role should become more of a backseat coach and safety net for the leaders in your change effort.

1.1c—Ensure Compatibility and Understanding

The tentative facilitator and school district engage in a brief courtship to make sure they are compatible with each other and to build working relationships. This process entails the facilitator meeting several times with all key formal and informal stakeholder leaders to get to know each other and build trust. Objectives of these meetings could also include (a) helping leaders of all stakeholder groups understand the role of the facilitator (not to tell them what changes to make, but to help them decide what changes to make) and the responsibilities of the leaders and other participants in the district, and (b) building political support for the change process from the leaders of all the stakeholder groups, including the school board. This process culminates in all leaders (not just the superintendent) and the facilitator signing a contract to initiate the change process (just for step 1.2 [page 166] at this point), including responsibilities, resource needs, and funding. The contract for step 1.2 should include the following.

- Desired outcomes

- Expectations (process activities and timelines)

- A stipend for the facilitator

- Human resource needs and participation roles and responsibilities of the leaders

- Money for retreats and participant time

- Anticipated problems and how to deal with them

- Instructions on how to revise or terminate the contract

Step 1.2—Form a Prelaunch Team and Build District Capacity

Forming a prelaunch team that will lead the early phases of transformation is the next step in the process. It involves several activities related to building this team and increasing the district's capacity for change.

1.2a—Form the Prelaunch Team

The facilitator helps to form a small prelaunch team whose members typically include the superintendent, an influential school board member, the head of the teachers' association, an influential principal, a powerful central office staff member who is likely to become the assistant superintendent for transformation (see 1.2g—Select Assistant Superintendent for Transformation), a highly respected nonteaching staff member, and an influential parent leader. This team should not be larger than seven or eight people, no matter the size of your district.

1.2b—Develop Team Culture and Capacity

The prelaunch team does not make any decisions about the nature of their ideal vision of PCBE. Instead, it lays the foundation for the change process, beginning by developing its own culture and capacity for systemic transformation that can survive the team's later expansion into a roughly thirty-member leadership team in phase 2. Forming such a large team at once would likely result in a team culture and dynamic detrimental to the paradigm change process. Culture includes adopting a set of norms and values for the transformation process. Capacity includes understanding systems thinking, the paradigm change process, systems design, dialogue, and small-group facilitation. Periodic one- or two-day retreats are far more efficient than two-hour meetings—one two-day retreat (about fifteen hours) can accomplish more than a school year of monthly two-hour meetings. It is helpful for the prelaunch team to find and create learning tools that it can reuse as new people join the change process.

1.2c—Enhance District Readiness

The prelaunch team and the facilitator address any of the remaining district readiness issues identified by the facilitator in step 1.1 (page 163).

1.2d—Conduct a Political Assessment and Community Analysis

The prelaunch team then engages in three activities: (1) it conducts a political assessment of top formal and opinion leaders in the district; (2) it conducts a community analysis to locate resources and support for the change initiative and cultivates support from those organizations and individuals; and (3) it designs strategies for communicating with each political group. It may be helpful to classify people as what Block (1991) calls *allies* (high trust, high agreement), *bedfellows* (low trust, high agreement), *opponents* (high trust, low agreement), *adversaries* (low trust, low agreement), and *fence-sitters* (undecided where they stand).

1.2e—Develop School Board Culture and Capacity

The prelaunch team helps the school board develop a culture and capacity for systemic transformation. The board should formally commit to the paradigm change process regardless of personnel changes, establish criteria for selecting a new superintendent who will support the transformation to PCBE (in case the superintendent leaves before the process is well established), and participate in annual retreats.

1.2f—Secure External and Internal Funding

The prelaunch team helps the top leadership in the district secure external funding, if possible, and reallocates some internal funds for the paradigm change effort. This greatly speeds up the change process, making changes in district leadership less likely (understanding that such changes can derail the transformation process), and it makes the process less onerous for participants.

1.2g—Select the Assistant Superintendent for Transformation

The facilitator helps the prelaunch team with the selection of someone within the district to lead the transformation process. It should be someone who is charismatic, well-liked, and highly respected—who already knows the important people and operations of the district and has not made enemies in the district or community. The superintendent is seldom able to devote the time needed to perform this function, except perhaps in the smallest of school districts. We suggest you give this person an impressive title to show the importance of this position—something like *assistant superintendent for transformation*. The facilitator further develops that person's capacity to coordinate and inspire transformation to PCBE, and the superintendent places all current change efforts under that person's purview. If possible, this person should be on the prelaunch team from the beginning. Initially, this could be a part-time responsibility, but it should transition to full-time as the transformation process accelerates. This person should be one of the most powerful and highly respected people in the central office.

1.2h—Form a District Facilitation Team

The facilitator helps the prelaunch team to form a small district facilitation team—primarily made up of central office staff, who can all allocate some time to help the assistant superintendent—and develops its culture and capacity for systemic transformation. Institutionalizing the change process in this manner helps to build political support, provide logistical help, and ensure sustainability of the change process.

1.2i—Sign a Contract for Phase 2

Finally, the facilitator and prelaunch team assess how well their relationship is working, and if all is well, they both sign a contract with the school board for step 2 (page 169), including responsibilities, resource needs, and funding. Figure 9.2 displays the map of the change process with these latest activities added to phase 1.

Phase 1. Prepare for the Change Process
Step 1.1. Initiate the change process.
1.1a   Ensure sufficient district readiness.
1.1b   Select an external facilitator.
1.1c   Ensure compatibility and understanding.
Step 1.2. Form a prelaunch team and build district capacity.
1.2a   Form the prelaunch team.
1.2b   Develop team culture and capacity.
1.2c   Enhance district readiness.
1.2d   Conduct a political assessment and community analysis.
1.2e   Develop school board culture and capacity.
1.2f   Secure external and internal funding.
1.2g   Select assistant superintendent for transformation.
1.2h   Form a district facilitation team.
1.2i   Sign a contract for phase 2.
Phase 2. Create a Shared Vision and Develop Capacity and a Strategy for Change
Phase 3. Choose a School or Schools to Pioneer PCBE
Phase 4. Create a Shared Ideal School Vision
Phase 5. Create a Separate District Administrative Structure
Phase 6. Implement and Evolve the School Vision
Phase 7. Expand to Additional Schools
Phase 8. Evolve the Ideal Visions

Figure 9.2: The change process, phase 1.

Phase 2: Create a Shared Ideal District Vision and Develop Capacity and a Strategy for Change

Building on the enhanced capacity from phase 1, in this phase, the facilitator helps the prelaunch team expand into a district leadership team, which envisions an ideal future for its school district (with broad stakeholder input). To do so, it must first develop its culture, norms, and capacity for transformation. Then it decides on a strategy for designing and implementing its PCBE vision, and develops the capacity of school teams to design and implement compatible visions of PCBE in their schools. Throughout phase 2, the district leadership team and board should be applying for external funding to help support the rest of the change process. Such funding speeds up the paradigm change process and thereby greatly enhances its chances of success. The following sections describe the activities associated with this phase.

Visioning Toolkit

The KnowledgeWorks Foundation (2018) has created a Visioning Toolkit that provides the following resources to help you begin and sustain the work of implementing personalized learning.

1. Guidance on crafting a systemwide vision for personalized learning, incorporating diverse stakeholder voices

2. Questions and considerations for finding the right people to champion the work of personalizing learning

3. Direction on how to identify factors that may impact implementation

4. Help with creating messages to introduce your vision with key audiences and sustaining enthusiasm for personalized learning (KnowledgeWorks Foundation, p. 2)

Step 2. Develop a Districtwide Ideal Vision and Expand Capacity

This step includes several activities related to expanding leadership and gathering input.

2a—Expand the Prelaunch Team Into the District Leadership Team

The facilitator helps the prelaunch team expand into a district leadership team of about thirty people and develop its culture and capacity for paradigm change. Its functions include (1) build a convincing case for the need and opportunity for paradigm change to PCBE, (2) identify best practices and exemplary PCBE schools, (3) find external funding for the next step, and (4) affirm the need to create a separate district administration in some form. The district leadership team's composition should include one teacher from each level (elementary, middle, and high) in each feeder system (a single high school and all the schools that feed students into it), one principal from each level in each feeder system, nonteaching staff, board members, parents, community leaders, union president, and central office administrators (including the chief financial officer and the publicity person), as well as all the prelaunch team members. Consider adding a representative from a local post-secondary education institution where your graduates go.

During this team expansion, the prelaunch team transforms into a steering committee within the leadership team. Its members must meet far more often than the leadership team and must commit to attending every meeting. The steering committee begins by assimilating the new members into the norms, culture, and capacity that it had developed as the prelaunch team—building their ownership of the norms, culture, and capacity. Throughout the transformation process, the facilitator guides the steering committee and develops its capacity to facilitate the leadership team such that less and less support is needed from the facilitator.

2b—Initiate a Campaign to Help Stakeholders
Change Their Thinking About Education

The district facilitation team initiates a massive multi-year campaign to change the way community members and educators think about education (Wolk, 2016, January 6). We recommend that this begins with organizing and conducting what Francis Duffy (2003) calls a *community engagement conference* (see Community Engagement Conference). Invite all stakeholder groups in the district (teachers, administrators, non-teaching staff, parents, employers, local politicians, and state education agency representatives). The purpose of this meeting is to build understanding of PCBE, evidence of its benefits, why it requires fundamental paradigm change, why systemic thinking is essential to paradigm change, and why their involvement in the change process is important. The district facilitation team then develops a strategic plan for sharing the new mental model of education with as many stakeholders as possible. Garnering broad public and educator support is crucial to the sustainability of the transformation.

Community Engagement Conference

"An effective tool for building external political support is what I call the Community Engagement Conference. This is a special three-day event organized and conducted using principles of Open Space Technology developed by [Harrison] Owen (1991, 1993). Up to 1,000 people from the community, including school board members and state department of education representatives, can be brought into one room (a large one, of course), and then they are guided through a process in which they self-organize into smaller discussion groups, focusing on topics related to the main theme of the conference. . . . Notes from the discussion groups are entered into laptop computers at the end of each session. At the end of the third day of the conference, you will have a deep and broad database full of wonderfully creative ideas for redesigning your district, a collection of needs and concerns expressed by community members, and an idea of how much political support exists for continuing the redesign process. Most important, you will have demonstrated an authentic interest in the needs, views, and perceptions of a broad sample of your external stakeholders" (Duffy, 2003, p. 179).

2c—Form Input Groups for the Leadership Team

The steering committee, with guidance from the facilitator, helps the district facilitation team to organize interested participants from the community engagement conference into input groups. Each input group should include two leadership team members to share what happens in district leadership team meetings with other stakeholders and get input from the other stakeholders to take back to the next leadership team meeting. This provides more input for the leadership team's visioning process, and it helps expand the opportunity for mindset change and consensus-building.

2d—Develop Transformational Leaders for Schools and Districts

The facilitator helps the district facilitation team to develop all school and district leaders into transformational leaders (also known as participatory leaders or servant leaders or developmental leaders). To do so, they help develop their culture and capacity for paradigm change and provide two-way communication between individual leaders and the leadership team. All leaders can thereby provide input for the PCBE vision and evolve their mindsets in tandem with leadership team members. This could be done by forming a collaborative team for similar-type leaders. For example, principals could meet regularly to discuss what they are doing to change from the supervisory paradigm of leadership to the transformational paradigm, what has worked well, what problems they have encountered, and what solutions might work well. The following are some topics that might be addressed with leaders.

- Ways PCBE is different from the standardized, time-based, sorting-focused paradigm of education

- Why PCBE is better for meeting the needs of students and the community

- Ways that paradigm change is different from typical reform, including the importance of learning and broad stakeholder involvement and ownership of the change process

- The differences between the supervisory (command-and-control) paradigm of leadership and the transformational (empowerment) paradigm, including their decision-making processes

- Tools for transformational leadership, such as developing and using a shared vision to provide direction and motivation, leading consensus building, building trust, empowering and supporting their staff, supporting customized professional development, and so forth

At the same time, the district facilitation team creates reusable learning tools to support continuous learning by new participants as they are oriented to the change process. These tools include workshops and forums and may include videos, readings, and activities for use in those workshops and forums, and learning in collaborative teams and individual learning.

2e—Identify Exemplary PCBE Schools and Practices

The district facilitation team (as always, with coaching from the steering committee and the facilitator) identifies best practices and exemplary PCBE schools. The leadership team studies information about these practices and schools, and a few leadership team members visit two or more exemplary schools. They take pictures, videos, copies of school documents, and extensive notes that they will use to prepare a report for the other leadership team members and other change process participants.

2f—Conduct a System Engagement Conference

After sufficient learning has taken place in the leadership team, input groups, and among other leaders, then the leadership team (with help from the district facilitation team and facilitator) organizes and conducts a system engagement conference (Duffy, 2002, 2003). At this conference, all members of the leadership team, input groups, and other leaders develop a districtwide ideal vision for the school district. This typically occurs in a two-day retreat. Participants in this conference should only be those who have been involved in the process to date, because understanding of PCBE is key. This vision includes features for three key subsystems and for how the district interacts with its community (Duffy, 2003, 2006). The three key subsystems are (1) the district's core work processes (teaching and learning), (2) its supporting work processes (administration and support services such as transportation and food services), and (3) its internal social infrastructure (such as culture, policies, roles, and communications). The core work processes should include both content (the essential learnings for students) and method (the best ways to learn and assess those essentials and other content). The vision should be general enough that different schools can implement it in different ways. Detailed designs should be left to each school to create.

2g—Use Results to Draft the Ideal Vision

The leadership team takes the results of the system engagement conference and formulates them as the first draft of the ideal vision for the district, with additional input from the input groups and other leaders. Later in this process (see step 5.2, page 180), you will address the constraints that prevent you from implementing your ideal vision now. You will need to make some compromises in your first step toward that ideal. But for now, it is important to create an ideal vision, ignoring current constraints that may be possible to overcome in the foreseeable future. Understand that the ideal vision can, should, and will evolve over time. We even recommend that, after about ten years from implementation, you should form a new district leadership team to create a new ideal vision, given that educational needs and tools are likely to change a lot by then. As always, the facilitator guides all activities, but with the goal of building the capacity of participants to play that role, so they become less dependent upon the facilitator.

2h—Hold Community Forums to Build Ownership of the Vision

The district facilitation team, with guidance from the leadership team, organizes a series of school-based community forums to develop broad stakeholder ownership of and commitment to the ideal district vision. This means allowing forum participants to offer suggestions for revising the vision, after which the leadership team makes any appropriate revisions to the ideal vision, publicizes those revisions, and orchestrates a public ceremony to affirm the vision.

2i—Review and Coordinate All Current Change Efforts

The assistant superintendent for transformation and the district facilitation team assume responsibility for all current PCBE change efforts in the district, decide which ones to let go of (due to lack of alignment with the ideal vision), and align each remaining one with the ideal vision as much as possible.

2j—Sign a Contract for Phase 3

Finally, the facilitator signs a contract with the leadership team and school board for phase 3 (described next) of this change process, complete with responsibilities, resource needs, and budget. Figure 9.3 displays the map of the change process with these latest activities added to phase 2.

Phase 1. Prepare for the Change Process
Step 1.1. Initiate the change process.
Step 1.2. Develop a prelaunch team and district capacity.
Phase 2. Create a Shared Vision and Develop Capacity and a Strategy for Change
Step 2. Develop a districtwide ideal vision and expand capacity.
2a Expand the prelaunch team into the district leadership team.
2b Initiate a campaign to change stakeholders' thinking about education.
2c Form input groups for the leadership team.
2d Develop transformational leaders for schools and district.
2e Identify exemplary PCBE schools and practices.
2f Conduct a system engagement conference.
2g Use results to draft the ideal vision.
2h Hold community forums to build ownership of the vision.
2i Review and coordinate all current change efforts.
2j Sign a contract for phase 3.
Phase 3. Choose a School or Schools to Pioneer PCBE
Phase 4. Create a Shared Ideal School Vision
Phase 5. Create a Separate District Administrative Structure
Phase 6. Implement and Evolve the School Vision
Phase 7. Expand to Additional Schools
Phase 8. Evolve the Ideal Visions

Figure 9.3: The change process, phase 2.

Phase 3: Choose a School or Schools to Pioneer PCBE

Now that the district has built capacity and envisioned its model, it is time to bring it into the schools. In this phase, teachers implement and improve the vision, as well as prepare to expand the implementation to higher developmental levels or other schools in the following year. To decide how fast to expand, keep in mind that transformation is a resource-intensive process. Also, teachers are no different from administrators, parents, and the general public in that they fall on a continuum from early adopters to resisters (Rogers, 2003) and some may resist or even try to sabotage attempts at change. We recommend you be strategic in how you deploy scarce transformational resources and avoid transforming too many classrooms and schools in a district to PCBE at once, unless it is a small district or you have large external funding. However, it is difficult for students to move from one paradigm of education to another (either Education 2.0 to 3.0, or vice versa), so it is important to view the core work process (teaching and learning) as a preK–12 process. Therefore, the leadership team should first develop a strategy for how many schools, which schools, and which teachers (classrooms) will be involved in the first round of transformation.

Step 3.1—Develop a Strategy for District Transformation

Developing a strategy for district transformation involves decisions about how implementation of PCBE will proceed, as described in the following activities.

3.1a—Decide Whether to Start With One Feeder System or the Whole District

In a school district that has two or more high schools, there is typically a feeder system. So, one strategy is to achieve preK–12 consistency by having one feeder system transform at a time and encouraging teachers most interested in PCBE to transfer into that system, while others transfer out. This feeder-system strategy does not require all schools and teachers in the feeder system to change at once (see 3.1b—Decide on a School-Within-a-Building or Whole-Building Strategy). Also, the PCBE school or schools must have a totally independent administrative system on both the school and district levels (excepting the superintendent, unless it is a large school district).

Separate District Administration System

Since PCBE is incompatible with the current system, it is important to design a separate district administration system to support the PCBE schools, operating independently from the current district administration system and its teacher-centered schools. Ted Kolderie, a co-founder of Education Evolving, called this the split-screen strategy (Kolderie, 2014). Ron Wolk, the founding editor of *Education Week*, talked about it as "parallel tracks" (Wolk, 2011). Additionally, Robert Schwartz spoke of "multiple pathways" (Schwartz, 2013). This parallel district system will be designed later in the change process.

3.1b—Decide on a School-Within-a-Building or Whole-Building Strategy

Whether or not you choose the feeder-system strategy, a strategy that works well in large schools is to divide the building into two smaller schools (not necessarily the same size)—one that transforms to PCBE and one that doesn't. Teachers and students most interested in transformation would join the PCBE school. This school-within-a-building strategy allows the teachers who are innovators and early adopters to blaze the trail for the other teachers to follow later, with the advantage that pioneers have more motivation and dedication to overcome the many difficulties they will encounter at first. However, in such cases, it is important to take steps to avoid an us-versus-them culture. The PCBE school within the building must be endorsed by all as blazing a trail for the others to follow. Again, PCBE schools must have totally independent administrative systems on both the school and district levels (excepting the superintendent). If the school buildings are small enough, it is usually better to transform whole buildings, but allow teachers to transfer in or out based on their enthusiasm for implementing PCBE.

Step 3.2—Choose a School or Schools

Having decided on a districtwide strategy for transformation, the next step is to carry out that strategy by selecting the school or schools and grade levels that will pioneer the transformation to PCBE. For both the schools-within-a-building strategy and the whole-building strategy, we recommend starting by transforming a minimum of grades preK–3 and a maximum of grades preK–6 at once, depending on resources available, and then transforming one progressively higher grade level each year of the ensuing change process. This not only helps ensure sufficient resources for the change process, but also alleviates the problems associated with students switching between paradigms. Under this progressive approach to transformation, young students, who are not yet conditioned to Education 2.0, are the first to take on PCBE, and no students are required to revert to the teacher-centered paradigm once they have experienced PCBE. Also, lower grade levels tend naturally to be more learner-centered and flexible, so it is easier and quicker to transform multiple grades at once on those levels. Following is some detailed guidance for this step.

3.2a—Decide How Many Schools to Transform and Help All to Form Self-Assessment Teams

The district facilitation team decides how many schools it can afford to support in the transformation process during the first round of changes, and it helps every school in the district to form a small self-assessment team. The self-assessment teams each conduct a school readiness analysis, develop a readiness enhancement plan, and work to enhance their schools' readiness, primarily through community forums and workshops.

3.2b—Select the Initial Schools Based on Self-Assessment Results

The leadership team selects the schools that will comprise the cluster of schools that will transform during the first round of transformation. We use the term *cluster of schools* to refer to all those schools that are transforming to PCBE—either the schools-within-a-building or the whole-school buildings. The selection should be based primarily on readiness for paradigm change as reflected by the self-assessment results. It is often helpful to have schools apply for transformation and address the criteria for readiness in their applications. Schools that are less ready could apply for help to enhance their readiness. The Teacher-Powered Schools initiative describes ten different ways that those schools could secure autonomy within the district (www.teacherpowered.org/inventory/arrangements).

3.2c—Form and Develop a Cluster Design Team With Representatives From the Selected Schools

The leadership team forms a cluster design team with representatives from all the schools that were selected to transform. It should have two committees—one for the core work processes and one for the supporting work processes. The design of the central administration that will oversee that cluster will be addressed in phase 5 (page 179). A larger school district could form three separate cluster design teams, but it is important for them to coordinate often. The design of the core work processes will strongly influence the design of the supporting work processes, and both will influence the nature of the administrative support needed.

3.2d—For the Feeder-System Strategy, Conduct a Cluster Engagement Conference

For a large district using the feeder-system strategy, the cluster design team (with assistance from the district facilitation team) should conduct a cluster engagement conference to develop an ideal vision preK–12 for the cluster that is aligned with the district ideal vision. Then community forums are conducted in each school in the feeder system to review and suggest revisions for the cluster ideal vision. (If there was large cluster participation in developing the district's ideal vision, this step could be skipped.)

3.2e—Develop a Cluster Strategy for School Transformation

The cluster design team, with help from the district facilitation team, develops a cluster strategy for school transformation, which addresses such questions as the following.

- When will each school and supporting-work-unit within the cluster begin to transform?

- Which grade levels will transform first?

- Will the remaining grade levels gradually transform, one level per year?

- How much time will be devoted to design, development, and teacher training before implementation begins?

If more than one cluster is transforming (very rare), the leadership team develops a district strategy for school transformation, primarily by helping the cluster design teams decide when each cluster will begin to transform itself. Meanwhile, the district facilitation team develops its own capacity and mechanisms to support the schools in their redesign process.

3.2f—Sign a Contract for Phases 4 and 5

Finally, the facilitator signs a contract with the leadership team and school board for phases 4 and 5, complete with responsibilities, resource needs, and budget. Phases 4 and 5 occur simultaneously, but they don't have to be started at exactly the same time.

Since quite a few teams are involved in the change process, we list here all the teams that are formed at some point during the process.

- **District-level teams**
  - Prelaunch team—becomes steering committee
  - District facilitation team (with a steering committee)
  - Leadership team
  - Input groups (for leadership team)
- **Cluster-level teams**
  - Cluster design teams
- **School-level teams**
  - School self-assessment teams—become school design teams
  - Learning communities (for school design teams)
  - Task forces (for school design teams)

Figure 9.4 displays the map of the change process with these latest activities added to phase 3.

Phase 1. Prepare for the Change Process
Step 1.1. Initiate the change process.
Step 1.2. Develop a prelaunch team and district capacity.
Phase 2. Create a Shared Vision and Develop Capacity and a Strategy for Change
Step 2. Develop a districtwide ideal vision and expand capacity.
Phase 3. Choose a School or Schools to Pioneer PCBE
Step 3.1. Develop a strategy for district transformation.
3.1a Decide whether to start with one feeder system.
3.1b Decide on a school-within-a building or whole-building strategy.
Step 3.2. Choose a school or schools.
3.2a Decide how many schools to transform and help all to form self-assessment teams.
3.2b Select the initial schools based on self-assessment results.
3.2c Form and develop a cluster design team with representatives from the selected schools.
3.2d For the feeder-system strategy, conduct a cluster engagement conference.
3.2e Develop a cluster strategy for school transformation.
3.2f Sign a contract for phases 4 and 5.
Phase 4. Create a Shared Ideal School Vision
Phase 5. Create a Separate District Administrative Structure
Phase 6. Implement and Evolve the School Vision
Phase 7. Expand to Additional Schools
Phase 8. Evolve the Ideal Visions

Figure 9.4: The change process, phase 3.

Phase 4: Create a Shared Ideal School Vision

Once the district has a plan and selects schools to transform, the process shifts to schools themselves. As this phase consists of school-level activities, we provide detailed guidance in chapter 10 under phase 1 (page 191) and phase 2 (page 196). The following sections provide a brief summary of the relevant steps.

Step 4.1—Initiate the School Change Process

This step (1.1 in chapter 10, page 192) involves choosing a facilitator for the school change process, enhancing the school's readiness, building leadership support on the school level, and signing a compact (not a formal contract) between the school and the district leadership team for the school-level change process.

Step 4.2—Form a Prelaunch Team and Build School Capacity

In this step (1.2 in chapter 10, page 194), the school prelaunch team builds capacity on the school level, conducts a political assessment and community analysis, designs strategies for communicating with each stakeholder group, secures external and internal funds, selects a leader for the school-level transformation effort, and signs a broader compact for the school-level transformation effort.

Step 4.3—Develop an Ideal Vision and Expand Capacity

This step (2.1 in chapter 10, page 196) expands the school's prelaunch team into a school leadership team and develops its culture and capacity. Then the school leadership team conducts a community engagement conference, forms input groups, works with school leaders to develop their capacity for transformation, learns about exemplary PCBE schools, develops a shared ideal vision for the school, and places all current school change efforts under the purview of the leader for the school's transformation effort.

Step 4.4—Develop a Strategy for Implementing the School Vision

In this step (2.2 in chapter 10, page 199), the school leadership team develops a strategy for how much of the school, which grade levels, and which teachers will be involved in the first round of transformation.

Step 4.5—Further Develop the Vision

In this step (2.3 in chapter 10, page 200), the school decides on ways to compromise on the ideal vision to meet practical constraints, and it develops more details for this first step toward the ideal vision, including detailed designs for the studios (classrooms) of all teachers involved in the first implementation.

Figure 9.5 displays the map of the change process with these latest activities added to phase 4.

Phase 1. Prepare for the Change Process
Step 1.1. Initiate the change process.
Step 1.2. Develop a prelaunch team and district capacity.
Phase 2. Create a Shared Vision and Develop Capacity and a Strategy for Change
Step 2. Develop a districtwide ideal vision and expand capacity.
Phase 3. Choose a School or Schools to Pioneer PCBE
Step 3.1. Develop a strategy for district transformation.
Step 3.2. Choose a school or schools.
Phase 4. Create a Shared Ideal School Vision
Step 4.1. Initiate the school change process.
Step 4.2. Form a prelaunch team and build school capacity.
Step 4.3. Develop an ideal vision and expand capacity.
Step 4.4. Develop a strategy for implementing the school vision.
Step 4.5. Further develop the vision.
Phase 5. Create a Separate District Administrative Structure
Phase 6. Implement and Evolve the School Vision
Phase 7. Expand to Additional Schools
Phase 8. Evolve the Ideal Visions

Figure 9.5: The change process, phase 4.

Phase 5: Create a Separate District Administrative Structure

Once you have a vision for PCBE schools, you must design a district administrative structure that can meet their needs, which are very different from those of Education 2.0 schools. In this phase, the assistant superintendent for transformation and the district facilitation team help all stakeholders create a shared ideal vision of a new district administrative structure, they develop an implementation plan for the new administrative structure, and they implement and improve the first step toward their ideal vision.

Step 5.1—Create a Shared Ideal Vision of the New Administrative Structure

Creating a shared vision for PCBE administration involves several activities related to gathering input and drafting the structure.

5.1a—Conduct a Community Engagement Conference

The district facilitation team organizes and conducts a second community engagement conference (see step 2.1, page 196) for all stakeholder groups in the district to explore and build understanding of alternative administrative structures, with a particular focus on professional organizational structures (see principles V, W, and X in chapter 6, page 103), including pros and cons of each. Discussions might center around the structures described in chapter 6, such as the following.

- A large building divided into small schools that operate independently of each other
- Teachers choosing their own school leader
- Teachers hiring and firing their own fellow staff members
- Teachers managing their school's budget
- The role of the district office redefined as supporting rather than controlling the schools
- The kinds of supports that the district office should provide to the schools

5.1b—Form Input Groups

Interested participants from the community engagement conference are organized into input groups. Each input group should include two leadership team members who share what happens in each leadership team meeting and get input from the other stakeholders to take back to the next leadership team meeting. This provides more input for the leadership team's visioning process, and it helps expand the opportunity for mindset change and consensus-building.

5.1c—Identify Exemplary Teacher-Led Schools and Practices

The district facilitation team identifies best practices, several exemplary teacher-led schools, and within-district school choice programs, and the district leadership team studies information about them. A few leadership team members visit two or more schools, taking photos, videos, copies of school documents, and extensive notes that they use to prepare a report for the other leadership team members and other change process participants.

5.1d—Conduct a System Engagement Conference

After sufficient learning has taken place in the leadership team and input groups, the leadership team (with help from the district facilitation team) organizes and conducts a system engagement conference for all members of the leadership team, input groups, and other leaders to develop a districtwide ideal vision for the new administrative structure, preferably in a two-day retreat. Participants in this conference should only be those who have been involved in the process to date, because understanding of alternative administrative structures is key.

5.1e—Use Results to Draft the Ideal Vision

The leadership team takes the results of the system engagement conference and formulates them as the first draft of the ideal vision for the new district administrative structures (Vision 1.0), with additional input from the input groups and other leaders. As with the district's vision for the PCBE system as a whole, this vision of the administrative structures will evolve over time and require compromise for initial implementation. But for now, it is important to create an ideal vision, ignoring current constraints that may be possible to overcome in the foreseeable future.

5.1f—Hold Community Forums to Build Ownership of the Vision

Unless you are certain that you already have enough public and political support, the district facilitation team, with guidance from the district leadership team, organizes a series of school-based community forums to develop broad stakeholder ownership of, and commitment to, the ideal vision for this new administrative structure. This means allowing forum participants to offer revisions to the vision, after which the leadership team makes any appropriate revisions to the ideal vision, publicizes those revisions, and orchestrates a public ceremony to affirm the vision.

5.1g—Assign Implementation to the Assistant Superintendent for Transformation

The assistant superintendent for transformation and the district facilitation team assume responsibility for leading the implementation of the new administrative structure.

Step 5.2—Develop an Implementation Plan for the New Administrative Structure

5.2a—Decide Which Functions to Implement First

The assistant superintendent for transformation and the district facilitation team review the functions called for by the ideal vision and decide which functions can and should be implemented right away (given the importance of starting with high-leverage changes), which ones may take a year or two to implement, and which ones will take longer. Based on this analysis, they prepare a description of the new administration system that describes the initial structure for each school (leaving plenty of leeway for the teachers in each school to decide on their own structures) and the initial structure for the district office.

5.2b—Decide Who Should Carry Out Each of the Initial Functions

The assistant superintendent for transformation and the district facilitation team decide who should carry out each of the initial functions for the district office. They also help each school leadership team decide who should carry out each of their school's initial administrative functions. Keep in mind that Education 2.0 administrative functions will still need to be carried out for schools that are not transforming yet. Some of the central office functions for the new schools could be done by the same people who perform similar functions for the Education 2.0 system, but there is danger in that because the command-and-control orientation of administrators' work with schools in Education 2.0 and the service orientation in Education 3.0 make it difficult for an administrator to switch back and forth. Hence, whenever possible, it is wise to have different people working in completely separate administrative systems, with just a few exceptions, such as the following.

- Special education services
- Government reporting
- Transportation
- Food services
- Maintenance

5.2c—Prepare People, Administrative Tools, and Policies

Hire and train the appropriate people for this very different administrative role (service-oriented), procure appropriate administrative tools, and formulate and implement relevant policies, procedures, and practices.

Step 5.3—Implement the First Step Toward the Ideal Vision of the New Administrative Structure

5.3a—Carry Out the Functions

Carry out the functions for the new administrative system. As this is done, continuously look for ways to improve the system. Given their role of serving rather than controlling the schools, administrators should seek frequent feedback from those they serve to find ways to improve their services. They can begin to perform some of these functions before the first PCBE school begins operations (phase 6, page 182). One such early function is to work on waivers of state requirements requested by the transforming school(s).

Figure 9.6 (page 182) displays the map of the change process with these latest activities added to phase 5.

Phase 1. Prepare for the Change Process
Step 1.1. Initiate the change process.
Step 1.2. Develop a prelaunch team and district capacity.
Phase 2. Create a Shared Vision and Develop Capacity and a Strategy for Change
Step 2. Develop a districtwide ideal vision and expand capacity.
Phase 3. Choose a School or Schools to Pioneer PCBE
Step 3.1. Develop a strategy for district transformation.
Step 3.2. Choose a school or schools.
Phase 4. Create a Shared Ideal School Vision
Step 4.1. Initiate the school change process.
Step 4.2. Form a prelaunch team and build school capacity.
Step 4.3. Develop an ideal vision and expand capacity.
Step 4.4. Develop a strategy for implementing the school vision.
Step 4.5. Further develop the vision.
Phase 5. Create a Separate District Administrative Structure
Step 5.1. Create a shared ideal vision of the new administrative structure.
5.1a   Conduct a community engagement conference.
5.1b   Form input groups.
5.1c   Identify exemplary teacher-led schools and practices.
5.1d   Conduct a system engagement conference.
5.1e   Use results to draft the ideal vision of the new administrative structure.
5.1f   Hold community forums to build ownership of the vision.
5.1g   Assign implementation to the assistant superintendent for transformation.
Step 5.2. Develop an implementation plan for the new administrative structure.
5.2a   Decide which functions to implement first.
5.2b   Decide who should carry out each of the initial functions.
5.2c   Prepare people, administrative tools, and policies.
Step 5.3. Implement the first step toward the ideal vision of the new administrative structure.
5.3a   Carry out and improve the functions.
Phase 6. Implement and Evolve the School Vision
Phase 7. Expand to Additional Schools
Phase 8. Evolve the Ideal Visions

Figure 9.6: The change process, phase 5.

Phase 6: Implement and Evolve the School Vision

Building on the school-level vision from phase 4, this phase focuses on how to make it happen. As this is a school-level activity, we provide detailed guidance in chapter 10 under phase 3 (page 203) and phase 4 (page 205). The following sections provide a brief summary of the relevant steps.

Step 6.1—Implement and Improve the Initial Vision

6.1a—Prepare

In this step (3.1 in chapter 10, page 203), teachers select a principal for each new school, and the school leadership team recruits students, conducts student and parent orientations, supervises renovations, procures equipment and materials, and has teachers trained.

6.1b—Implement

Then all staff implement, formatively evaluate, and improve this first step toward the ideal vision.

Step 6.2—Expand the Implementation

6.2a—Recruit and Train New Teachers

In this step (3.2 in chapter 10, page 204) the school leadership team recruits and organizes additional teachers from Education 2.0 schools into a new task force to expand PCBE to the next-higher age level—and perhaps even to additional studios (classrooms) at the current developmental levels. Also, the current teachers train the new ones, sometimes with the help of outside experts.

6.2b—Continue the Expansion

This expansion continues each year until the entire school (building) has been transformed.

Step 6.3—Evolve the Implementation

6.3a—Evaluate and Improve

In this step (phase 4 in chapter 10, page 205) each task force continually evaluates and improves its practical vision each year, to evolve closer to the school's ideal vision. The school leadership team coordinates those improvements.

6.3b—Sign a Contract for Phase 7

Finally, the facilitator signs a contract with the district leadership team and school board for phase 7, complete with responsibilities, resource needs, and budget.

Figure 9.7 displays the map of the change process with these latest activities added to phase 6.

Phase 1. Prepare for the Change Process
Step 1.1. Initiate the change process.
Step 1.2. Develop a prelaunch team and district capacity.
Phase 2. Create a Shared Vision and Develop Capacity and a Strategy for Change
Step 2. Develop a districtwide ideal vision and expand capacity.

Figure 9.7: The change process, phase 6.

continued →

Phase 3. Choose a School or Schools to Pioneer PCBE
Step 3.1. Develop a strategy for district transformation.
Step 3.2. Choose a school or schools.
Phase 4. Create a Shared Ideal School Vision
Step 4.1. Initiate the school change process.
Step 4.2. Form a prelaunch team and build school capacity.
Step 4.3. Develop an ideal vision and expand capacity.
Step 4.4. Develop a strategy for implementing the school vision.
Step 4.5. Further develop the vision.
Phase 5. Create a Separate District Administrative Structure
Step 5.2. Develop an implementation plan for the new administrative structure.
Step 5.3. Implement the first step toward the ideal vision of the new administrative structure.
Phase 6. Implement and Evolve the School Vision
Step 6.1. Implement and improve the initial vision.
6.1a   Prepare.
6.1b   Implement.
Step 6.2. Expand the implementation.
6.2a   Recruit and train new teachers.
6.2b   Continue the expansion.
Step 6.3. Evolve the implementation.
6.3a   Evaluate and improve.
6.3b   Sign a contract for phase 7.
Phase 7. Expand to Additional Schools
Phase 8. Evolve the Ideal Visions

Phase 7: Expand to Additional Schools

Step 7.1—Select Additional Schools

Continue to carry out your district and cluster strategies for transformation by repeating appropriate parts of step 3.2 (see Step 3.2—Choose a School or Schools, page 174). Decide how many more schools you can afford to support in the transformation process now, given school and community receptiveness, your funds, and other resources available, and use school self-assessments to select the schools at the highest levels of readiness.

Step 7.2—Help Each School Create a Shared Ideal Vision

Repeat phase 4 (phases 1 and 2 in chapter 10, pages 191 and 196).

Step 7.3—Help Each School Implement and Evolve Its Vision

Repeat phase 6 (phases 3 and 4 in chapter 10, pages 203 and 205).

Figure 9.8 displays the map of the change process with these latest activities added to phase 7.

Phase 1. Prepare for the Change Process
Step 1.1. Initiate the change process.
Step 1.2. Develop a prelaunch team and district capacity.
Phase 2. Create a Shared Vision and Develop Capacity and a Strategy for Change
Step 2. Develop a districtwide ideal vision and expand capacity.
Phase 3. Choose a School or Schools to Pioneer PCBE
Step 3.1. Develop a strategy for district transformation.
Step 3.2. Choose a school or schools.
Phase 4. Create a Shared Ideal School Vision
Step 4.1. Initiate the school change process.
Step 4.2. Form a prelaunch team and build school capacity.
Step 4.3. Develop an ideal vision and expand capacity.
Step 4.4. Develop a strategy for implementing the school vision.
Step 4.5. Further develop the vision.
Phase 5. Create a Separate District Administrative Structure.
Step 5.2. Develop an implementation plan for the new administrative structure.
Step 5.3. Implement the first step toward the ideal vision of the new administrative structure.
Phase 6. Implement and Evolve the School Vision
Step 6.1. Implement and improve the initial vision.
Step 6.2. Expand the implementation.
Step 6.3. Evolve the implementation.
Phase 7. Expand to Additional Schools
Step 7.1. Select additional schools.
Step 7.2 Help each school create a shared ideal vision.
Step 7.3 Help each school implement and evolve its vision.
Phase 8. Evolve the Ideal Visions

Figure 9.8: The change process, phase 7.

Phase 8: Evolve the Ideal Visions

Educational needs and tools change over time. After about ten years of expanding and continuously improving the school visions and the district administrative vision and their implementations, the district and schools should form new leadership teams to develop new ideal visions toward which they can continue to evolve. This entails repeating phases 1 through 7.

Figure 9.9 (page 186) summarizes the detailed guidance for all the phases of the district change process. The next chapter provides guidance for transforming a single school.

Phase 1. Prepare for the Change Process

Step 1.1. Initiate the change process.

1.1a   Ensure sufficient district readiness.

1.1b   Select an external facilitator.

1.1c   Ensure compatibility and understanding.

Step 1.2. Form a prelaunch team and build district capacity.

1.2a   Form the prelaunch team.

1.2b   Develop team culture and capacity.

1.2c   Enhance district readiness.

1.2d   Conduct a political assessment and community analysis.

1.2e   Develop school board culture and capacity.

1.2f   Secure external and internal funding.

1.2g   Select the assistant superintendent for transformation.

1.2h   Form a district facilitation team.

1.2i   Sign a contract for phase 2.

Phase 2. Create a Shared Ideal District Vision and Develop Capacity and a Strategy for Change

2a   Expand the prelaunch team into the district leadership team.

2b   Initiate a campaign to change stakeholders' thinking about education.

2c   Form input groups for the leadership team.

2d   Develop transformational leaders for schools and district.

2e   Identify exemplary PCBE schools and practices.

2f   Conduct a system engagement conference.

2g   Use results to draft the ideal vision.

2h   Hold community forums to build ownership of the vision.

2i   Review and coordinate all current change efforts.

2j   Sign a contract for phase 3.

Phase 3. Choose a School or Schools to Pioneer PCBE

Step 3.1. Develop a strategy for district transformation.

3.1a   Decide whether to start with one feeder system or the whole district.

3.1b   Decide on a school-within-a-building or whole-building strategy.

Step 3.2. Choose a school or schools.

3.2a   Decide how many schools to transform and help all to form self-assessment teams.

3.2b   Select the initial schools based on self-assessment results.

3.2c   Form and develop a cluster design team with representatives from the selected schools.

3.2d   For the feeder-system strategy, conduct a cluster engagement conference.

3.2e   Develop a cluster strategy for school transformation.

3.2f   Sign a contract for phases 4 and 5.

Phase 4. Create a Shared Ideal School Vision

> **Step 4.1. Initiate the school change process.**
>
> **Step 4.2. Form a prelaunch team and build school capacity.**
>
> **Step 4.3. Develop an ideal vision and expand capacity.**
>
> **Step 4.4. Develop a strategy for implementing the school vision.**
>
> **Step 4.5. Further develop the vision.**

Phase 5. Create a Separate District Administrative Structure

> **Step 5.1. Create a shared ideal vision of the new administrative structure.**
>
> 5.1a   Conduct a community engagement conference.
>
> 5.1b   Form input groups.
>
> 5.1c   Identify exemplary teacher-led schools and practices.
>
> 5.1d   Conduct a system engagement conference.
>
> 5.1e   Use results to draft the ideal vision of the new administrative structure.
>
> 5.1f   Hold community forums to build ownership of the vision.
>
> 5.1g   Assign implementation to the assistant superintendent for transformation.
>
> **Step 5.2. Develop an implementation plan for the new administrative structure.**
>
> 5.2a   Decide which functions to implement first.
>
> 5.2b   Decide who should carry out each of the initial functions.
>
> 5.2c   Prepare people, administrative tools, and policies.
>
> **Step 5.3. Implement the first step toward the ideal vision of the new administrative structure.**
>
> 5.3a   Carry out and improve the functions.

Phase 6. Implement and Evolve the School Vision

> **Step 6.1. Implement and improve the initial vision.**
>
> 6.1a   Prepare.
>
> 6.1b   Implement.
>
> **Step 6.2. Expand the implementation.**
>
> 6.2a   Recruit and train new teachers.
>
> 6.2b   Continue the expansion.
>
> **Step 6.3. Evolve the implementation.**
>
> 6.3a   Evaluate and improve.
>
> 6.3b   Sign a contract for phase 7.

Phase 7. Expand to Additional Schools

> **Step 7.1. Select additional schools (repeat step 3.2)**
>
> **Step 7.2. Help each school create a shared ideal vision (repeat phase 4)**
>
> **Step 7.3. Help each school implement and evolve its vision (repeat phase 6)**

Phase 8. Evolve the Ideal Visions

Figure 9.9: The phases of the change process for a district.

Change Process for an Independent School

All the values, principles, and continuous activities described in chapter 8 (page 147) apply to the change process for an independent school. Only the sequential activities are significantly different across the three scopes of change (classroom, school, and district). This chapter opens with an overview of the process for changing an independent school; it then provides detailed guidance for sequential activities.

This chapter is for schools that operate independently of a larger system's control. It includes some public charter schools, though not the ones that belong to networks that control important aspects of their school. It also applies to private independent schools. This process should not be used to change one school within a school district or centralized network, because the PCBE school would be incompatible with the rest of the system, would not be able to implement many of the crucial aspects of PCBE for it to be effective, and would not survive more than a few years. Schools within a district or centralized network must use the change process for a school district (see chapter 9, page 159).

In 2009, the average number of students in each of the following kinds of private schools was (Planty et al., 2009):

- Nonsectarian—88

- Catholic—283

- Other religious—112

In fall 2015, the average number of students in a public charter school was 406 (National Center for Education Statistics, 2018). The guidance we offer here is generally for smaller schools (around 150 students), but we also offer adjustments for larger schools when needed.

Similar to school districts, conditions often vary significantly from one school to another, and this requires variations in the change process. We encourage your change team to look for beneficial ways to adapt the process described herein, with the caution that careless adaptations can be detrimental to the change process. Your team must carefully consider adaptations with respect to the framework and common obstacles described in chapter 8 (page 147). In addition, we strongly encourage you to continually monitor, evaluate, and improve all aspects of your change process as it proceeds.

Overview of Sequential Activities for the Independent School Change Process

The following is an overview of four sequential activities for a school-level change process. The title of each phase sounds similar to those for the district-level change process, but there are important differences in how each is done.

1. **Prepare for the change process:** A building needs a foundation. So does the change process. Preparing a school for paradigm change is critical to successful implementation of PCBE. Kotter (2012) identified eight reasons for failed transformational change. Six of those eight reasons are linked to inadequate or short-circuited preparation of the system. It is important to choose a process facilitator, enhance school readiness, marshal leadership support, form and develop a small prelaunch team of leaders of all stakeholder groups, and enhance school capacity for paradigm change.

2. **Create a shared ideal vision, expand capacity, and develop a strategy for change:** Developing a shared vision of PCBE reduces resistance to change and promotes learning, mindset change, and commitment (Banathy, 1991; Hammonds, 2018; Jenlink et al., 1998; Senge, 2000; Theobald, 1987). The prelaunch team expands into a school leadership team that includes leaders of all stakeholder groups in the school to lead this activity. Each leader engages others in their stakeholder group (akin to pyramid groups), to share and evolve thinking and seek input to the vision. During this time, the leadership team develops the school's capacity for change. This primarily entails developing a culture for change, enhancing the change process skills of participants, engaging the community, forming input groups, and learning about existing PCBE schools. Next, the leadership team develops a strategy for the implementation approach (whole-building or school-within-a-building) and decides which grade levels to transform the first year of implementation. Then the leadership team decides on ways that the ideal needs to be scaled back for the initial implementation of PCBE in the school, taking into account the need to make sufficient high-leverage changes right away. Finally, they decide how many and which teachers will transform in this first iteration, and those teachers are formed into task forces that prepare detailed designs for the initial studios (classrooms) on each of the selected grade levels.

3. **Implement and improve the vision:** Time and money are allocated to procuring necessary resources, (for example, hands-on learning materials, digital tools, online tutorials and assessments), finding or designing projects and other activities for students, engaging teachers in professional development for effective use of the tools and design of the projects, and remodeling facilities. This is also the time to recruit students and hold a student orientation to prepare them for their new roles. A parent orientation is also held. Then the school implements high-leverage changes for its vision and makes other changes as the need emerges. Leaders continuously evaluate and improve the new system. Finally, recruit additional teachers each year and form task forces to expand the implementation to other classrooms on the same grade levels, as well as to the next higher grade level.

4. **Evolve the implementation:** The school makes additional changes as needed or desired in order to support the high-leverage changes. Formative evaluation is key. No summative evaluation should be done for about five years to give time for the evolution to overcome inevitable problems. Eventually, the school forms a new leadership team to develop and evolve toward a new ideal vision.

The following sections present detailed guidance for these sequential activities.

Detailed Guidance for the Sequential Activities

There are four phases to the change process for an independent school, as follows.

Phase 1. Prepare for the change process.

Phase 2. Create an ideal shared vision, expand capacity, and develop a strategy for change.

Phase 3. Implement and improve the vision.

Phase 4. Evolve the implementation.

Each phase consists of steps and activities that teachers, leaders, and teams should undertake. If you are a school within a district, you should use this process as a part of the broader process to transform the whole district (see chapter 9, page 159), while remembering that your changes will be unsustainable unless fundamental changes are made throughout the district, especially in the central office.

Phase 1: Prepare for the Change Process

There are two major steps in preparation for change: (1) initiating the effort and (2) developing a prelaunch team to lay the foundation for the change process. However, as with the phases, the steps and the activities that make up each step should not be thought of as a lockstep sequence. Instead, they should be perceived as a set of flowing activities that converge, diverge, and backflow from time to time, and do so repeatedly throughout the phase. Also, activities during a step often need to be adapted to local conditions. Some activities listed here may not be needed, while some activities not listed here may be needed. However, extreme care and thought should precede any changes to these guidelines.

Step 1.1—Initiate the Change Process

The first step in the transformation process for a school involves several activities related to readiness and preparation for change.

1.1a—Select a Process Facilitator

The principal and other instigators of the change to PCBE choose a facilitator for the change process. Often schools have a history of working with consultants in a "solve the problem for us" capacity or doctor-patient relationship wherein the consultant provides a diagnosis and prescribes a treatment. Facilitation differs from consultation in that the facilitator is not the expert but a process guide. Whereas consultation calls for an expert knowledge base on one or a few areas of education, facilitation calls for expertise in the following areas (see appendix C, page 217, for more detail).

- Interpersonal skills
- Group-process skills
- Deep-listening skills
- Motivational and inspirational skills
- Suspension of personal biases and judgments
- Conflict-management skills
- Systems-thinking skills
- Dialogue and consensus-building skills
- Promotion of individual, team, and organizational learning
- Skills for building and sustaining community
- Skills for disclosing one's lack of agreement
- Trust-building skills
- Political neutrality
- Charisma
- Support for the values of the change process

Facilitating this process is time consuming. If you choose someone from your school staff, you should provide some release time from other daily obligations, and make sure this person is viewed as neutral and does not have any bad relationships with stakeholders. An external facilitator is more likely to meet these criteria, but knowledge of the school and good relationships with its stakeholders are important criteria that an external facilitator would lack.

1.1b—Ensure Sufficient School Readiness

The facilitator makes sure the school is at a sufficient level of readiness to embark on the journey. The following are the most important criteria.

- **Is the board of trustees supportive of the change to PCBE?** If not, the facilitator should meet individually with each trustee to win his or her support. Without the board's full support, the change effort should be abandoned.

- **Is the principal a transformational leader?** If not, the facilitator should work with the principal to cultivate those skills and attitudes.

- **What is the quality of the relationships among the teachers, between the teachers and the principal, and between the principal and the teachers' union (if any)?** If the quality of any of these relationships is poor, the facilitator should work to improve those relationships, primarily by facilitating communication, openness, and trust-building.

- **What is the school's history with change?** Are the teachers exhausted from frequent change efforts? Do they believe that "this too shall pass" and largely ignore change initiatives? If attitudes about change are negative, the facilitator should work with teachers, individually if needed, to help them see that this change is different and how PCBE can benefit them and their students.

1.1c—Ensure Leadership Support and Understanding

The facilitator builds leadership support for the change to PCBE. This includes (a) ensuring political support for the change process from the leaders of all the school's stakeholder groups, and (b) ensuring that those leaders understand the role of the facilitator and the leaders' responsibilities. Subsequently, all leaders, the board of trustees, and the facilitator sign a compact (not a formal legal contract) to initiate the change process (just for step 1.2 at this point), including responsibilities, resource needs, and funding. The compact should include the following for step 1.2.

- Desired outcomes

- Expectations (process activities and timelines)

- Release time for the facilitator

- Human resource needs, participation roles, and access for all parties

- Money for retreats and participant time

- Anticipated problems and how to deal with them

- Instructions on how to revise or terminate the compact

If the facilitator is hired from outside the school, a formal contract is also needed that addresses the same points.

Step 1.2—Form a Prelaunch Team and Build School Capacity

The next step in the process is to form the team that will lead the initial phases and the development of school capacity, as described in the following activities.

1.2a—Form the Prelaunch Team

This step begins with the facilitator forming a small prelaunch team whose members typically include an influential member of the board of trustees, the principal, at least one influential teacher leader, a teachers' association representative (if any), an assistant principal (if any), a highly respected nonteaching staff member, and an influential parent leader. This team should not be larger than seven or eight people, no matter the size of your school.

1.2b—Develop Team Culture and Capacity, Conduct a Political Assessment and Community Analysis, and Design Strategies for Communicating With Stakeholders

The prelaunch team does not make any decisions about the ideal vision for PCBE. Instead, it serves four purposes related to preparing the school for the change process. One is to develop its own culture and capacity for systemic transformation that can survive the team's later expansion into a roughly fifteen-member leadership team (more or less, depending on the size of the school—see step 2.1). Forming such a large team at once would likely result in a team culture and dynamic that may be detrimental to the change process. Culture includes adopting a set of norms and values for the transformation process. Capacity includes understanding systems thinking, the paradigm change process, systems design, dialogue, and small-group facilitation. Periodic one- or two-day retreats are far more efficient than two-hour meetings. Your team can accomplish more in a two-day retreat (about fifteen hours) than in a school year of monthly two-hour meetings. It is helpful for the prelaunch team to find and create learning tools that it can reuse as new people join the change process.

Additional purposes of the prelaunch team are (1) conduct a political assessment of top formal and opinion leaders in the school, (2) conduct a community analysis to identify where resources and support can be found for the change initiative, and (3) design strategies for communicating with each stakeholder group. It may be helpful to classify people as what Block (1991) calls *allies* (high trust, high agreement), *bedfellows* (low trust, high agreement), *opponents* (high trust, low agreement), *adversaries* (low trust, low agreement), and *fence-sitters* (undecided where they stand). In a small school, this will be a quick process.

1.2c—Secure External and Internal Funding

The prelaunch team, with guidance from the facilitator, helps the principal and board of trustees secure external funding, if possible, and reallocate some internal funds to the change process. Sufficient funds will greatly speed up the process, making changes in school leadership less likely (understanding that such changes can derail the transformation process), and it makes the process less onerous for participants.

1.2d—Select an Assistant Principal for Transformation

The prelaunch team (as always, with guidance from the facilitator) selects someone already in the school to lead the transformation process. This should be a charismatic, well-liked, and highly respected leader who is committed to PCBE and knows the important people and operations of the school. We suggest you give this person an impressive title to show the importance of this position—something like *assistant principal for transformation* (or *director of transformation* in a small school). In a small school, the principal is often a good choice. The facilitator further develops that person's capacity to coordinate and inspire systemic transformation to PCBE, and the principal places all current change efforts under that person's purview. If possible, this person should be on the prelaunch team from the beginning. Initially, this could be a quarter-time responsibility (assign fewer students to their classroom at the elementary level, or give a reduced course load in a middle or high school), but plans should be made for it to become half-time (or more for a large school) as the transformation process accelerates.

1.2e—Sign a Compact for Phase 2

Finally, the facilitator signs a compact with the prelaunch team and board of trustees for phase 2, including responsibilities, resource needs, and funding. If the facilitator is external, a formal contract is also needed.

Figure 10.1 displays a map of the change process with these activities included in phase 1.

Phase 1. Prepare for the Change Process

Step 1.1. Initiate the change process.

- 1.1a Select a process facilitator.
- 1.1b Ensure sufficient school readiness.
- 1.1c Ensure leadership support and understanding.

Step 1.2. Form a prelaunch team and build school capacity.

- 1.2a Form a prelaunch team.
- 1.2b Develop team culture and capacity, conduct a political assessment and community analysis, and design strategies for communicating with stakeholders.
- 1.2c Secure external and internal funding.
- 1.2d Select an assistant principal for transformation.
- 1.2e Sign a compact for phase 2.

Phase 2. Create a Shared Ideal Vision, Expand Capacity, and Develop a Strategy for Change

Phase 3. Implement and Improve the School Vision

Phase 4. Evolve the Implementation

Figure 10.1: The change process for a school, phase 1.

Phase 2: Create a Shared Ideal Vision, Expand Capacity, and Develop a Strategy for Change

Once stakeholders are on board, it is time to plan in more detail. In this phase, the prelaunch team expands into the school leadership team, and it envisions an ideal future for their school (with broad stakeholder input). The team also expands its capacity for transformation, decides on a strategy for designing and implementing their PCBE vision, and adapts the ideal vision for practical implementation.

Step 2.1—Develop an Ideal Vision and Expand Capacity

This step includes several activities related to expanding leadership and gathering input.

2.1a—Expand the Prelaunch Team Into the School Leadership Team, Develop Its Capacity, and Transform the Prelaunch Team Into a Steering Committee

The facilitator helps the prelaunch team expand into a school leadership team and develops its culture and capacity for paradigm change. This team should be small enough to function effectively but large enough to bring in the many necessary perspectives to create a plan that will have broad buy-in. In a small school, membership may total only ten members, while in a larger school it may be fifteen to twenty. Its functions include (a) building a convincing case for the needs and opportunities for paradigm change to PCBE, (b) identifying best practices and several exemplary PCBE schools, and (c) finding external funding for the next step. The leadership team's composition typically includes more teachers (at least one from each grade level), more nonteaching staff, more parents, and several community leaders, as well as all the prelaunch team members. Consider adding a representative from an educational institution that many of your graduates attend, which could be a higher-level school or a postsecondary institution.

Experience Learning to Redesign Schools

Transcend, in collaboration with Excellent Schools New Mexico (https://excellentschoolsnm.org/coming-soon/), convened five small teams of teachers, coaches, and administrators in Santa Fe for six months to figure out how to redesign their schools. They have gained key insights about educators' key roles on school design teams, including:

1. Educator-designers look at problems as design issues.

2. Educator-designers need agency.

3. We need a new type of professional learning experience that gives design teams the tools, processes, time, space, and networks to redesign their schools.

One participant stated, "This collaborative is helping me find the passion I had when I first started teaching and is motivating me to think bigger and bolder for the future of education. I have not felt this hopeful about my abilities to enact systemic change as an educator in a long time and am so thankful that someone is helping to do this necessary work to reimagine education and that I get to be a part of it" (Bhatt, 2019).

During this team expansion, the prelaunch team transforms into a steering committee within the leadership team. Members must meet far more often than the whole leadership team and must commit to attending every meeting. Throughout the transformation process, the facilitator guides the steering committee and develops its capacity to facilitate the leadership team with as little direct facilitation as possible by the facilitator.

2.1b—Initiate a Campaign to Help Stakeholders Change Their Thinking About Education

The assistant principal for transformation and the facilitator organize and conduct a community engagement conference (Duffy, 2002, 2003) for all the school's stakeholder groups (teachers, administrators, nonteaching staff, parents, employers, local politicians, and perhaps even a state education agency representative—see Community Engagement Conference, page 170). The purpose of this meeting is to build understanding of PCBE, evidence of its benefits, why it requires fundamental paradigm change, why systemic thinking is essential to paradigm change, and why stakeholders' involvement in the change process is important. If the school is relatively large and a relatively small percent of stakeholders participated in the community engagement conference, then the leadership team develops a strategic plan for sharing the new mental model of education with as many stakeholders as possible.

2.1c—Form Input Groups for the Leadership Team

The leadership team and assistant principal for transformation organize interested participants from the community engagement conference into input groups, each of which should include two school leadership team members who share what happens in each leadership team meeting and seek input from the other stakeholders to take back to the next leadership team meeting. Input groups expand the opportunity for mindset change and consensus-building, and they provide more input for the leadership team's visioning process.

2.1d—Develop Transformational Leaders Throughout the School

For a large school, the facilitator helps the assistant principal for transformation to develop all school leaders (for example, department heads) into transformational leaders (also known as participatory leaders, servant leaders, or developmental leaders). This includes developing their culture and capacity for paradigm change, and establishing two-way communication between them and the leadership team. All leaders can thereby provide input for the PCBE vision and work to evolve their mindsets in tandem with leadership team members. This could be done by forming a collaborative team for those leaders. For example, department heads could meet regularly to discuss what they are doing to change from the supervisory paradigm of leadership to the transformational paradigm, what has worked well, what problems they have encountered, and what solutions might work well. The following are some topics that might be addressed with these leaders.

- Ways PCBE is different from the standardized, time-based, sorting-focused paradigm of education

- Why PCBE is better for meeting the needs of students and the community

- Ways that paradigm change is different from typical reform, including the importance of learning and broad stakeholder involvement and ownership of the change process

- Differences between the supervisory (command-and-control) paradigm of leadership and the transformational (empowerment) paradigm, including their decision-making processes

- Tools for transformational leadership, such as developing and using a shared vision to provide direction and motivation, leading consensus building, building trust, empowering and supporting their staff, supporting customized professional development, and so forth

During this step, the assistant principal for transformation and facilitator create reusable learning tools to support new participants' continuous learning of these and other ideas and skills as they are oriented to the change process and its progress. These tools include workshops and forums and may include videos, readings, and activities for use in those workshops and forums, and learning in collaborative teams and individual learning.

2.1e—Identify Exemplary PCBE Schools and Practices

The leadership team (as always, with support from the steering committee and the facilitator) identifies best practices and exemplary PCBE schools. The leadership team studies information about these practices and schools, and a few team members visit two or more exemplary schools. They take pictures, videos, copies of school documents, and extensive notes that they use to prepare a report for the other leadership team members and other change process participants.

2.1f—Conduct a System Engagement Conference to Develop an Ideal Vision for the School

After sufficient learning has taken place in the leadership team, input groups, and among other leaders, then the leadership team, assistant principal for transformation, and facilitator organize and conduct a system engagement conference—preferably in a two-day retreat (Duffy, 2002, 2003). At this conference, all members of the leadership team, input groups, and other leaders develop an ideal vision for the school. Participants in this conference should only be those who have been involved in the process to date, because understanding of PCBE is key. This vision includes features for three key subsystems and for how the school interacts with its community. The three key subsystems are (1) the school's core work processes (teaching and learning), (2) its supporting work processes (administration and support services such as transportation and food services), and (3) its internal social infrastructure, such as culture, policies, roles, and communications (Duffy, 2003, 2006). The core work processes should include both content (the essential learnings for the students) and method (the best ways to learn and assess those essentials and other content).

2.1g—Use Results to Draft the Ideal Vision

The leadership team takes the results of the system engagement conference and formulates them as the first draft of the ideal vision for the school, with additional input from the input groups and other leaders. Later in this process, you will address the constraints that prevent you from implementing the ideal right now. You will need to make some compromises in your first step toward the ideal. But for now, it is important to create an ideal vision, ignoring current constraints that may be possible to overcome in the foreseeable future. Because educational needs and tools change over time, schools should create a new ideal vision after about ten years and continue evolving toward it. As always, the facilitator guides all activities, but with the goal of building the capacity of participants to play that role, so they become less dependent upon the facilitator.

2.1h—Hold Community Forums to Build Ownership of the Vision

The assistant principal for transformation, with guidance from the leadership team, organizes a few community forums to develop broad stakeholder ownership of and commitment to the ideal vision. Forum participants offer revisions to the vision, after which the leadership team makes any appropriate revisions to the ideal vision, publicizes those revisions, and orchestrates a public ceremony to affirm the vision.

2.1i—Review and Coordinate All Current Change Efforts

The assistant principal for transformation assumes responsibility for all current PCBE change efforts in the school and aligns each with the ideal vision as much as possible.

Throughout this step, the leadership team and board should be applying for external funding to help support the rest of the change process.

Step 2.2—Develop a Strategy for Implementing the Ideal Vision

In this step, the school leadership team selects a strategy for starting to implement the vision and transform to PCBE. Transformation is a resource-intensive process, so it may not be advisable to change a large school all at once. However, it is difficult for students to move from one paradigm of education to another (either Education 2.0 to 3.0, or vice versa), so it is important to view the core work process (teaching and learning) as a preK–12 process.

2.2a—Decide on a School-Within-a-Building or a Whole-Building Strategy

The leadership team should develop a strategy for how much of the school will be involved in the first round of transformation. One strategy is to transform the whole building. This option is best if the school is quite small. In this strategy, it is wise to help teachers who are not enthusiastic about PCBE to find a job in a different school. A second strategy is to divide the school into two schools-within-the-building (not necessarily the same size), one of which will transform now and one which will follow later. In this case, encourage teachers and students most interested in PCBE to join the one transforming now. This allows the most enthusiastic teachers to blaze the trail for the other teachers to follow later, with the advantage that those pioneers have more motivation and dedication to overcome the many difficulties they will initially encounter. However, in this strategy, it is important to prevent a culture of competition between the two schools (an attitude of "us versus them") by developing a buildingwide understanding that the entire building will eventually transform to PCBE. In the meantime, however, the PCBE school must have a totally independent administrative system (a different principal, budget, and so on), due to the incompatibility of Education 3.0 with Education 2.0.

2.2b—Decide Which Grade Levels and How Many and Which Teachers Will Transform First

The leadership team and assistant principal for transformation decide which grade levels and teachers will be involved in the first round of transformation, with considerable input from the teachers. As students advance in grade levels, it becomes progressively harder for them to switch to PCBE, because they have become conditioned to traditional teacher-centered education. Similarly, it is frustrating for students who have experienced PCBE to go back to the teacher-centered, time-based system. Therefore, for both the schools-within-a-building strategy and the whole-building strategy, it is wise to first implement the changes in lower grades—at minimum, grades preK–2 and at most, grades preK–5—and then convert one higher grade each year thereafter. This progressive approach also helps prevent spreading resources for change too thinly. Furthermore, lower grade levels tend naturally to be more learner-centered and flexible, so transformation is easier and quicker on those levels.

For a whole-building approach, all teachers at the selected levels will be involved. For a school-within-the-building approach, you should ask for volunteers for the PCBE school, because the first year will be the toughest and teacher enthusiasm and commitment will be key to a successful implementation. You should also select roughly equal numbers of teachers at each level that you decide to change now so the students in the PCBE school will be able to stay in the PCBE system each new school year.

Step 2.3—Further Develop the Vision and Resources

Now that you know whether you will initially transform a school-within-the-building or the whole building and which grade levels will go first, you can decide on initial compromises to the ideal vision and then develop more details for the first step of implementation. This is not the ideal vision; it is a practical vision that represents the first step toward the ideal.

2.3a—Compromise on the Ideal as Needed and Select High-Leverage Changes for Implementation

The leadership team decides what compromises need to be made on the ideal, and selects the most effective high-leverage changes to make it happen. The following are some typical high-leverage changes to start with.

- Replacing the current report card with a list of competencies whereby each student must reach the criteria for mastery of a set of competencies before progressing to the next set of competencies

- Requiring a personal learning plan for every student whereby each student can immediately progress to the next set of competencies that is appropriate for him or her after mastering the current set

- Changing to multi-year mentoring and multi-age grouping

- Changing to project-based learning in which the teacher's role is a coach or facilitator

- Including parents in student goal setting and the learning process

2.3b—Organize Teachers Into Task Forces to Design Each Developmental Level

All the teachers selected for the PCBE school join a task force for their developmental level (formerly, a group of grade levels). The leadership team must provide release time for each task force to plan its initial implementation and develop the necessary learning resources. At least one parent and one leadership team member should join each task force. Each task force designs the initial studios (classrooms) for its developmental level, and the leadership team helps task forces coordinate those designs so they fit seamlessly with each other. The plans should include details about the following.

- **Outcomes:** What goals are important? What kinds of student learning, school climate, teacher satisfaction, parent and community participation, and so forth do we want to see in our school?

- **Criteria:** What criteria should be used to assess each outcome?

- **Content:** What specific competencies (learning targets) should be required and optional at each developmental level? (See chapter 3 [page 57]. Also, Perkins [2014] provides stimulating thoughts for your task forces to consider.)

- **Means:** What are the methods, practices, and interventions by which we will achieve and assess the outcomes? (See chapters 1 [page 15] and 2 [page 27].)

- **Tools and facilities:** What equipment and materials will optimize the means, and what should the facilities be like?

This activity requires considerable time and money to identify existing programs and resources, and identify gaps where you must design and develop your own. Each task force should design and develop the systems for their developmental level, which are likely to include measurement topics and proficiency scales, an assessment system, a record-keeping system, instructional resources, and a learning management system. Marzano and colleagues (2017) provide some guidance for this in *A Handbook for Personalized Competency-Based Education*. It is also helpful to work with institutions where your students go after graduation to identify and improve the extent to which your students will be prepared to meet their expectations.

2.3c—Sign a Compact for Phase 3

The facilitator signs a compact with the leadership team and board for phase 3, complete with responsibilities, resource needs, and budget.

Figure 10.2 displays the map of the change process with these latest activities added to phase 2.

Phase 1. Prepare for the Change Process
Step 1.1. Initiate the change process.
Step 1.2. Form a prelaunch team and build school capacity.

Phase 2. Create a Shared Ideal Vision, Expand Capacity, and Develop a Strategy for Change

Step 2.1. Develop an ideal vision and expand capacity.

2.1a   Expand the prelaunch team into the school leadership team, develop its capacity, and transform the prelaunch team into a steering committee.

2.1b   Initiate a campaign to help stakeholders change their thinking about education.

2.1c   Form input groups for the leadership team.

2.1d   Develop transformational leaders throughout the school.

2.1e   Identify exemplary PCBE schools and practices.

2.1f   Conduct a system engagement conference to develop an ideal vision for the school.

2.1g   Use results to draft the ideal vision.

2.1h   Hold community forums to build ownership of the vision.

2.1i   Review and coordinate all current change efforts.

Step 2.2. Develop a strategy for implementing the ideal vision.

2.2a   Decide on a school-within-a-building or a whole-building strategy.

2.2b   Decide which grade levels and how many and which teachers will transform first.

Step 2.3. Further develop the vision and resources.

2.3a   Compromise on the ideal as needed and select high-leverage changes for implementation.

2.3b   Organize teachers into task forces to design each developmental level.

2.3c   Sign a compact for phase 3.

Phase 3. Implement and Improve the School Vision
Phase 4. Evolve the Implementation

Figure 10.2: The change process for a school, phase 2.

Phase 3: Implement and Improve the Vision

After designing a vision and strategies to implement it in phase 2, phase 3 focuses on making it happen. In this phase, teachers in the transforming developmental levels implement and improve the initial practical vision and prepare to expand the implementation to higher developmental levels in the following year.

Step 3.1—Implement and Improve the Initial Vision

The first step in implementing the vision involves several activities related to preparing the school, the teachers, the students, and their parents for the first year of PCBE. At this point, the facilitator advises the leadership team's steering committee, and the leadership team advises and coordinates the teacher task forces.

3.1a—Select a Principal, Renovate Facilities, Acquire Equipment and Materials, and Prepare Teachers

In the school-within-the-building approach, the teachers select a principal—typically the assistant principal for transformation. During the summer, planned renovations (if any) of the facilities take place, equipment and materials are ordered and installed, and teachers receive training in effective use of the equipment, materials, and facilities. Each task force functions as a collaborative team.

3.1b—Recruit Students

The task forces recruit students for the PCBE school's transformed developmental levels using flyers and informational meetings. Leaders should offer a parent information session to explain the PCBE system. If more students are interested than there is room for, a lottery system is appropriate, possibly with a built-in algorithm to balance representation in terms of gender, race, ethnicity, and socioeconomic status, if the community so desires and laws allow. Of course, recruiting methods targeting traditionally underrepresented and underserved populations can and should also be used to help achieve a balanced representation of the broader community.

3.1c—Orient Students and Parents

Since the procedures and culture of a PCBE school are so different from what students are used to, during the first few weeks of implementation of the PCBE school, teachers should devote considerable attention to preparing the students for the transition from passive learners to active, self-directed learners. This includes orienting them to the studio, developing norms, establishing routines, and fostering a collaborative culture. This is an important part of building a student-centered and empowered culture in the studios, and will likely take up to six weeks. Parents will also need an orientation. The teacher should explain classroom routines and expectations, share ways the parents can and should be involved in their child's education, and inform parents about the types of questions to ask their child to have conversations about their day at school.

3.1d—Implement the New PCBE System

The content and methods of the initial vision are fully implemented in the studios, and the task forces meet weekly to evaluate what is working well and what changes might improve the system. These formative evaluations are shared with the leadership team and principal (for the school-within-the-building approach) or assistant principal for transformation (for the whole-building approach). The task forces make changes as they identify them, in an emergent manner. The leadership team should take on a supportive rather than controlling role, while also making sure the emergent changes are as consistent as feasible with the ideal vision and are compatible with what other task forces are doing.

Step 3.2—Expand the Implementation

The next step of implementation is to expand it (scale up). The following activities relate to adding progressively more grade levels and teachers to the PCBE system.

3.2a—Prepare to Transform the Next-Higher Grade Level in the Following Year

At the beginning of the first year of implementation, the leadership team should begin recruiting additional teachers at the next-higher grade level to join the PCBE system in the following year. These teachers organize into a new task force with parent and leadership team representation. Note that, for a new developmental level, a multi-age classroom will begin as a single-age classroom with more students joining as the implementation progresses by one grade level each year. Thus, it is important that the task force includes teachers for all years of that developmental level, even though some won't switch to PCBE until a year or two later.

3.2b—Recruit and Prepare a Second Wave of Teachers to Adopt PCBE at Developmental Levels That Have Already Transformed

In the school-within-the-building approach, leaders should (resources permitting) also recruit more teachers for developmental levels that have already transformed to PCBE. That is, rather than transforming one school-within-a-building now and the other several years later, teachers gradually join the PCBE school until the entire building has transformed. These secondary (and tertiary, and so on) adopters can see a clear image of what PCBE will be like for them because it is already happening in their building. Again, it is important to recruit equal numbers of teachers for each developmental level, so that students will not have to alternate between PCBE and traditional education. The newly recruited teachers should sit in on the task force meetings for their respective developmental levels prior to shifting to PCBE.

Step 3.2 continues until the entire school has transformed. For a large school building, we recommend you consider dividing the PCBE school, as it grows, into two or more schools to retain the benefits of small schools (strong relationships among teachers and students, increased opportunities for teacher-led schools, and so on; see Principle U: Small School Size, page 104).

To see the map of the change process with these latest activities added to phase 3, see figure 10.3.

Phase 4: Evolve the Implementation

Each task force continually evaluates and improves their practical vision each year to evolve ever closer to the school's ideal vision. This entails formative evaluation, but recall that no summative evaluation should be done for about five years, to give time for the evolution to overcome inevitable problems. Because new educational needs and tools will demand further changes, it is wise for the school to form a new leadership team after about ten years and develop a new ideal vision for the school, toward which it can continue to evolve.

To summarize the phases of school transformation, figure 10.3 lists each phase and its associated steps and activities.

Phase 1. Prepare for the Change Process

Step 1.1. Initiate the change process.

1.1a Select a process facilitator.

1.1b Ensure sufficient school readiness.

1.1c Ensure leadership support and understanding.

Step 1.2. Form a prelaunch team and build school capacity.

1.2a Form a prelaunch team.

1.2b Develop team culture and capacity, conduct a political assessment and community analysis, and design strategies for communicating with stakeholders.

1.2c Secure external and internal funding.

1.2d Select an assistant principal for transformation.

1.2e Sign a compact for phase 2.

Phase 2. Create a Shared Ideal Vision, Expand Capacity, and Develop a Strategy for Change

Step 2.1. Develop an ideal vision and expand capacity.

2.1a Expand the prelaunch team into the school leadership team, develop its capacity, and transform the prelaunch team into a steering committee.

2.1b Initiate a campaign to help stakeholders change their thinking about education.

2.1c Form input groups for the leadership team.

2.1d Develop transformational leaders throughout the school.

2.1e Identify exemplary PCBE schools and practices.

2.1f Conduct a system engagement conference to develop an ideal vision for the school.

2.1g Use results to draft the ideal vision.

2.1h Hold community forums to build ownership of the vision.

2.1i Review and coordinate all current change efforts.

Figure 10.3: The change process for a school.

continued ➔

Step 2.2. Develop a strategy for implementing the ideal vision.

2.2a   Decide on a school-within-a-building or a whole-building strategy.

2.2b   Decide which grade levels and how many and which teachers will transform first.

Step 2.3. Further develop the vision.

2.3a   Compromise on the ideal as needed and select high-leverage changes for implementation.

2.3b   Organize teachers into task forces to design each developmental level.

2.3c   Sign a compact for phase 3.

Phase 3. Implement and Improve the Vision

Step 3.1. Implement and improve the initial vision.

3.1a   Select a principal, renovate facilities, acquire equipment and materials, and prepare teachers.

3.1b   Recruit students.

3.1c   Orient students and parents.

3.1d   Implement the new PCBE system.

Step 3.2. Expand the Implementation.

3.2a   Prepare to transform the next-higher grade level in the following year.

3.2b   Recruit and prepare a second wave of teachers to adopt PCBE at developmental levels that have already transformed.

Phase 4. Evolve the Implementation

Transforming Education

Transforming your school or district from Education 2.0 to Education 3.0 is far more difficult than piecemeal reforms, which themselves are seldom easy. In our view, however, there is nothing more important than the shift to PCBE. In our introduction, we highlighted several serious problems related to the United States educational systems.

- **Equity:** Educational quality is often dependent on local socioeconomic conditions, increasing economic inequality and diminishing the potential of both individuals and society.

- **Survival:** Some constituents feel it would be simpler to abandon public education in favor of a privatized system; this would only exacerbate inequality and segregation.

- **Ethics:** In an era characterized by apparent increases in corruption and morally bankrupt behavior, schools are uniquely positioned to contribute to the ethical development of our youth.

- **New needs:** Given changes in workforce needs and society at large, educational systems must shift their priorities in order to effectively prepare students for the current era.

- **A devaluing of teaching:** The challenges of teaching, along with low compensation compared to other professions, has led to teacher shortages and high turnover, directly impairing the quality of education.

As a society, we cannot meet these challenges without a well-educated citizenry. Education is the key to meeting many of these challenges—but not if it is Education 2.0! Hopefully, the six research-based core ideas described in part I provide a window on how the transformation of your educational system can effectively address many of these serious problems. Transforming education to improve our world is key to the future health of our communities and society at large.

Your commitment to undertaking this difficult journey is crucial. Change will not happen without the time, effort, and dedication of educators and like-minded citizens. The sooner your planning for change begins, the easier it will be for your community to come together and surmount the challenges you face. We hope this book will help your team navigate this journey. These are proven ideas and methods both for a *vision* of personalized competency-based education and for the *action* (or process) for transforming your system to that vision. Schools, districts, and their communities differ widely, and so we hope the advice, scenarios, and variety of resources presented here will guide you to customize your vision to your situation, both in the nature of your new PCBE system (Education 3.0) and in the transformation process. Proceed with a full understanding of the systemic interdependencies and repercussions for every decision and change you make.

Don't try to do it alone. Seek outside help from expert organizations (see appendices B and D, pages 211 and 225). Marshal enough resources for your transformation process to succeed. Planning and collaboration are essential. If you think there is some way we can help, please do not hesitate to contact us. If your experience forges tools or guidance that could be helpful to others, we encourage you share them with us as well.

Charles M. Reigeluth
reigelut@indiana.edu

Jennifer R. Karnopp
jrkarnopp@gmail.com

Ideas for New Curricula

The U.S. Department of Labor convened the **Secretary's Commission on Achieving Necessary Skills (SCANS)**, which issued a report in 1991 (Secretary's Commission on Achieving Necessary Skills, 1991) on the skills and knowledge that students would need to be successful in the workplace. Their job performance skills include five broad competencies, which offer guidance on authentic tasks that are relevant to students' current and future lives: using resources, using interpersonal skills, using information, using systems, and using technology.

The Partnership for 21st Century Learning (n.d.) developed their Framework for 21st Century Learning with input from teachers, education experts, and business leaders to define and illustrate the skills and knowledge students need to succeed in work, life, and citizenship. Their learning outcomes fall into four categories: key subjects and 21st century themes; learning and innovation skills; information, media, and technology skills; and life and career skills.

Author **Tony Wagner** (2012) describes seven survival skills that he believes are important for students' current and future lives: critical thinking and problem solving, collaboration across networks and leading by influence, agility and adaptability, initiative and entrepreneurialism, effective oral and written communication, accessing and analyzing information, and curiosity and imagination.

Professor **David Perkins** (2014) at Harvard University provided guidance for readers to clarify their own goals and priorities for what he describes as *lifeworthy learning*, a truly enlightening journey. The major topics he describes include learning agendas, big understandings, big questions, life-ready learning, the seven seas of knowledge, ways of knowing, and big know-how.

The **William and Flora Hewlett Foundation** (2013) funded the Deeper Learning initiative (Watkins et al., 2018), which identified the following set of six interrelated competencies.

1. Mastering rigorous academic content

2. Learning how to think critically and solve problems

3. Working collaboratively

4. Communicating effectively

5.   Directing one's own learning

6.   Developing an academic mindset—a belief in one's ability to grow

Professor **Alan Collins** (2017) took an even broader approach to updating what students learn. He proposed a passion-based curriculum derived largely from elements at Central Park East Secondary School, High Tech Schools, Summit Public Schools, and AltSchools. It entails each student choosing about eight to ten curricular topics over his or her entire preK–12 experience. The student must be passionate about each of those topics and pursue only about two of them for a two- to three-year stretch, so they can engage in truly deep learning. The goal is to embed only truly useful elements of the current curriculum, along with new elements like finance, health, economics, the environment, law, strategic thinking, creative thinking, social and emotional learning, and much more, in projects the student works on in each curricular topic.

MyWays (myways.nextgenlearning.org) is an initiative spearheaded by **Next Generation Learning Challenges** (2019) to help educators fully prepare the students of today for a challenging, unpredictable tomorrow. The first of four major areas that MyWays addresses is innovative definitions of student success—guidelines about what is important for students to learn. MyWays integrates numerous curriculum frameworks into twenty competencies that are grouped into four categories: content knowledge, habits of success, creative know-how, and wayfinding abilities.

Mark Prensky (2016) observed that up until now education has been about improving individuals. He argued that now it needs to be about improving the world and having students improve in that process. The curriculum should be focused on helping students to develop the individual and collective passion to make their world a better place, including civic education and responsibilities in a democratic society. Prensky (2016) described the current academic model of individual achievement in a narrow range of subjects as being organized around progressions in four main pillars of the curriculum: math, English (or language arts), social studies, and science (MESS). He proposed that the Empowerment to Better Their World model should be organized around progressions in four different pillars: effective accomplishing, effective thinking, effective action, and effective relationships. He provided suggestions for specific content under each of those four categories. Parts of the academic model (and indeed, of each of the other frameworks just described) are plugged into those pillars—primarily the effective thinking pillar—when and if appropriate.

Helpful Resources for the Vision

APPENDIX
B

This appendix contains lists of some resources that we are aware of, but not all information, products, or services will apply to your situation. You can visit www.reigeluth.net /organizations-supporting to view additional resources. You should carefully investigate what each resource has to offer. Also, there are undoubtedly many other fine resources that we are not aware of yet. We encourage them to contact us for inclusion in our website. This appendix has two sections: one on the organizations that can help you with the vision, and another on schools that you can visit to see powerful visions in action.

Organizations That Help With the Vision

The following organizations offer advice about what your vision should be like. Many provide assistance for both what your vision should be like and the process of creating and implementing it. Here we describe a few of the organizations that have a greater focus on the vision.

- **2Revolutions** (www.2revolutions.net) is an education design lab considering questions about the future of the American education system. Using design thinking to generate creative ideas, it seeks to respond to the forces of social and economic change to build new systems of learning that will prepare students for the future.

- **Aurora Institute** (www.inacol.org) drives the transformation of education systems and accelerates the advancement of breakthrough policies and practices to advance powerful, personalized, learner-centered experiences. Priorities are to create personalized competency-based education systems, redesign systems of assessment to align with student-centered learning, rethink accountability for continuous improvement, create innovation zones and pilots, and build infrastructure for new learning models.

- **Center for Collaborative Education** or CCE (cce.org) partners with public schools and districts to help them transform in a way that ensures all students succeed. Projects include performance assessments to replace standardized

211

tests in New Hampshire and Massachusetts and a credential program customized to serve high-need schools in Los Angeles.

- **Center for Innovation in Education** (education.uky.edu/engagement/cie/) is housed at the University of Kentucky and partners with states and local agencies. Its work is based on the idea that all students should become lifelong learners and graduate with the knowledge and skills needed to begin a career and participate in civic life.

- **Center on Reinventing Public Education** or CRPE (www.crpe.org) is a nonpartisan research center that conducts rigorous research and policy analysis to help educators, policymakers, civic and community leaders, parents, and students themselves reimagine education systems and structures. It analyzes complex trends and data, communicates new possibilities for system change, and provides guidance and thought leadership to support that change.

- **CompetencyWorks** (www.competencyworks.org) houses a wealth of resources related to competency-based education. Research papers, articles, and tools give K–12 educators the information they need to understand PCBE and apply those concepts. The website includes a blog and a wiki, which allow practitioners and innovators to share experiences, tools, samples, and lessons learned. Users can also subscribe to a monthly newsletter highlighting key resources and news.

- **Education Elements** (www.edelements.com) helps schools to create new instructional model designs: competency-based learning, blended learning, personalized learning, project-based learning, and more. Other services include strategy development, professional development and support, school leadership development, finding open educational resources, and others.

- **Education Reimagined** (education-reimagined.org) is dedicated to accelerating the growth and impact of the learner-centered education (LCE) movement in the United States by promoting LCE among education stakeholder groups, supporting learner-centered leaders, and helping those leaders to collaborate, innovate, and advocate together.

- **Highlander Institute** (highlanderinstitute.org) contributes to the goal of an equitable education system by providing services, programs, resources, and events related to personalized learning.

- **Khan Academy** (www.khanacademy.org/about) is an open educational resource with lessons, activities, and mastery assessments organized into courses. It is personalized and enables users to learn at their own pace. It also allows teachers and parents to view student performance.

- **KnowledgeWorks Foundation** (knowledgeworks.org) recognizes that students have varying backgrounds and perspectives; thus, their educational experiences must vary as well. The foundation develops policy recommendations and works with educators to increase their abilities related to personalized learning and competency-based education. Their website shares teacher-friendly articles, videos, infographics, and other resources created by experts.

- **Leap Innovations** (www.leapinnovations.org) emphasizes tailoring the learning experience for each individual student's strengths and interests. They provide professional development, partner with schools that want to redesign their systems, and manage a network of teachers who pilot personalized learning innovations. On their website, educators can access research reports and tools for various content areas and grade levels.

- **Learning Accelerator** (learningaccelerator.org) is a catalyst to transform American K–12 education to make it personalized, informed by data, and mastery-based through blended learning on a national scale. It views blended learning as a key mechanism for making this vision possible for every child, in every school, throughout the country.

- **Marzano Resources** (www.marzanoresources.com) provides educators with consulting, professional development workshops and conferences, books, and videos to help them transform to personalized competency-based education.

- **Next Generation Learning Challenges** or NGLC (www.nextgenlearning .org) is a nonprofit organization that works on developing resources and sharing information to address challenges in public education. Their work is organized around specific challenges such as designing for equity, reimagining assessment, building community, and so on. NGLC believes that educators themselves should be the ones who lead the shift toward the future of education. In service of these goals, it funds innovative designs, builds networks of educators, shares content and tools, and advocates for student-centered, research-based systems.

- **PBLWorks** (pblworks.org) helps educators improve student learning outcomes by making PBL accessible by teachers in grades K–12 and all subject areas. It provides resources for educators, as well as on-site professional development services for teachers, school leaders, and district leaders.

- **Teacher-Powered Schools** (www.teacherpowered.org) highlights schools that are run by their teachers. Teacher leadership and professional partnership arrangements put authority and the ability to enact change in the hands of classroom teachers, who are most familiar with what their students need. Teacher Powered Schools spreads awareness of the teacher-powered model, supports teachers who want to design and run their own schools, and educates teachers unions, administrators, and policymakers. They assert that this model benefits both teachers and students.

- **Transcend Education** (www.transcendeducation.org) partners with visionary school communities to design their own educational models. Rather than prescribing a defined model, Transcend offers eight "great leaps" (each presented as a shift from the old model to the future) that communities should consider as they develop local solutions.

Schools to Consider Visiting to See Their PCBE Visions Implemented

Please keep in mind that the Education 3.0 paradigm (PCBE) is still in the early stages of development, much like air transportation as a new paradigm of transportation during the 1930s. PCBE is already more effective than Education 2.0, but great advances will continue to be made for decades. The following are a few of the schools and school networks that offer varying visions of PCBE in action, and they are all in a state of continual improvement. Additional schools and networks are listed on our website, www .reigeluth.net/pcbe-school-systems. Visits to a few of these schools can be a huge help in developing your ideal vision of PCBE. Undoubtedly, we are unaware of many additional schools, districts, and networks that are well into the PCBE paradigm. We encourage such school systems to contact us for inclusion on our website.

- **Compass Montessori School** (www.compassmontessori.org) is a preK–12 public charter school in Colorado. In keeping with the Montessori philosophy, the school nurtures the whole child. With its small, caring community, Compass emphasizes respect for self, others, and the environment. Students learn in multi-age classrooms and master learning progressions at their own pace. Traditional Montessori materials and methods help learners develop independence, solve problems, and become lifelong learners. Compass also includes a small farm, kitchen, and store that provide experiential learning opportunities in an interdependent microeconomy.

- **Da Vinci Schools** (www.davincischools.org) is a public charter school network serving 2,300 students in four high schools, a K–8 home-school-hybrid model, and a college completion pathway program. The schools emphasize real-world learning: curricula at all grade levels are centered around projects, high schools offer career and technical courses, and Da Vinci partners with companies to offer students internships and work experience. Mastery-based grading helps students focus on learning, rather than earning grade points. Students do not earn credit for a course if they have not demonstrated mastery of enough of the content.

- **Lindsay Unified School District** (www.lindsay.k12.ca.us) is described in detail in chapter 7 (page 133).

- **Met High School** (www.themethighschool.org) is a network of high schools in Rhode Island that offers career and technical education in a highly personalized model. Learning beyond the classroom is essential. Students select fields of interest and work with mentors in their fields to complete projects and internships. Teachers take on the role of advisors, working with students and their families to create individual learning plans. The Met also prioritizes planning for career or education beyond high school and requires all students to apply to college or other post-secondary programs. The Met was the first Big Picture Learning school.

- **Minnesota New Country School** (www.newcountryschool.com) is described in detail in chapter 7 (page 121).

- **Montessori Schools** (www.montessori.edu) are based on the teachings of Maria Montessori, who observed that children are natural and spontaneous learners. In Montessori environments, students direct their own learning, and thus become creative, lifelong learners. Teachers prepare the learning environment, provide materials, and nurture exploration. Multi-age grouping is essential to Montessori schools, and students work together and learn from each other. There are no class periods; students can work on a chosen activity as long as desired.

- **Sanborn Regional School District** (www.sau17.org) in New Hampshire has been undergoing a transformation to PCBE since 2009, with impressive results. Their transformation is based on three Cs: Collaboration (PLCs, small learning communities, collaborative learning), Competency (competency-based, whole child), and Culture and climate (student engagement, PBL, community engagement, flexible grouping; Sanborn Regional School District, 2015).

- **Summit Public Schools** (summitps.org) initially operated six charter schools in San Jose, California, and serve primarily low-income and immigrant families. In an area where only 39 percent of high school students complete the right courses to be eligible to attend four-year college, "almost all of Summit's twelfth graders have been accepted to at least one four-year college" (Childress & Benson, 2014, p. 35). They personalize learning by offering blended learning that features an individualized playlist showing what students have mastered and what they should do next, and providing access to a range of resources from Khan Academy, other open educational resource providers, and Summit teachers themselves. Student progress is competency-based, self-paced, and self-directed. The schools use expeditionary learning to promote critical thinking, and they offer a "Tutoring Bar," inspired by the Apple Genius Bar, to provide one-on-one tutoring on demand. With support from the Chan Zuckerberg Initiative, the Summit Learning Program is now being used in more than 380 schools with over 72,000 students. One of their schools is Summit Denali in the San Francisco Bay area.

- **Thrive Public Schools** (www.tworiverspcs.org) is two public charter schools (preK–8 and preK–3) in Washington, DC. It uses expeditionary learning, in which students learn by addressing complex, open-ended problems. Each expedition is a long-term, multidisciplinary opportunity to explore in-depth content around a specific theme. In addition to academic knowledge and skills, this approach to learning engenders critical thinking, problem solving, and social skills like kindness and acceptance. An expedition concludes with a showcase, in which students share their learning products and process.

- **Two Rivers Public Charter School** (www.tworiverspcs.org) is two public charter schools (preK–8 and preK–3) in Washington, DC. It uses expeditionary learning, in which students learn by addressing complex, open-ended problems. At the completion of learning expeditions, students participate in a showcase to present the results of their expeditions. It also uses the Responsive Classroom approach to create a safe environment where children are able to take risks, both academic and social, to help children understand the importance of kindness toward and acceptance of all people, to celebrate differences in people and cultures, and to learn important social skills such as empathy and problem solving.

- **Valor Collegiate Academies** (valorcollegiate.org) is a public charter school network in Nashville, TN. It has broadened the vision for education by placing whole-child development at the core of its model, called the Compass Framework, but not at the expense of developing intellectual prowess. The points of the Compass are body, heart, mind, and spirit. Students develop these areas through experiential tasks in defined curricula similar to badges in many Scouting programs. Valor promotes strong relationships and community through Circle, a small-group meeting of diverse students and a faculty mentor who support each other in their Compass work.

District Readiness Criteria

APPENDIX
C

Rate your district in question on each area of consideration.

Scale

10 = Outstanding readiness

5 = Requires work before a successful paradigm change effort can begin

0 = No signs of readiness

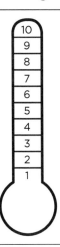

A. Our Need and Purpose for Change

Do we recognize the need for paradigm change? If so:

- Why do we think we need paradigm change?

- What are the strengths and weaknesses of our reasons?

- Are there any factors that make us hesitant to engage in paradigm change?

Some reasons are stronger than others, such as a concern that your children's needs or your community's needs are not being met by the schools. Weaker reasons include that everyone else is restructuring or it's a good way to get grant moneys. If your district feels that your schools are already doing a fine job, and you simply want to stay on the cutting edge, you may lack the will to take risks necessary to succeed in paradigm change.

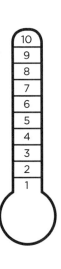

B. Our Commitment to Change

- **History:** How much money have we spent on change in the last five years? What types of professional development efforts have occurred? What were the driving forces for these expenditures and efforts?

- **Future:** How much time are our board and superintendent willing to commit to the PCBE effort? Are our board and administration willing to commit hard money to the change effort? Are we willing to suspend current change efforts to provide the necessary space and resources? Are we willing to go to the public to ask for support?

A paradigm change effort is time consuming, threatening, and often discouraging. Strong support and encouragement from the leadership are essential to sustain the effort. Commitment to professional development may be one indicator of such support and encouragement, depending on the nature of the professional development. Willingness of the leadership to take risks and not punish failures are also important.

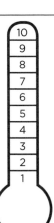

C. Scope of the Change Effort

- Are we interested in a districtwide effort or just school-based efforts?

A school-based effort, if it is indeed systemic, will require changes on the district level for it to succeed and endure. This will likely mean changes in vocational-technical, special education, and alternative education programs, as well as regular or general education.

- Are we willing to engage in a long-term effort?

Paradigm change requires time—a lot of it! If your district is looking for a quick fix, you have a problem.

D. Flexibility of the Board and Administration

- How willing are we to engage in negotiations for release time for professionals?

It is not as important that you be willing to give release time right away as it is for you to be willing to negotiate about the idea.

- How willing are we to engage students and the community in the change effort? Are we willing to allow shared decision making? Do we view leadership as helping or directing?

Such willingness is a reflection of your values about leadership and authority.

- Are we willing to experiment with changes and forgive "failures"?

Risk-taking is essential to a paradigm change effort, and with risks inevitably come some failures. To be willing to undertake risks, teachers and others will need the confidence that they will be supported, not criticized, in the face of failures.

- How do we handle problems? How will they be handled in our effort? Have we traditionally handled problems by casting blame, or by providing collaboration and support to overcome them?

- How willing are we to examine current district policy and develop and implement new policies aligned with a paradigm change effort and PCBE?

This will clear the way for entering into a paradigm change process and be a visible statement of priority and commitment.

Potential problems: *Board members and superintendents have a tendency to not state unequivocally what their positions are on these issues, leaving the door open for them to act later in ways that are detrimental to the change effort.*

10
9
8
7
6
5
4
3
2
1

E. Attitude Toward an External Facilitator

- How willing are our school board and superintendent to allow an external facilitator to become a part of our school community and have access to all people in it?

If the facilitator does not become a part of the school community and culture, that person's effectiveness and credibility will suffer. Also, without access to all people, it will be difficult for the facilitator to understand your mindsets and engage you in the kind of dialogue that can influence your mindsets and sense of ownership in the process.

- How well do our key leaders (board, superintendent, union leadership, business leaders, and so on) get along with the facilitator?

If they do not get along well personally, it will be difficult to have the kind of collaboration necessary for a paradigm change effort to succeed.

- What role do we see the facilitator playing?

If you see the facilitator as one who facilitates meetings, rather than facilitating the change process, you will be less likely to consider the facilitator's advice regarding the larger process issues. And if you see the facilitator as an expert with preformed solutions, you may be disappointed in his or her focus on process without predetermined outcomes. And if you don't see the facilitator as neutral and overtly involved in the process, you may want to co-opt her or him to be your advocate or messenger.

Potential problems: *If a personality conflict arises between the facilitator and a leader in your district, that leader may not communicate that to the facilitator, but instead may undermine the facilitator's efforts.*

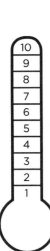

F. Attitude Toward Ourselves and the Community

- How well do the various stakeholders within our district get along with each other? Are there apparent serious conflicts that have a history?

- How well do our district and community get along? Is there a strong community involvement in the schools, or are there apparent boundary issues and negative dynamics?

- How willing are our school board and superintendent (and other leaders) to examine our organizational/system attitudes about change and other dynamic conflicts that present serious obstacles to a paradigm change effort?

Potential problems: *Attitudes toward the facilitator and toward themselves as a school district and community may be indicators of internal conflict and struggles that stand in the path of a successful relationship and endanger a paradigm change process. These attitude problems may not be immediately observable, and a school board or superintendent may be reluctant to disclose the underlying issues for fear of the facilitator not coming on board.*

Vision and Action © 2020 Marzano Resources • MarzanoResources.com
Visit **MarzanoResources.com/reproducibles** to download this free reproducible.

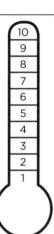

G. Stability of Leadership in the Community

- The superintendent, principals, other administrators, school board, teachers' union, parents' organization—how frequently are their leaders changing?

The more rapidly the leadership changes, the more difficult the change process will be, because new leaders will have to start at ground zero regarding mindset, beliefs, conceptual knowledge, and procedural knowledge about the change effort. Furthermore, they may enter with an antagonistic view of the effort that could be difficult or impossible to overcome.

- How harmonious are the relationships within groups (among individuals)?

If there is divisiveness within the district administrative council or the teachers' union or the school board, then it is much more difficult for consensus to be reached among those groups, leadership is less likely to be stable, and there is likely to be more pressure for the facilitator to take sides.

Potential problems: *You may not be aware of imminent changes in leadership.*

H. Communications

- How extensive and frequent are the communications among the various groups in our school community, and what are the tone and quality of those communications?

The quantity and quality of communication are essential to respect, openness, trust, and consensus, especially two-way communication.

Potential problems: *This is a difficult criterion to assess, particularly since communication may be excellent between two people or groups but not between others.*

I. Language of Change

- What observable language of change are our people using when interacting with each other? Do people seem to have a grasp of the language, and how compatible is the language with paradigm change?

Potential problems: *You may use the language appropriated from readings to convey that you are in alignment with paradigm change, but still lack the literacy for systems thinking.*

J. Harmony Among and Within Groups and Individuals

- How harmonious are the relationships among the following groups?

  – Teachers' union and district administration

  – Teachers and building principal

  – Schools and local businesses

  – Schools and parents

  – Schools and the community

  – Local and state education agencies

A major goal of a change effort is to build mutual understanding and consensus among groups. If there are adversarial relationships among groups, this task is made much more difficult.

- How harmonious are the relationships within each of those groups and among leaders of different groups?

If there are personality conflicts or antagonisms, they will make it much more difficult to build mutual understanding and consensus among the groups.

- Does the superintendent (or board) not want the facilitator to talk with certain people, and if so, why? And who does each want the facilitator to talk with, and why?

This reveals antagonisms, favoritisms, and communication problems involving the superintendent (or board).

Potential problems: *Unless they are severe, problems are often difficult to detect. Some stakeholders may give the impression that problems are the fault of another group, when in fact the blame is shared.*

K. Resources and Financial Stability of the School System

- How sound is our system's financial standing?

If it is weak, it will likely be more difficult for you to negotiate the release time and other resources that are essential to the change effort. It will also be more difficult to sustain the effort over time.

- How good are our nonmonetary resources available for the transformation process (expertise, space, and so on)?

For an effort that is to be owned and run by the stakeholders, the talents of those stakeholders will have a considerable impact on the success of the effort.

- Do we have a successful grant-writing officer? How successful has our school system been in obtaining grants?

A history of success is an indicator of your school system's frame of mind regarding self-determination and initiative for overcoming your problems.

Potential problems: *There may be a tendency for leaders to paint a rosier picture than reality if they are excited about the transformation to PCBE.*

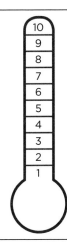

L. Business Support for Change in the Schools

- How willing are our local chamber of commerce and local businesses and foundations in general to commit resources to a paradigm change effort?

To the extent that they are interested in paradigm change in the schools, the change effort will be more likely to get the resources it needs to succeed.

Potential problems: *Businesses may not see education as their problem, so it may be necessary to educate them about the benefits to them of a strong educational system. Or, they may have their own agenda and try to co-opt you and the change effort to meet conflicting needs.*

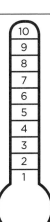

M. Facilitator Attitude Toward Us

- How much time is the facilitator willing to spend with us?

If it is not much, it may be difficult to sustain momentum. More facilitator time will be required early in the process, but over time the facilitator should be gradually making him- or herself unnecessary. Also, if your expectations are that the facilitator will work either more or less time per week with you than what you intended, it is important to reach a consensus.

- How well does the facilitator get along with us?

If you don't feel the facilitator can develop a good personal relationship with you, the transformation process will be more difficult and less likely to succeed.

Potential problems: *It is easy to underestimate the amount of time the facilitator will need to spend initially to get the change effort underway. It is also sometimes difficult to accurately assess the facilitator's competing time demands. Remember Murphy's Law on both counts!*

N. Feasibility of the Effort

- How big is our school system? How highly bureaucratized?

The larger and more bureaucratized your school system, the more difficult the change process is likely to be, all other things being equal.

- How much time will our district require of the facilitator?

The larger the district, the more time it is likely to require. Also, the further along you are in your thinking about change, the less time it is likely to require of the facilitator. In the beginning, much direct facilitation may be required, but as your capacity for change is built, the facilitator should increasingly work primarily in the background, providing scaffolding at a higher level. So, the time demands on the facilitator are likely to become less as the change process advances.

Source: Reigeluth, C. M., & Duffy, F. M. (2019). The school system transformation process: Guidance for paradigm change in school districts. In M. Spector, B. Lockee, & M. Childress (Eds.), Learning, Design, and Technology *(pp. 1–32). New York: Springer Nature. Used with permission.*

Helpful Resources for the Transformation Process

The following organizations offer advice or assistance for the transformation process. Many provide assistance for both what your vision should be like and the process of creating and implementing it. Here we describe a few of the organizations that have a greater focus on the transformation process. Additional organizations are listed on our website, www.reigeluth.net/pcbe-school-systems. Also, there are undoubtedly many other fine organizations that we are not aware of. We encourage such organizations to contact us for inclusion in our website.

- **2Revolutions** (www.2revolutions.net) is an education design lab considering questions about the future of the American education system. Using design thinking to generate creative ideas, it seeks to respond to the forces of social and economic change to build new systems of learning that will prepare students for the future.

- **Education Elements** (www.edelements.com) helps schools to create new instructional model designs: competency-based learning, blended learning, personalized learning, project-based learning, and more. Other services include strategy development, professional development and support, school leadership development, finding open educational resources, and others.

- **Education Reimagined** (education-reimagined.org) is dedicated to accelerating the growth and impact of the learner-centered education (LCE) movement in the United States by promoting LCE among education stakeholder groups, supporting learner-centered leaders, and helping those leaders to collaborate, innovate, and advocate together.

- **Highlander Institute** (highlanderinstitute.org) contributes to the goal of an equitable education system by providing services, programs, resources, and events related to personalized learning.

- **Institute for the Future of Learning** or IFL (www.the-ifl.org) offers workshops, coaching, and research for leaders seeking to transform the current rigid system of education. Their work incorporates an understanding of the human dynamics of meaningful and sustainable change.

- **Reinventing Schools Coalition** or RISC (www.reinventingschools.org) developed based on the founders' experience implementing competency-based education in their own district and a desire to help other districts do the same. Their Quality Schools Model includes shared vision, academic standards, instruction, aligned assessments, meaningful report cards, and sustainability.

- **Summit Learning** (www.summitlearning.org) shares a personalized instructional approach that involves mentoring, projects, and self-direction. As part of implementation, the Summit model also considers the individual needs of the entire community and customizes systems for local needs. Summit schools receive one-on-one training and support, as well as a complete curriculum, instructional resources, assessments, and a learning management system. Summit Learning currently serves more than 380 schools, nearly 3,800 educators, and more than 72,000 students across the United States.

- **Transcend Education** (www.transcendeducation.org) partners with visionary school communities to design their own educational models. Rather than prescribing a defined model, Transcend offers eight "great leaps" (each presented as a shift from the old model to the future) that communities should consider as they develop local solutions.

- **Transforming Learning Collaborative** (services.nextgenlearning.org /transforming-learning-collaborative) is a partnership founded by Next Generation Learning Challenges, Da Vinci Schools, and Schools That Can. The schools in the network serve as exemplars of innovation in education, and the collaborative offers conferences and a yearlong incubator for educators and schools wishing to transform. The following mentor schools and districts have joined the collaborative to provide learning and design experiences, mentoring, and training: Building 21, Distinctive Schools, Lindsay Unified School District, Valor Collegiate Academy, Vista Unified School District, and Workshop School.

REFERENCES AND RESOURCES

Ackoff, R. L. (1981). *Creating the corporate future: Plan or be planned for.* New York: John Wiley & Sons.

American Institutes for Research. (1999). *An educator's guide to schoolwide reform.* Arlington, VA: American Association of School Administrators.

American Psychological Association. (1993). *Learner-centered psychological principles: Guidelines for school redesign and reform.* Washington, DC: Author.

Anderson, C. (2016, January 26). Resolving the charter school debate. *Education Week.* Accessed at www.edweek.org/ew/articles/2016/01/27/resolving-the-charter-school-debate .html on April 9, 2019.

Anderson, G., Boud, D., & Sampson, J. (1996). *Learning contracts: A practical guide.* London: Kogan Page.

Anderson, S. E. (1990). *Project excellence: A case study of a student-centred secondary school.* Toronto, Canada: Ministry of Education.

Annenberg Institute for School Reform. (2002). *The Annenberg challenge: Lessons and reflections on public school reform.* Accessed at http://annenberginstitute.org/sites/default/files /product/252/files/Lessons_Report.pdf on April 9, 2019.

Ash Center for Democratic Governance and Innovation. (2017). *Citizen voices, community solutions: Designing better transparency and accountability approaches to improve health.* Cambridge, MA: Author. Accessed at www.ash.harvard.edu/files/ash/files/citizen_voices _community_solutions.pdf on April 9, 2019.

Aslan, S., & Reigeluth, C. M. (2015). Examining the challenges of learner-centered education. *Phi Delta Kappan, 97*(4), 63–68.

Aslan, S., & Reigeluth, C. M. (2016). Investigating "the coolest school in America": How technology is used in a learner-centered school. *Educational Technology Research & Development, 64*(6), 1107-1133. doi:10.1007/s11423-016-9450-9

Aslan, S., Reigeluth, C. M., & Thomas, D. (2014). Transforming education with self-directed project-based learning: The Minnesota New Country School. *Educational Technology, 54*(3), 39–42.

Ausubel, D. P. (1968). *Educational psychology: A cognitive view.* New York: Holt, Rinehart & Winston.

Banathy, B. H. (1991). *Systems design of education: A journey to create the future.* Englewood Cliffs, NJ: Educational Technology Publications.

Banathy, B. H. (1996). *Designing social systems in a changing world.* New York: Plenum Press.

Bandura, A. (1977). *Social learning theory.* New York: General Learning Press.

Bandura, A. (1986). *Social foundations of thought and action*. Englewood Cliffs, NJ: Prentice-Hall.

Battelle for Kids. (n.d.). *Battelle for kids*. Accessed at www.battelleforkids.org/networks /p21 on July 17, 2019.

Battistich, V., Solomon, D., Watson, M., & Schaps, E. (1997). Caring school communities. *Educational Psychologist, 32*(3), 137–151.

Betts, F. (1992). How systems thinking applies to education. *Educational Leadership, 50*(3), 38–41.

Bhatt, S. (2019, May 22). Teachers are great at designing classrooms. Let's get them redesigning schools. *EdSurge*. Accessed at www.edsurge.com/news/2019-05-22 -teachers-are-great-at-designing-classrooms-let-s-get-them-redesigning-schools on November 18, 2019.

Block, P. (1991). *The empowered manager: Positive political skills at work*. San Francisco: Jossey-Bass.

Bloom, B. S. (1984). The 2 sigma problem: The search for methods of group instruction as effective as one-to-one tutoring. *Educational Researcher, 13*(6), 4–16.

Borba, Michele. (2018, October). Nine competencies for teaching empathy. *Educational Leadership*. Accessed at http://www.educationalleadership-digital.com/educational leadership/2018xx/MobilePagedArticle.action?articleId=1429755#articleId1429755 on November 11, 2019.

Boss, S., & Larmer, J. (2018). *Project based teaching: How to create rigorous and engaging learning experiences*. Alexandria, VA: Association for Supervision and Curriculum Development.

Bower, M., Howe, C., McCredie, N., Robinson, A., & Grover, D. (2014). Augmented Reality in education—cases, places and potentials. *Educational Media International, 51*(1), 1–15. doi:10.1080/09523987.2014.889400

Bransford, J. D., Brown, A. L., & Cocking, R. R. (Eds.). (2000). *How people learn: Brain, mind, experience, and school*. Washington, DC: National Academies Press.

Brown, J. S., & Burton, R. R. (1978). Diagnostic models for procedural bugs in basic mathematical skills. *Cognitive Science, 2*(2), 155-192.

Bryk, A. S., Gomez, L. M., Grunow, A., & LeMahieu, P. G. (2015). *Learning to improve: How America's schools can get better at getting better*. Cambridge, MA: Harvard Education Press.

Burnette, D. (2017). States waive regulations, create innovation zones. *Education Week, 37*(12), 12–14.

Bushweller, K. (2017). Turning state law into classroom reality. *Education Week, 37*(12), 18–21.

Cabrera, D., & Cabrera, L. (2015). *Systems thinking made simple: New hope for solving wicked problems*. Ithaca, NY: Odyssean Press.

Casey, K. (2018). *Moving toward mastery: Growing, developing and sustaining educators for competency-based education*. Accessed at www.inacol.org/wp-content/uploads/2018/11 /Moving-Toward-Mastery.pdf on September 13, 2019.

Checkland, P. (1984). *Systems thinking, systems practice*. New York: John Wiley & Sons.

Chen, Z., & Reigeluth, C. M. (2010). Communication in a leadership team for systemic change in a school district. *Contemporary Educational Technology, 1*(3), 233–254.

Childress, S., & Benson, S. (2014). Personalized learning for every student every day. *Phi Delta Kappan, 95*(8), 33–38.

Choice Schools Associates. (2016, August 25). 14 easy ways to create the whole child approach in your classroom. *Choice Schools Associates.* Accessed at https://choiceschools.com/14 -easy-ways-create-whole-child-approach-classroom/ on November 11, 2019.

Collins, A. (2017). *What's worth teaching? Rethinking curriculum in the age of technology.* New York: Teachers College Press.

Corrigan, R., & Denton, P. (1996). Causal understanding as a developmental primitive. *Developmental Review, 16*(2), 162–202.

Csíkszentmihályi, M. (1990). *Flow: The psychology of optimal experience.* New York: Harper & Row.

Damon, W., Menon, J., & Bronk, K. C. (2003). The development of purpose during adolescence. *Applied Developmental Science, 7*(3), 119–128.

Darling-Hammond, L., & Cook-Harvey, C. M. (2018). *Educating the whole child: Improving school climate to support student success.* Accessed at https://learningpolicyinstitute.org/sites /default/files/product-files/Educating_Whole_Child_REPORT.pdf on April 9, 2019.

Darling-Hammond, L., Cook-Harvey, C. M., Flook, L., Gardner, M., & Melnick, H. (2018). *With the whole child in mind: Insights from the Comer School Development Program.* Alexandria, VA: Association for Supervision and Curriculum Development.

Deci, E. L., & Ryan, R. M. (1985). *Intrinsic motivation and self-determination in human behavior.* New York: Plenum Press.

Desautels, L. (2018, September 25). *Teaching self-regulation in the early grades.* Accessed at www.edutopia.org on April 9, 2019.

Design Kit. (2015). *The field guide to human-centered design.* San Francisco: IDEO.

DiMartino, J., Clarke, J., & Wolk, D. (2003). *Personalized learning: Preparing high school students to shape their futures.* New York: Scarecrow Press.

Dintersmith, T. (2018, April 30). What's actually working in the classroom? *Education Week.* Accessed at www.edweek.org/ew/articles/2018/05/02/whats-actually-working-in-the -classroom.html on April 9, 2019.

Dirkswager, E. J. (Ed.). (2002). *Teachers as owners: A key to revitalizing public education.* Lanham, MD: Scarecrow Press.

Duffy, F. M. (2002). *Step-up-to-excellence: An innovative approach to managing and rewarding performance in school systems.* Lanham, MD: Scarecrow Education.

Duffy, F. M. (2003). *Courage, passion, and vision: A guide to leading systemic school improvement.* Lanham, MD: Scarecrow Education.

Duffy, F. M. (2004). *Moving upward together: Creating strategic alignment to sustain systemic school improvement.* Lanham, MD: Scarecrow Education.

Duffy, F. M. (2006). *Power, politics, and ethics in school districts: Dynamic leadership for systemic change.* Lanham, MD: Rowman & Littlefield Education.

Duffy, F. M. (2010). *Dream! Create! Sustain! Mastering the art and science of transforming school systems.* Lanham, MD: Rowman & Littlefield Education.

Duffy, F. M., & Chance, P. L. (2007). *Strategic communication during whole-system change: Advice and guidance for school district leaders and PR specialists.* Lanham, MD: Rowman & Littlefield Education.

Duffy, F. M., & Reigeluth, C. M. (2008). The school system transformation (SST) protocol. *Educational Technology, 48*(4), 41–49.

Duffy, F. M., Rogerson, L. G., & Blick, C. (2000). *Redesigning America's schools: A systems approach to improvement.* Norwood, MA: Christopher-Gordon.

DuFour, R., DuFour, R., Eaker, R., Many, T., & Mattos, M. (2016). *Learning by doing: A handbook for professional learning communities at work* (3rd ed.). Bloomington, IN: Solution Tree Press.

Durlak, J. A., Weissberg, R. P., Dymnicki, A. B., Taylor, R. D., & Schellinger, K. B. (2011). The impact of enhancing students' social and emotional learning: A meta-analysis of school-based universal interventions. *Child Development, 82*(1), 405–432.

Dutta, P. (2013). *Personalized Integrated Educational System (PIES) for the learner-centered information-age paradigm of education: A study to improve the design of the functions and features of PIES.* Unpublished doctoral dissertation, Indiana University, Bloomington.

Dweck, C. S. (2016). *Mindset: The new psychology of success.* New York: Ballantine Books.

Dyjur, P., & Lindstrom, G. (2017). Perceptions and uses of digital badges for professional learning development in higher education. *TechTrends, 61*(4), 386–392.

Eckel, P., Hill, B., & Green, M. (1998). *En route to transformation. On change: An occasional paper series of the ACE Project on Leadership and Institutional Transformation.* Washington, DC: American Council on Education.

Educate the Whole Child. (n.d.). *What is whole child education?* Accessed at www.educatethewholechild.org/what-is-it/ on July 25, 2019.

Educational Impact. (n.d.). *Deconstructing standards practice: Developing learning targets: Mastering curriculum mapping.* Accessed at www.educationalimpact.com/resources/mcm/pdf/MCM_1B_Activity4_DevelopingLearnDev_Targets.pdf on April 9, 2019.

Edwards, C. P. (2006). Montessori education and its scientific basis. *Applied Developmental Psychology, 27*(2), 183–187.

Egol, M. (2003). *The education revolution: Spectacular learning at lower cost.* Tenafly, NJ: Wisdom Dynamics.

Elias, M. J., Zins, J. E., Weissberg, R. P., Frey, K. S., Greenberg, M. T., & Haynes, N. M. (1997). *Promoting social and emotional learning: Guidelines for educators.* Alexandria, VA: Association for Supervision and Curriculum Development.

Emery, M., & Purser, R. E. (1996). *The Search Conference: A powerful method for planning organizational change and community action.* San Francisco: Jossey-Bass.

Erikson, E. H. (1968). *Identity: Youth and crisis.* New York: W. W. Norton.

FairTest. (2019). More than 1000 accredited colleges and universities that do not use ACT/SAT scores to admit substantial numbers of students into bachelor-degree programs. Accessed at www.fairtest.org/university/optional on April 9, 2019.

Farris-Berg, K., & Dirkswager, E. J. (2013). *Trusting teachers with school success: What happens when teachers call the shots.* Lanham, MD: Rowman & Littlefield Education.

Ferguson, D. L., Ralph, G., Meyer, G., Lester, J., Droege, C., Gudjonsdottir, H., et al. (2001). *Designing personalized learning for every student.* Alexandria, VA: Association for Supervision and Curriculum Development.

Finn-Stevenson, M., Desimone, L., & Chung, A.-M. (1998). Linking child care and support services with the school: Pilot evaluation of the school of the 21st century. *Children and Youth Services Review, 20*(3), 177–205.

Fishman, B. J., Marx, R. W., Best, S., & Tal, R. T. (2003). Linking teacher and student learning to improve professional development in systemic reform. *Teaching and Teacher Education, 19*(6), 643–658.

Flippo, T. (2016). *Social and emotional learning in action: Experiential activities to positively impact school climate.* Lanham, MD: Rowman & Littlefield.

Forrester, J. W. (1999). *Systems dynamics: The foundation under systems thinking.* Accessed at http://sysdyn.mit.edu/sdep/papers/D-4828.html on April 9, 2019.

Freeman, S., Eddy, S. L., McDonough, M., Smith, M. K., Okoroafor, N., Jordt, H., et al. (2014). Active learning increases student performance in science, engineering, and mathematics. Accessed at www.pnas.org/content/111/23/8410 on April 9, 2019.

Frey, N., Fisher, D., & Smith, D. (2019). *All learning is social and emotional: Helping students develop essential skills for the classroom and beyond.* Alexandria, VA: Association for Supervision and Curriculum Development.

Freina, L., & Ott, M. (n.d.). *A literature review on immersive virtual reality in education: State of the art and perspectives.* Accessed at https://ppm.itd.cnr.it/download/eLSE%202015 %20Freina%20Ott%20Paper.pdf on September 13, 2019.

Fried, R. L. (2001). Passionate learners and the challenge of schooling. *Phi Delta Kappan, 83*(2), 124–136.

Frost, D., & Worthen, M. (2017). *iNACOL issue brief: State policy & K–12 competency-based education.* Accessed at www.inacol.org/wp-content/uploads/2017/08/iNACOL -IssueBrief-StatePolicy-K12CBE.pdf on September 13, 2019.

Fullan, M. (2001). *Leading in a culture of change.* San Francisco: Jossey-Bass.

Fullan, M. (2003). *Change forces with a vengeance.* New York: Routledge.

Fullan, M. G., & Stiegelbauer, S. M. (1991). *The new meaning of educational change* (2nd ed.). New York: Teachers College Press.

Gallagher, C. J. (2003). Reconciling a tradition of testing with a new learning paradigm. *Educational Psychology Review, 15*(1), 83–99.

Gardner, H. (2011). *Frames of mind: The theory of multiple intelligences.* New York: Basic Books.

Gewertz, C. (2018, February 6). Do student projects have a role in college admissions? *Education Week.* Accessed at www.edweek.org/ew/articles/2018/2002/2007/do-student -projects-have-a-role-in.html on September 13, 2019.

Gokhale, A. A. (1995). Collaborative learning enhances critical thinking. *Journal of Technology Education, 7*(1), 22–30.

Goleman, D. (1995). *Emotional intelligence: Why it can matter more than IQ.* New York: Bantam Books.

Goleman, D. (1998). *Working with emotional intelligence.* New York: Bantam Books.

Goodlad, S., & Hirst, B. (1989). *Peer tutoring: A guide to learning by teaching.* New York: Kogan Page.

Gordon, E. E. (2005). *Peer tutoring: A teacher's resource guide.* Lanham, MD: Scarecrow Education.

Grant, S., & Shawgo, K. E. (2013). Digital badges: An annotated research bibliography v1. Accessed at www.hastac.org/digital-badges-bibliography on April 9, 2019.

Great Schools Partnership. (2014). The glossary of education reform for journalists, parents, and community members. Accessed at www.edglossary.org/personal-learning-plan on September 13, 2019.

Greene, R. W. (2014). *Lost at school: Why our kids with behavioral challenges are falling through the cracks and how we can help them.* New York: Scribner.

Guskey, T. R., & Gates, S. L. (1986). Synthesis of research on the effects of mastery learning in elementary and secondary classrooms. *Educational Leadership, 43*(8), 73–80.

Hall, G. E., & Hord, S. M. (1987). *Change in schools: Facilitating the process.* Albany: State University of New York Press.

Hall, G. E., & Hord, S. M. (2001). *Implementing change: Patterns, principles, and potholes.* Boston: Allyn & Bacon.

Hallermann, S., Larmer, J., & Mergendoller, J. R. (2011). *PBL in the elementary grades: Step- by-step guidance, tools and tips for standards-focused K–5 projects.* Novato, CA: Buck Institute for Education.

Hammonds, V. (2018). *Visioning toolkit: Laying the groundwork for a community-wide vision for personalized learning.* Accessed at https://knowledgeworks.org/resources/toolkit-community-wide-vision-personalized-learning on April 9, 2019.

Hampton, F. M., Mumford, D. A., & Bond, L. (1998). Parent involvement in inner-city schools: The Project FAST extended family approach to success. *Urban Education, 33*(3), 410–427.

Han, S., Capraro, R., & Capraro, M. M. (2015). How science, technology, engineering, and mathematics (STEM) project-based learning (PBL) affects high, middle, and low achievers differently: The impact of student factors on achievement. *International Journal of Science and Mathematics Education, 13*(5), 1089–1113.

Hanover Research. (2015). *Personalized learning and student achievement.* Accessed at www.gssaweb.org/wp-content/uploads/2015/11/Personalized-Learning-and-Student-Achievement.pdf on April 9, 2019.

Haynes, E., Zeiser, K., Surr, W., Hauser, A., Clymer, L., Walston, J., et al. (2016). *Looking under the hood of competency-based education: The relationship between competency-based education practices and students' learning skills, behaviors, and dispositions.* Quincy, MA: Nellie Mae Education Foundation. Accessed at www.nmefoundation.org/getattachment/Resources/Competency-Based-Pathways/Looking-Under-The-Hood-Of-Competency-Based-Educati/CBE-Study-Full-Report-FINAL-(2).pdf?lang=en-US&ext=.pdf on April 9, 2019.

Haystead, M. W. (2010). *RISC vs. non-RISC schools: A comparison of student proficiencies for reading, writing, and mathematics.* Centennial, CO: Marzano Research. Accessed at www.marzanoresearch.com/research/reports/risc-vs-non-risc-schools-a-comparison-of-student-proficiencies-for-reading-writing-and-mathematics on April 9, 2019.

Herdman, P. (2016, January 5). With ESSA passage, Delaware offers lessons. *Education Week.* Accessed at www.edweek.org/ew/articles/2016/01/06/with-essa-passage-delaware-offers-lessons.html on April 9, 2019.

Herold, B. (2017a, March 28). Curriculum "playlists": A take on personalized learning. *Education Week.* Accessed at www.edweek.org/ew/articles/2017/03/29/curriculum-playlists-a-take-on-personalized-learning.html on April 9, 2019.

Herold, B. (2017b, November 7). The case(s) against personalized learning. *Education Week.* Accessed at www.edweek.org/ew/articles/2017/11/08/the-cases-against-personalized -learning.html on April 9, 2019.

Horn, M. B. (2015). The rise of altschool and other micro-schools. *Education Next, 15*(3). Accessed at www.educationnext.org/rise-micro-schools on April 9, 2019.

Hudson, E. (2018, October 17). *How to design a competency-based assessment.* Accessed at https://globalonlineacademy.org/insights/articles/how-to-design-a-competency-based -assessment on April 9, 2019.

Huh, Y., & Reigeluth, C. M. (2017a). Designing instruction for self-regulated learning. In C. M. Reigeluth, B. J. Beatty, & R. D. Myers (Eds.), *Instructional-design theories and models: The learner-centered paradigm of education* (Vol. 4, pp. 243–267). New York: Routledge.

Huh, Y., & Reigeluth, C. M. (2017b). Online K–12 teachers' perceptions and practices of supporting self-regulated learning. *Journal of Educational Computing Research, 55*(8), 1129–1153.

Huh, Y., & Reigeluth, C. M. (2017c). Self-regulated learning: The continuous-change conceptual framework and a vision of new paradigm, technology system, and pedagogical support. *Journal of Educational Technology Systems, 46*(2), 191–214.

Hutchins, C. L. (1996). *Systemic thinking: Solving complex problems.* Aurora, CO: Professional Development Systems.

Hybert, F. (2018). To connect classes to careers, consider erasing grade levels *Ed Surge.* Accessed at https://www.edsurge.com/news/2018-03-17-to-connect-classes-to-careers -consider-erasing-grade-levels on September 13, 2019.

IDEO. (2015). *The field guide to human-centered design.* San Francisco: Author. Accessed at https://bestgraz.org/wp-content/uploads/2015/09/Field-Guide-to-Human-Centered -Design_IDEOorg.pdf on September 13, 2019.

Iowa Department of Education. (n.d.). *Iowa CBE collaborative.* Accessed at https:// educateiowa.gov/pk-12/standards-and-curriculum/competency-based-pathways/iowa -cbe-collaborative on April 9, 2019.

Jacobson, R., Villarreal, L., Muñoz, J., & Mahaffey, R. (2018). It takes a community. *Phi Delta Kappan, 99*(5), 8–14.

Jenkins, J. M., & Keefe, J. W. (2002). Two schools: Two approaches to personalized learning. *Phi Delta Kappan, 83*(6), 449-456.

Jenlink, P. M., Reigeluth, C. M., Carr, A. A., & Nelson, L. M. (1996). An expedition for change. *TechTrends, 41*(1), 21–30.

Jenlink, P. M., Reigeluth, C. M., Carr, A. A., & Nelson, L. M. (1998). Guidelines for facilitating systemic change in school districts. *Systems Research and Behavioral Science, 15*(3), 217–233.

Johnson, D. W., & Johnson, R. (1989). *Cooperation and competition: Theory and research.* Edina, MN: Interaction Book Company.

Johnson, D. W., & Johnson, R. (2005). New developments in social interdependence theory. *Psychology Monographs, 131*(4), 285–358.

Jonassen, D. H. (2011). *Learning to solve problems: A handbook for designing problem-solving learning environments.* New York: Routledge.

Jong, C., Thomas, J. N., Fisher, M. H., Schack, E. O., Davis, M. A., & Bickett, M. E. (2017). Decimal dilemmas: Interpreting and addressing misconceptions. *Ohio Journal of School Mathematics, 75,* 13–21.

Joseph, R., & Reigeluth, C. M. (2005). Formative research on an early stage of the systemic change process in a small school district. *British Journal of Educational Technology, 36*(6), 937–956.

Jung, E., Reigeluth, C. M., Kim, M., & Trepper, S. (2019). An investigation into state-level paradigm change and politics in education: Ohio's Transformational Dialogue for Public Education. In J. M. Spector, B. Lockee, & M. Childress (Eds.), *Learning, design, and technology: An international compendium of theory, research, practice, and policy* (pp. 1–34). New York: Springer.

Junge, A., & Farris-Berg, K. (2015). *15 areas of autonomy secured by teams of teachers designing and running teacher-powered schools.* Accessed at www.teacherpowered.org/files /Teacher-Powered-Autonomies-Detailed.pdf on September 13, 2019.

Kamradt, T. F., & Kamradt, E. J. (1999). Structured design for attitudinal instruction. In C. M. Reigeluth (Ed.), *Instructional-design theories and models: A new paradigm of instructional theory* (Vol. 2, pp. 563–590). Mahwah, NJ: Lawrence Erlbaum.

Keefe, J. W. (2000). *Personalized instruction: Changing classroom practice.* Larchmont, NY: Eye on Education.

Keefe, J. W. (2007). What is personalization? *Phi Delta Kappan, 89*(3), 217–223.

Keefe, J. W. (2008). *Personalized instruction: The key to student achievement.* Lanham, MD: Rowman & Littlefield Education.

Keller, J. M. (1983). Motivational design of instruction. In C. M. Reigeluth (Ed.), *Instructional-design theories and models: An overview of their current status* (pp. 386–429). Hillsdale, NJ: Lawrence Erlbaum.

Keller, J. M. (2010). *Motivational design for learning and performance: The ARCS model approach.* New York: Springer.

Kerzner, H. R. (2009). *Project management: A systems approach to planning, scheduling, and controlling* (10th ed.). Hoboken, NJ: John Wiley & Sons.

Khan Academy. (n.d.). How do I master a topic in Missions? Accessed at https://khanacademy .zendesk.com/hc/en-us/articles/202755500-How-do-I-master-a-topic on April 9, 2019.

Kim, D. H. (2014). Transformational dialogue for public education: Moving from tweaking to transforming at the state level. *Educational Technology, 54*(3), 22–28.

Kirschner, P. A., Sweller, J., & Clark, R. E. (2006). Why minimal guidance during instruction does not work: An analysis of the failure of constructivist, discovery, problem-based, experiential, and inquiry-based teaching. *Educational Psychologist, 41*(2), 75–86.

Klein, A. (2018a, February 2). Betsy DeVos opens up ESSA pilot allowing federal money to follow students. *Education Week.* Accessed at http://blogs.edweek.org/edweek/campaign -k-12/2018/02/essa_weighted_student_funding_pilot_devos.html on September 13, 2019.

Klein, A. (2018b, May 8). "Continuous improvement" model woven into ESSA plans: States seek systemic route to steady gains. *Education Week.* Accessed at www.edweek.org/ew /articles/2018/05/07/continuous-improvement-model-woven-into-state-essa.html on April 9, 2019.

KnowledgeWorks Foundation. (2018). *Laying the groundwork for a community-wide vision for personalized learning.* Accessed at https://knowledgeworks.org/wp-content/uploads/2018/02/visioning-toolkit.pdf on July 22, 2019.

KnowledgeWorks Foundation. (2019). What happens when second graders plan for the future. Accessed at https://knowledgeworks.org/resources/students-goals-primary-school on September 13, 2019.

Kohn, A. (1990). *The brighter side of human nature: Altruism and empathy in everyday life.* New York: Basic Books.

Kolderie, T. (2014). *The split screen strategy: Improvement + innovation: How to get education changing the way successful systems change.* Edina, MN: Beaver's Pond Press.

Kolderie, T. (2018). *Thinking out the how.* Edina, MN: Beaver's Pond Press.

Kolderie, T. (2019). How the state can deal with the school boards' inertia. Accessed at http://bit.ly/SchoolBoardsInertia on September 13, 2019.

Kolderie, T., Dirkswager, E. J., Farris-Berg, K., & Schroeder, J. (2003). *Teacher professional partnerships: A different way to help teachers and teaching.* Saint Paul, MN: Education Evolving.

Kotter, J. P. (2012). *Leading change.* Cambridge, MA: Harvard Business Review Press.

Kulik, C.-L. C., Kulik, J. A., Bangert-Drowns, R. L., & Slavin, R. E. (1990). Effectiveness of mastery learning programs: A meta-analysis. *Review of Educational Research, 60*(2), 265–299.

Lambert, N. M., & McCombs, B. L. (Eds.). (1998). *How students learn: Reforming schools through learner-centered education.* Washington, DC: American Psychological Association.

Lash, D., & Belfiore, G. (2017). *Introduction and overview of the MyWays Student Success Series.* Accessed at https://s3.amazonaws.com/nglc/resource-files/MyWays_00Introduction.pdf on April 9, 2019.

Lee, D., Huh, Y., Lin, C.-Y., & Reigeluth, C. M. (2018). Technology functions for personalized learning in learner-centered schools. *Educational Technology Research and Development, 66*(5), 1269–1302.

Lee, S., & Reigeluth, C. M. (2007). Community involvement in Decatur's Journey Toward Excellence. In F. M. Duffy & P. Chance (Eds.), *Strategic communication during whole-system change: Advice and guidance for school district leaders and PR specialists* (pp. 213–231). Lanham, MD: Rowman & Littlefield.

Lewis, C., Schaps, E., & Watson, M. (1995). Beyond the pendulum: Creating challenging *and* caring schools. *Phi Delta Kappan, 76*(7), 547–554.

Lewis, C., Watson, M., & Schaps, E. (1999). Recapturing education's full mission: Educating for social, ethical, and intellectual development. In C. M. Reigeluth (Ed.), *Instructional-design theories and models: A new paradigm of instructional theory* (Vol. 2, pp. 511–536). Mahwah, NJ: Lawrence Erlbaum.

Lickona, T. (1991). *Educating for character: How our schools can teach respect and responsibility.* New York: Bantam Books.

Lillard, A. S. (2006). The early years: Evaluating Montessori education. *Science, 313*(5795), 1893-1894. doi:10.1126/science.1132362

Lillard, A. S. (2016). *Montessori: The science behind the genius* (3rd ed.). Oxford, England: Oxford University Press.

Lillard, A. S., & Else-Quest, N. M. (2006). Evaluating Montessori education. *Science, 313*(5795), 1893–1894.

Lindsay Unified School District. (2017). *Beyond reform: Systemic shifts toward personalized learning.* Bloomington, IN: Marzano Resources.

Lytle, J. H. (2002). Whole-school reform from the inside. *Phi Delta Kappan, 84*(2), 164–167.

Mahoney, J. L., Durlak, J. A., & Weissberg, R. P. (2018). An update on social and emotional learning outcome research. *Phi Delta Kappan, 100*(4), 18-23.

Mahoney, J. L., & Weissberg, R. P. (2018). SEL: What the research says. *Educational Leadership, 76*(2), 34–35.

Marklein, M. B. (2013, February 27). Grades pointless? Some colleges don't care about GPAs. *USA Today.* Accessed at www.usatoday.com/story/news/nation/2013/02/27/college-grade-point-averages/1947415 on April 9, 2019.

Marzano, R. J. (2006). *Classroom assessment and grading that work.* Alexandria, VA: Association for Supervision and Curriculum Development.

Marzano, R. J. (2010). *Formative assessment and standards-based grading.* Bloomington, IN: Marzano Resources.

Marzano, R. J. (2017). *The new art and science of teaching.* Bloomington, IN: Solution Tree.

Marzano, R. J., Norford, J. S., Finn, M., & Finn, D., III. (2017). *A handbook for personalized competency-based education.* Bloomington, IN: Marzano Resources.

Marzano, R. J., Scott, D., Boogren, T. H., & Newcomb, M. L. (2017). *Motivating and inspiring students: Strategies to awaken the learner.* Bloomington, IN: Marzano Resources.

Maslow, A. H. (1954). *Motivation and personality.* New York: Harper & Row.

McClelland, D. C. (1987). *Human motivation.* Cambridge, England: Cambridge University Press.

McCombs, B. L. (1994). *Development and validation of the learner-centered psychological principles.* Aurora, CO: Mid-continent Regional Educational Laboratory.

McCombs, B. L. (2013). The learner-centered model: Implications for research approaches. In J. H. D. Cornelius-White, R. Motschnig-Pitrik, & M. Lux (Eds.), *Interdisciplinary handbook of the person-centered approach: Research and theory* (pp. 335–352). New York: Springer.

McCombs, B. L., & Miller, L. (2007). *Learner-centered classroom practices and assessments: Maximizing student motivation, learning, and achievement.* Thousand Oaks, CA: Corwin Press.

McCombs, B. L., & Whisler, J. S. (1997). *The learner-centered classroom and school: Strategies for increasing student motivation and achievement.* San Francisco: Jossey-Bass.

McPartland, J. M., & Nettles, S. M. (1991). Using community adults as advocates or mentors for at-risk middle-school students: A two-year evaluation of Project RAISE. *American Journal of Education, 99*(4), 568–586.

Means, B., Yoyama, Y., Murphy, R., Bakia, M., & Jones, K. (2009). *Evaluation of evidence-based practices in online learning: A meta-analysis and review of online learning studies.* Oxford, England: Association for Learning Technology. Accessed at http://repository.alt.ac.uk/629 on April 9, 2019.

Merrell, K. W., & Gueldner, B. A. (2010). *Social and emotional learning in the classroom: Promoting mental health and academic success.* New York: Guilford Press.

Merrill, M. D. (2013). *First principles of instruction: Identifying and designing effective, efficient, and engaging instruction.* San Francisco: Pfeiffer.

Miliband, D. (2006). Choice and voice in personalised learning. In *Schooling for tomorrow: Personalising education* (pp. 21–30). Paris: Organisation for Economic Co-operation and Development.

Miller, D. N., George, M. P., & Fogt, J. B. (2005). Establishing and sustaining research-based practices at Centennial School: A descriptive case study of systemic change. *Psychology in the Schools, 42*(5), 553–567.

Minero, E. (2019). 10 powerful community-building ideas *Edutopia.* Accessed at www .edutopia.org/article/10-powerful-community-building-ideas on September 13, 2019.

Montessori, M. (1912). *The Montessori method: Scientific pedagogy as applied to child education in "The children's houses" with additions and revisions by the author.* New York: Frederick A. Stokes.

Montessori, M. (1917). *The advanced Montessori method* (Vol. 1). New York: Frederick A. Stokes.

Montessori, M. (1964). *The Montessori method.* New York: Schocken Books.

Montessori, M. (1967). *The absorbent mind.* New York: Dell.

Montessori, M. (1973). *From childhood to adolescence: Including Erdkinder and the function of the university.* New York: Schocken Books.

Muilenberg, L. Y., & Berge, Z. L. (Eds.). (2016). *Digital badges in education: Trends, issues, and cases.* New York: Routledge.

Murphy, R., Gallagher, L., Krumm, A., Mislevy, J., & Hafter, A. (2014). *Research on the use of Khan Academy in schools.* Menlo Park, CA: SRI International. Accessed at www.sri.com /sites/default/files/publications/2014-03-07_implementation_briefing.pdf on April 9, 2019.

Myers, R. D., & Reigeluth, C. M. (2017). Designing games for learning. In C. M. Reigeluth, B. J. Beatty, & R. D. Myers (Eds.), *Instructional-design theories and models, Vol. IV: The learner-centered paradigm of education* (pp. 205-242). New York: Rougledge.

National Academies of Sciences, Engineering, and Medicine. (2018). *How people learn II: Learners, contexts, and cultures.* Washington, DC: National Academies Press.

National Center for Education Statistics. (2018). *Public charter school enrollment.* Accessed at https://nces.ed.gov/programs/coe/indicator_cgb.asp on April 9, 2019.

National Center on Education and the Economy. (2007). *Tough choices, tough times: The report of the New Commission on the Skills of the American Workforce—Executive summary.* Washington, DC: Author. Accessed at www.ncee.org/wp-content/uploads/2010/04 /Executive-Summary.pdf on April 9, 2019.

Nevis, E. C., Lancourt, J., & Vassallo, H. G. (1996). *Intentional revolutions: A seven-point strategy for transforming organizations.* San Francisco: Jossey-Bass.

New Commission on the Skills of the American Workforce. (2007). *Tough choices, tough times: The report of the new commission on the skills of the American workforce: Executive summary.* Washington, DC: Author.

New Hampshire Department of Education. (n.d.). *Performance assessment of competency education (PACE).* Accessed at www.education.nh.gov/assessment-systems/pace. htm#convening on April 9, 2019.

New Hampshire Department of Education. (2016). *Moving from good to great in New Hampshire: Performance assessment of competency education (PACE)*. Accessed at www.education.nh.gov/assessment-systems/documents/overview.pdf on April 9, 2019.

Newell, R. J. (2003). *Passion for learning: How project-based learning meets the needs of 21st-century students*. Lanham, MD: Rowman & Littlefield Education.

Newman, M. (2003). *A pilot systematic review and meta-analysis on the effectiveness of problem-based learning*. Accessed at https://eric.ed.gov/?id=ED476146 on April 9, 2019.

Next Generation Learning Challenges. (2019). *NGLA MyWays*. Accessed at https://myways.nextgenlearning.org/ on November 8, 2019.

Niguidula, D. (2019). *Demonstrating student mastery with digital badges and portfolios*. Alexandria, VA: Association for Supervision and Curriculum Development.

Nowack, K. M., & Wimer, S. (1997). Coaching for human performance. *Training and Development, 51*(10), 28–32.

O'Connor, K., Jung, L. A., & Reeves, D. (2018). Gearing up for FAST grading and reporting. *Phi Delta Kappan, 99*(8), 67–71.

Office of Educational Technology. (2010). *Transforming American education: Learning powered by technology—National Education Technology Plan 2010*. Accessed at www.ed.gov/sites/default/files/netp2010.pdf on April 9, 2019.

Office of Educational Technology. (2017). *Reimagining the role of technology in education: 2017 National Education Technology Plan update*. Accessed at https://tech.ed.gov/files/2017/01/NETP17.pdf on April 9, 2019.

Osher, D., Cantor, P., Berg, J., Steyer, L., & Rose, T. (2018). Drivers of human development: How relationships and context shape learning and development. *Applied Developmental Science*. Accessed at www.tandfonline.com/doi/full/10.1080/10888691.2017.1398650 on April 9, 2019.

Owen, H. (1991). *Riding the tiger: Doing business in a transforming world*. Bloomington, IN: Abbott Press.

Owen, H. (1993). *Open space technology: A user's guide* (1st ed.). Bloomington, IN: Abbott Press.

Pane, J. F., Steiner, E. D., Baird, M. D., Hamilton, L. S., & Pane, J. D. (2017). *Informing progress: Insights on personalized learning implementation and effects*. Santa Monica, CA: RAND Corporation. Accessed at www.rand.org/content/dam/rand/pubs/research_reports/RR2000/RR2042/RAND_RR2042.pdf on April 9, 2019.

Partnership for 21st Century Learning. (n.d.). *Learning for the 21st century*. Accessed at www.p21.org/storage/documents/P21_Report.pdf on April 9, 2019.

Pasmore, W. A. (1988). *Designing effective organizations: The sociotechnical systems perspective*. New York: John Wiley & Sons.

Patrick, S., Worthen, M., Frost, D., & Gentz, S. (2016). *Promising state policies for personalized learning*. Vienna, VA: iNACOL. Accessed at www.inacol.org/resource/promising-state-policies-for-personalized-learning on April 9, 2019.

Patrick, S., Worthen, M., & Truong, N. (2019). *iNACOL 2019 state policy priorities*. Accessed at www.inacol.org/wp-content/uploads/2018/09/2019-inacol-policy-priorities.pdf on September 13, 2019.

Perkins, D. N. (2014). *Future wise: Educating our children for a changing world.* San Francisco: Jossey-Bass.

Perkins, D. N., & Grotzer, T. A. (2005). Dimensions of causal understanding: The role of complex causal models in students' understanding of science. *Studies in Science Education, 41*(1), 117–165.

Perkins, D. N., & Unger, C. (1999). Teaching and learning for understanding. In C. M. Reigeluth (Ed.), *Instructional-design theories and models: A new paradigm of instructional theory* (Vol. 2, pp. 91–114). Mahwah, NJ: Lawrence Erlbaum.

Pettigrew, T. F. (1998). Intergroup contact theory. *Annual Review of Psychology, 49*(1), 65–85.

Pettigrew, T. F., & Tropp, L. R. (2008). How does intergroup contact reduce prejudice? Meta-analytic tests of three mediators. *European Journal of Social Psychology, 38*(6), 922–934.

Piaget, J. (1952). *The origins of intelligence in children.* New York: International Universities Press.

Piaget, J. (1977). *The essential Piaget: An interpretative reference and guide.* New York: Basic Books.

Pinchot, G., & Pinchot, E. (1993). *The end of bureaucracy and the rise of the intelligent organization.* San Francisco: Berrett-Koehler.

Planty, M., Hussar, W., Snyder, T., Kena, G., KewalRamani, A., Kemp, J., et al. (2009). *The condition of education 2009* (NCES 2009-081). Washington, DC: National Center for Education Statistics. Accessed at https://nces.ed.gov/pubs2009/2009081.pdf on April 9, 2019.

Poon, J. D. (2018, September 11). What do you mean when you say "student agency"? *Education Reimagined.* Accessed at https://education-reimagined.org/what-do-you-mean -when-you-say-student-agency on April 9, 2019.

Preeti, B., Ashish, A., & Shriram, G. (2013). Problem-based learning (PBL): An effective approach to improve learning outcomes in medical teaching. *Journal of Clinical & Diagnostic Research, 7*(12), 2896–2897.

Prensky, M. (2016). *Education to better their world: Unleashing the power of 21st-century kids.* New York: Teachers College Press.

Priest, N., Rudenstine, A., Weisstein, E., & Gerwin, C. (2012). Making mastery work: A close-up view of competency education. *Competency works* Accessed at https://www .competencyworks.org/resources/making-mastery-work/ on September 13, 2019.

Project Management Institute. (2013). *A guide to the project management body of knowledge: PMBOK Guide* (5th ed.). Newtown Square, PA: Author.

Prothero, A. (2016, January 26). "Micro schools" could be the new competition for private K–12. *Education Week.* Accessed at www.edweek.org/ew/articles/2016/01/27/micro -schools-could-be-new-competition-for.html on April 9, 2019.

Putman, M. (2018, June 8). *Using playlists to personalize learning* [Blog post]. Accessed at www.literacyworldwide.org/blog/literacy-daily/2018/06/08/using-playlists-to-personalize -learning on April 9, 2019.

Raemer, D., Anderson, M., Cheng, A., Fanning, R., Nadkarni, V., & Savoldelli, G. (2011). Research regarding debriefing as part of the learning process. *Simulation in Healthcare, 6,* S52–S57.

Rebora, A. (2018). Links between SEL and achievement start early. *Educational Leadership, 76*(2), 8.

Reigeluth, C. M. (1983). Meaningfulness and instruction: Relating what is being learned to what a student knows. *Instructional Science, 12*(3), 197–218.

Reigeluth, C. M. (1993). Principles of educational systems design. *International Journal of Educational Research, 19*(2), 117–131.

Reigeluth, C. M. (1995). A conversation on guidelines for the process of facilitating systemic change in education. *Systems Practice, 8*(3), 315–328.

Reigeluth, C. M. (1999). The elaboration theory: Guidance for scope and sequence decisions. In C. M. Reigeluth (Ed.), *Instructional-design theories and models: A new paradigm of instructional theory* (Vol. 2, pp. 425–453). Mahwah, NJ: Lawrence Erlbaum.

Reigeluth, C. M. (2006). A leveraged emergent approach to systemic transformation. *TechTrends, 50*(2), 46–47.

Reigeluth, C. M. (2007). Order, first step to mastery: An introduction to sequencing in instructional design. In F. E. Ritter, J. Nerb, E. Lehtinen, & T. O'Shea (Eds.), *In order to learn: How the sequence of topics influences learning* (pp. 19–40). New York: Oxford University Press.

Reigeluth, C. M. (2008). Chaos theory and the sciences of complexity: Foundations for transforming education. In B. Després (Ed.), *Systems thinkers in action: A field guide for effective change leadership in education* (pp. 24–38). New York: Rowman & Littlefield Education.

Reigeluth, C. M. (2018). *Teacher empowerment, student choice, and equity in school districts: A non-bureaucratic alternative for school organization and accountability*. Accessed at https://docs.wixstatic.com/ugd/4d4aa4_6eb61d665c044d3e8b693fa14c8592f5.pdf on April 9, 2019.

Reigeluth, C. M., Aslan, S., Chen, Z., Dutta, P., Huh, Y., Lee, D., et al. (2015). Personalized integrated educational system (PIES): Technology functions for the learner-centered paradigm of education. *Journal of Educational Computing Research, 53*(3), 459–496.

Reigeluth, C. M., Beatty, B. J., & Myers, R. D. (Eds.). (2017). *Instructional-design theories and models: The learner-centered paradigm of education* (Vol. 4). New York: Routledge.

Reigeluth, C. M., & Duffy, F. M. (2019). The school system transformation process: Guidance for paradigm change in school districts. In J. M. Spector, B. Lockee, & M. Childress (Eds.), *Learning, design, and technology: An international compendium of theory, research, practice, and policy*. New York: Springer.

Reigeluth, C. M., & Karnopp, J. R. (2013). *Reinventing schools: It's time to break the mold.* Lanham, MD: Rowman & Littlefield Education.

Reigeluth, C. M., Myers, R. D., & Lee, D. (2017). The learner-centered paradigm of education. In C. M. Reigeluth, B. J. Beatty, & R. D. Myers (Eds.), *Instructional-design theories and models: The learner-centered paradigm of education* (Vol. 4, pp. 5–32). New York: Routledge.

Reigeluth, C. M., & Rodgers, C. A. (1980). The elaboration theory of instruction: Prescriptions for task analysis and design. *NSPI Journal, 19*(1), 16–26.

Reigeluth, C. M., & Schwartz, E. (1989). An instructional theory for the design of computer-based simulations. *Journal of Computer-Based Instruction, 16*(1), 1–10.

Reigeluth, C. M., & Stinson, D. (2007a). The Decatur story: Reinvention of a school corporation—collaboration—developing partners in education. *The Indiana School Boards Association Journal, 53*(3), 13–15.

Reigeluth, C. M., & Stinson, D. (2007b). The Decatur story: Reinvention of a school corporation—culture and climate—the personality of school governance. *The Indiana School Boards Association Journal, 53*(4), 11–13.

Reigeluth, C. M., & Stinson, D. (2007c). The Decatur story: Reinvention of a school corporation—leadership and empowerment in Decatur's school transformation. *The Indiana School Boards Association Journal, 53*(2), 13–15.

Reigeluth, C. M., & Stinson, D. (2007d). The Decatur story: Reinvention of a school corporation—mission and values for Decatur's school transformation. *The Indiana School Boards Association Journal, 53*(1), 17–19.

Reigeluth, C. M., & Vogt, K. (2018). *How next generation schools define success.* Accessed at https://s3.amazonaws.com/nglc/resource-files/MyWays_InPractice.pdf on April 9, 2019.

Richter, K. B. (2007). *Integration of a decision-making process and a learning process in a newly formed leadership team for systemic transformation of a school district.* Unpublished doctoral dissertation, Indiana University, Bloomington.

Richter, K. B., & Reigeluth, C. M. (2006). A systemic change experience in Decatur Township. *Tech Trends, 50*(2), 35–36.

Richter, K. B., & Reigeluth, C. M. (2010). Systemic transformation in public school systems. In F. M. Duffy (Ed.), *Dream! Create! Sustain! Mastering the art and science of transforming school systems* (pp. 288–315). Lanham, MD: Rowman & Littlefield Education.

Ringers, J., Jr., & Decker, L. E. (1995). *School community centers: Guidelines for interagency planners.* Charlottesville, VA: Mid-Atlantic Center for Community Education.

Rogers, E. M. (2003). *Diffusion of innovations* (5th ed.). New York: Free Press.

Roseth, C. J., Johnson, D. W., & Johnson, R. T. (2008). Promoting early adolescents' achievement and peer relationships: The effects of cooperative, competitive, and individualistic goal structures. *Psychological Bulletin, 134*(2), 223–246.

Rowan, B., & Miller, R. J. (2007). Organizational strategies for promoting instructional change: Implementation dynamics in schools working with comprehensive school reform providers. *American Educational Research Journal, 44*(2), 252–297.

Rubin, S. C., & Sanford, C. (2018). *Pathways to personalization: A framework for school change.* Cambridge, MA: Harvard Education Press.

Ruyle, M. (2018). *Leading the evolution: How to make personalized competency-based education a reality.* Bloomington, IN: Marzano Resources.

Sanborn Regional School District. (2015). *Competency-based grading and reporting guide.* Accessed at www.thompsonschools.org/cms/lib/CO01900772/Centricity/Domain/2080 /Sanborn%20CCompetenc%20Handbook.pdf on April 9, 2019.

Sarason, S. B. (1995). *Parental involvement and the political principle: Why the existing governance structure of schools should be abolished* (1st ed.). San Francisco: Jossey-Bass.

Savery, J. R. (2009). Problem-based approach to instruction. In C. M. Reigeluth & A. A. Carr-Chellman (Eds.), *Instructional-design theories and models: Building a common knowledge base* (Vol. 3, pp. 143–165). New York: Routledge.

Schank, R. C., Berman, T. R., & Macpherson, K. A. (1999). Learning by doing. In C. M. Reigeluth (Ed.), *Instructional-design theories and models: A new paradigm of instructional theory* (Vol. 2, pp. 161–182). Mahwah, NJ: Lawrence Erlbaum.

Schlechty, P. C. (2001). *Shaking up the school house: How to support and sustain educational innovation.* San Francisco: Jossey-Bass.

Schlechty, P. C. (2005). *Creating great schools: Six critical systems at the heart of educational innovation.* San Francisco: Jossey-Bass.

Schön, D. A. (1995). *The reflective practitioner: How professionals think in action.* Aldershot, England: Arena Press.

Schunk, D. H. (1990). Goal setting and self-efficacy during self-regulated learning. *Educational Psychologist, 25*(1), 71–86.

Schutz, P. A., & Lanehart, S. L. (1994). Long-term educational goals, subgoals, learning strategies use and the academic performance of college students. *Learning and Individual Differences, 6*(4), 399–412.

Schwartz, R. B. (2013). Pathways, not tracks: An American perspective. In K. Baker (Ed.), *14–18: A new vision for secondary education* (pp. 71–84). New York: Bloomsbury Academic.

Secretary's Commission on Achieving Necessary Skills. (1991). *What work requires of schools: A SCANS report for America 2000.* Accessed at https://wdr.doleta.gov/scans/whatwork /whatwork.pdf on September 13, 2019.

Senge, P. M. (1990). *The fifth discipline: The art and practice of the learning organization* (1st ed.). New York: Doubleday.

Senge, P. M. (2000). *Schools that learn: A fifth discipline fieldbook for educators, parents, and everyone who cares about education* (1st ed.). New York: Doubleday.

Shaia, W. E., & Finigan-Carr, N. (2018). Moving from survival to fulfillment: A planning framework for community schools. *Phi Delta Kappan, 99*(5), 15–18.

Simms, J. A. (2016, August 8). *The critical concepts.* Accessed at www.marzanoresearch.com/ the-critical-concepts on June 24, 2019.

Singmaster, H. (2015, July 9). Why we need apprenticeship programs for high school students [Blog post]. Accessed at https://blogs.edweek.org/edweek/global_learning/2015/07/why _we_need_an_apprenticeship_program_for_high_school_students.html on April 9, 2019.

Smith, G. A., & Sobel, D. (2010). *Place- and community-based education in schools.* New York: Routledge.

Solomon, D., Watson, M., Battistich, V., Schaps, E., & Delucchi, K. (1992). Creating a caring community: Educational practices that promote children's prosocial development. In F. K. Oser, A. Dick, & J. L. Patry (Eds.), *Effective and responsible teaching: The new synthesis* (pp. 383–395). San Francisco: Jossey-Bass.

Sparks, S. D., & Harwin, A. (2018, May 29). A third of students need eye exams, study finds. *Education Week.* Accessed at www.edweek.org/ew/articles/2018/05/30/a-third-of-students -need-eye-exams.html?cmp=eml-enl-eu-news1-rm&M=58505383&U=1417327 on April 9, 2019.

Spillane, J. P. (2006). *Distributed leadership.* San Francisco: Jossey-Bass.

Srinivasan, L., & Archer, J. (2018). *From fragmentation to coherence: How more integrative ways of working could accelerate improvement and progress toward equity in education.* New York:

Carnegie Corporation of New York. Accessed at www.carnegie.org/media/filer_public /16/59/16592342-9aa0-4b1a-90fc-6242d1b09197/from_fragmentation_to_coherence _nov2018.pdf on April 9, 2019.

Stack, B. M., & Vander Els, J. G. (2017). *Breaking with tradition: The shift to competency-based learning in PLCs at work.* Bloomington, IN: Solution Tree Press.

Stanier, M. B. (2017, November 15). The 5 most powerful debrief questions and why they're important. *LinkedIn.* Accessed at https://www.linkedin.com/pulse/5-most-powerful -debrief-questions-why-theyre-michael-bungay-stanier on November 11, 2019.

Steiner, E. D., Hamilton, L. S., Stelitano, L., & Rudnick, M. (2017). *Designing innovative high schools: Implementation of the Opportunity by Design initiative after two years.* Santa Monica, CA: RAND Corporation. Accessed at www.rand.org/content/dam/rand/pubs /research_reports/RR2000/RR2005/RAND_RR2005.pdf on April 9, 2019.

Stone-McCown, K., & McCormick, A. H. (1999). Self-science: Emotional intelligence for children. In C. M. Reigeluth (Ed.), *Instructional-design theories and models: A new paradigm of instructional theory* (Vol. 2, pp. 537–562). Mahwah, NJ: Lawrence Erlbaum.

Strobel, J., & van Barneveld, A. (2009). When is PBL more effective? A meta-synthesis of meta-analyses comparing PBL to conventional classrooms. *Interdisciplinary Journal of Problem-Based Learning, 3*(1), 44–58.

Stroh, D. P. (2015). *Systems thinking for social change: A practical guide to solving complex problems, avoiding unintended consequences, and achieving lasting results.* White River Junction, VT: Chelsea Green.

Sturgis, C., & Casey, K. (2018). *Quality principles for competency-based education.* Vienna, VA: iNACOL.

Sturgis, C., & Patrick, S. (2010). When success is the only option: Designing competency-based pathways for next generation learning. Accessed at www.inacol.org/resource/when -success-is-the-only-option-designing-competency-based-pathways-for-next-generation -learning/ on September 13, 2019.

Sturgis, C., Patrick, S., & Pittenger, L. (2011). *It's not a matter of time: Highlights from the 2011 competency-based learning summit.* Accessed at www.inacol.org/wp-content /uploads/2015/02/iNACOL_Its_Not_A_Matter_of_Time_full_report.pdf on September 13, 2019.

Sturgis, C., & Vander Ark, T. (2018, December 12). The best academic schools in Tennessee feature the best character program in the country. *Getting Smart.* Accessed at www .gettingsmart.com/2018/12/the-best-academic-schools-in-tennessee-feature-the-best -character-program-in-the-country on April 9, 2019.

Sweller, J. (1994). Cognitive load theory, learning difficulty, and instructional design. *Learning and Instruction, 4*(4), 295–312.

Theobald, R. (1987). *The rapids of change: Social entrepreneurship in turbulent times.* Indianapolis, IN: Knowledge Systems.

Thomas, D., Enloe, W., & Newell, R. (Eds.). (2005). *"The coolest school in America": How small learning communities are changing everything.* Lanham, MD: Rowman & Littlefield Education.

Thompson, C. (2011, July 15). How Khan Academy is changing the rules of education. *Wired.* Accessed at www.wired.com/2011/07/ff_khan on April 9, 2019.

Togneri, W., & Anderson, S. E. (2003). *Beyond islands of excellence: What districts can do to improve instruction and achievement in all schools.* Alexandria, VA: Learning First Alliance.

Topping, K., & Ehly, S. (Eds.). (1998). *Peer-assisted learning.* Mahwah, NJ: Lawrence Erlbaum.

Transforming Education. (May 2019). Transforming Education's SEL integration approach for classroom educators. Accessed at https://www.transformingeducation.org on September 13, 2019.

Tyack, D. B., & Cuban, L. (1995). *Tinkering toward utopia: A century of public school reform.* Cambridge, MA: Harvard University Press.

Underwood, J., Baguley, T., Banyard, P., Coyne, E., Farrington-Flint, L., & Selwood, I. (2007). *Impact 2007: Personalising learning with technology.* Coventry, England: Becta. Accessed at libeprints.open.ac.uk/34533/1/Impact%202007.pdf on April 9, 2019.

Van Ryzin, M. J., & Roseth, C. J. (2018). The power of peer influence to address student behavioral problems. *Phi Delta Kappan, 99*(8), 62–66.

Vega, V. (2012, December 3). Project-based learning research review. *Edutopia.* Accessed at www.edutopia.org/pbl-research-learning-outcomes on April 9, 2019.

Wagner, T. (1994). *How schools change: Lessons learned from three communities revisited.* New York: RoutledgeFalmer.

Wagner, T. (2001). Leadership for learning: An action theory of school change. *Phi Delta Kappan, 82*(5), 378–383.

Wagner, T. (2012). *Creating innovators: The making of young people who will change the world.* New York: Scribner.

Wagner, T., & Dintersmith, T. (2015). *Most likely to succeed: Preparing our kids for the innovation era.* New York: Scribner.

Wagner, T., & Kegan, R. (2006). *Change leadership: A practical guide to transforming our schools.* San Francisco: Jossey-Bass.

Walker, A., & Leary, H. (2009). A problem-based learning meta analysis: Differences across problem types, implementation types, disciplines, and assessment levels. *Interdisciplinary Journal of Problem-Based Learning, 3*(1), 6–28.

Walsh, J. (1993, January 31). Is Saturn a failure? *The Star Tribune,* p. 1A.

Walter, F. (2018). School-based coordinators link students to community resources. *Phi Delta Kappan, 99*(5), 31–34.

Watkins, J., Peterson, A., & Mehta, J. (2018). The deeper learning dozen transforming school districts to support deeper learning for all: A hypothesis. *Academia.* Accessed at www.academia.edu/38674836/The_Deeper_Learning_Dozen_Transforming_School_Districts_to_Support_Deeper_Learning_for_All_A_Hypothesis on September 13, 2019.

Watson, S. L. (2008). *Somebody's gotta fight for them: A disadvantaged and marginalized alternative school's culture of learning and its case of change.* Unpublished doctoral dissertation, Indiana University, Bloomington.

Watson, S. L., & Reigeluth, C. M. (2008). Community members' perceptions on social, cultural changes and its implication for educational transformation in a small school district community. *Journal of Organisational Transformation and Social Change, 5*(1), 45–65.

Watson, S. L., & Reigeluth, C. M. (2013). Living the vision: A disadvantaged and marginalized alternative school's perspective on school culture and educational change. *International Journal of Education, 5*(2), 53–74.

Watson, W. R., & Watson, S. L. (2017). Principles for personalized instruction. In C. M. Reigeluth, B. J. Beatty, & R. D. Myers (Eds.), *Instructional-design theories and models: The learner-centered paradigm of education* (Vol. 4, pp. 93–120). New York: Routledge.

Weimer, M. (2002). *Learner-centered teaching: Five key changes to practice.* San Francisco: Jossey-Bass.

Weinzapfel, P. (2018). Districts embrace the community to benefit all students. *Phi Delta Kappan, 99*(5), 25–30.

Weyers, M. (2017, December 18). Project management for middle school: How one middle school teacher guides his students to managing their project-based learning groups like pros. *Edutopia.* Accessed at www.edutopia.org/article/project-management-middle-school on April 9, 2019.

Wiggins, G. (2017, June 29). Academic standards: Breaking whole things into broken bits. *Teacher Thought.* Accessed at www.teachthought.com/pedagogy/academic-standards -breaking-whole-things-into-broken-bits on April 9, 2019.

Wiggins, G., & McTighe, J. (2011). *The Understanding by Design guide to creating high-quality units.* Alexandria, VA: Association for Supervision and Curriculum Development.

Will, M. (2017, November 1). Students fare better when teachers have a say, study finds— but such teacher-leadership practices are rarely used. *Education Week.* Accessed at www .edweek.org/ew/articles/2017/11/01/students-fare-better-when-teachers-have-a.html on April 9, 2019.

William and Flora Hewlett Foundation. (2013). *Deeper learning competencies.* Accessed at https://hewlett.org/wp-content/uploads/2016/08/Deeper_Learning_Defined__April _2013.pdf on April 9, 2019.

Wiske, M. S. (Ed.). (1998). *Teaching for understanding: Linking research with practice.* San Francisco: Jossey-Bass.

Wolf, M. A. (2010). *Innovate to educate: System [re]design for personalized learning; A report from the 2010 Symposium.* Accessed at http://siia.net/pli/presentations/PerLearnPaper.pdf on September 13, 2019.

Wolk, R. A. (2011, March 7). Standards-based accountability's high stakes. *Education Week.* Accessed at www.edweek.org/ew/articles/2011/03/09/23wolk_ep.h30.html on April 9, 2019.

Wolk, R. A. (2016, January 5). To change education, change the message. *Education Week.* Accessed at www.edweek.org/ew/articles/2016/01/06/to-change-education-change-the -message.html on April 9, 2019.

Yonezawa, S., McClure, L., & Jones, M. (2012). *Personalization in schools.* Quincy, MA: Nellie Mae Education Foundation. Accessed at www.nmefoundation.org/research /personalization/personalization-in-schools on April 9, 2019.

Zimmerman, B. J. (2002). Becoming a self-regulated learner: An overview. *Theory into Practice, 41*(2), 64–70.

Zins, J. E., Weissberg, R. P., Wang, M. C., & Walberg, H. J. (2004). *Building academic success on social and emotional learning: What does the research say?* New York: Teachers College Press.

INDEX

A Handbook for Personalized Competency-Based Education
Robert J. Marzano, Jennifer S. Norford, Michelle Finn, and Douglas Finn III
Ensure all students master content by designing and implementing a personalized competency-based education (PCBE) system. Explore examples of how to use proficiency scales, standard operating procedures, behavior rubrics, personal tracking matrices, and other tools to aid in instruction and assessment.
BKL037

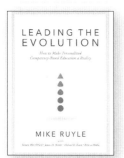

Leading the Evolution
Mike Ruyle with Tamera Weir O'Neill, Jeanie M. Iberlin, Michael D. Evans, and Rebecca Midles
Take action to evolve the existing model of schooling into one that is more innovative, relevant, and effective. *Leading the Evolution* introduces a three-pronged approach to driving substantive change—called the evolutionary triad—that connects transformational leadership, student engagement, and teacher optimism around personalized competency-based education.
BKL042

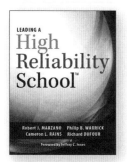

Leading a High Reliability School
Robert J. Marzano, Philip B. Warrick, Cameron L. Rains, and Richard DuFour
How do educators build High Reliability Schools (HRS) that consistently produce excellent results? The key is the PLC at Work™ process. This user-friendly resource will show you how to fully implement proven HRS and PLC structures that enable your school to become highly effective at promoting student learning.
BKF795

The Handbook for the New Art and Science of Teaching
Robert J. Marzano
Rely on this comprehensive guide to help you implement the teaching methods of Robert J. Marzano's *The New Art and Science of Teaching* framework, with over 330 instructional strategies. Each chapter outlines actionable steps, tips, and examples to help you succeed with this powerful model in your classroom.
BKF844

The New Art and Science of Teaching
Robert J. Marzano
This title is a greatly expanded volume of the original *The Art and Science of Teaching*, offering a framework for substantive change based on Dr. Marzano's fifty years of education research. While the previous model focused on teacher outcomes, the new version places focus on student outcomes.
BKF776

Solution Tree | Press
a division of

Solution Tree

Visit SolutionTree.com or call 800.733.6786 to order.

Professional Development Designed for Success

Empower your staff to tap into their full potential as educators. As an all-inclusive research-into-practice resource center, we are committed to helping your school or district become highly effective at preparing every student for his or her future.

Choose from our wide range of customized professional development opportunities for teachers, administrators, and district leaders. Each session offers hands-on support, personalized answers, and accessible strategies that can be put into practice immediately.

Bring Marzano Resources experts to your school for results-oriented training on:

- ▶ Assessment & Grading
- ▶ Curriculum
- ▶ Instruction
- ▶ School Leadership

- ▶ Teacher Effectiveness
- ▶ Student Engagement
- ▶ Vocabulary
- ▶ Competency-Based Education

LEARN MORE at MarzanoResources.com/PD